W9-BHI-230

Also by Leonard Silk

ECONOMICS IN PLAIN ENGLISH
THE ECONOMISTS
THE RESEARCH REVOLUTION
THE AMERICAN ESTABLISHMENT
(with Mark Silk)
CAPITALISM: THE MOVING TARGET
VEBLEN
NIXONOMICS
THE EDUCATION OF BUSINESSMEN
THE WORLD OF ECONOMICS
(with Phillip Saunders)
CONTEMPORARY ECONOMICS: PRINCIPLES AND ISSUES
A PRIMER ON BUSINESS FORECASTING
(with M. Louise Curley)
ETHICS AND PROFITS: THE CRISIS OF CONFIDENCE
IN AMERICAN BUSINESS
(with David Vogel)
IDEALS IN COLLISION: THE RELATIONSHIP BETWEEN BUSINESS
AND THE NEWS MEDIA
(with Rawleigh Warner)
SWEDEN PLANS FOR BETTER HOUSING
REAGAN THE MAN, THE PRESIDENT
(with Hedrick Smith, Adam Clymer, Robert Lindsey and
Richard Burt)

ECONOMICS IN THE REAL WORLD

by
Leonard Silk

SIMON AND SCHUSTER
New York

Copyright © 1984 by Leonard Silk
All rights reserved
including the right of reproduction
in whole or in part in any form
Published by Simon and Schuster
A Division of Simon & Schuster, Inc.
Simon & Schuster Building
Rockefeller Center
1230 Avenue of the Americas
New York, New York 10020

SIMON AND SCHUSTER and colophon are registered trademarks of
Simon & Schuster, Inc.

Designed by Irving Perkins
Manufactured in the United States of America

1   3   5   7   9   10   8   6   4   2

Library of Congress Cataloging in Publication Data

Silk, Leonard Solomon, date.
Economics in the real world.
Includes bibliographical references and index.
1.Economics.   I.Title.
HB71.S575   1984   330   84-13844
ISBN 0-671-25030-2

ACKNOWLEDGMENTS

For their good advice, warmth of spirit, and sustenance, I wish to thank Bernice Silk, Amelia North, Denisa Morgan, Soma Golden, Skip Miller, Herb Levine, Joe Spengler, Dick Mooney, Joe Pechman, George Perry, Herb Simon, Paul Davidson, Michael Korda, and John Herman.

For making my working life a joy, most of the time, I am grateful to *The New York Times,* a home away from home, a university on the run. I am indebted to my colleagues for their dedication, skepticism, and generosity.

I wish to thank the publisher of *The New York Times* for permitting me to draw upon my articles and columns in that newspaper. Acknowledgments are also due to the *Harvard Business*

Review for permission to use part of my review, "A Walk on the Supply Side," from the November–December 1981 issue; and to Harcourt, Brace, Jovanovich, Inc. for permission to quote from T. S. Eliot's "The Love Song of J. Alfred Prufrock."

TO ANDY

. . . looking over my shoulder

CONTENTS

8 CONTENTS

Statistical Appendices

Be assured, my young friend,
that there is a great deal of ruin in a nation.

—ADAM SMITH
(Letter to Sir John Sinclair)

ECONOMICS
IN THE REAL
WORLD

Chapter
1
INTRODUCTION

What *is* the real world? Ah, that is the question.

Is it what we can see and touch, or does it lie beyond our reach—like an invisible hand?

The philosopher Mortimer Adler says truth is not a matter of belief but of objective reality that is the same for all people, no matter what they think about it. You can label reality whatever you like—"Aaarghhh," he suggests—and it will not be affected in the slightest.

Does economics confront an objective reality? If so, what is it? Economists and statisticians trot out the so-called facts, the indicators, the signs: Hourly earnings of nonfarm production workers have risen X percent; rotary rigs running in oil fields in the lower 48 states have declined to Y; capacity utilization in manufacturing has risen to Z. And so on and on.

But what do all the signs mean? As another philosopher, Susanne Langer, said, all signs may be misunderstood. Wet streets are not a reliable sign of a recent rain if the sprinkler wagon has passed by. A shot may mean the start of a race, the rise of the sun, the sighting of danger. "Where we find the simplest form of error," said Miss Langer, "we may expect to find also, as its correlate, the simplest form of knowledge." It is the kind of knowledge, she said, that we share with animals.

The difference between economists and other animals, however, is that economists commonly have preconceptions of what things mean that grow out of the economic theories they learned as graduate students and have been building on ever since. Does this knowledge of theory affect their perception of the real world? They say it doesn't. Economists distinguish between "positive economics"—the description of reality, like it or not—and "normative economics"—the prescription of economic policies to achieve the values particular economists or their masters favor. Positive economics says what is, presumably for everyone; normative economics says what ought to be, according to a particular set of social, political, or interest-group aims.

But the analytically sharp line between positive and normative appears to vanish in the real world of political economy. Desire invades analysis.

Why does empirical evidence—the test of reality—not act as a checkrein on economists and politicians? One reason is that there are so many facts and so many ways of interrelating them that reality rarely assumes a firm and consistently clear shape. Another reason is that so many people—not just the economists and politicians but businessmen, bankers, workers, and others—are afraid that the perception of reality will affect the outcome of events: If a situation is described as dangerous, some businessmen and bankers fear it will worsen and accelerate the dangers. If a situation, inflation or unemployment, is described as bearable, people may fear they will be expected to go on bearing it too long.

And what is often in dispute is not present or past reality but the future, and the future is not "real." It does not yet exist. It cannot be described, in a way to which all honest people must assent, because the future is still to be created by a multitude of decisions, big and small, and by accidents or discoveries that cannot be known in advance.

Human beings cannot bear all that uncertainty. They feel they must know the future as a basis for rational actions, that is, actions designed to serve their self-interests.

Does all this mean there is no economic reality? Not at all. It is an extremely complex reality, difficult to work out. But truth is there to be deciphered as a basis for intelligent action—whether in the interests of the individual, the business, the nation, or the world. That is the creed of the economist as social scientist; or, to be normative, it ought to be, but, alas, in the real world, economic theories meant to describe and explain reality often become frozen into dogmas that distort or falsify it.

Has contemporary economics gone overboard into abstractions and drifted farther and farther away from the real world? That is not a new issue. Half a century ago John Maynard Keynes compared the economists of his day to Euclidian geometers living in a non-Euclidian world. Discovering that in experience straight lines apparently parallel often meet, Keynes said that the economists "rebuke the lines for not keeping straight—as the only remedy for the unfortunate collisions which are taking place."

What he meant was that his colleagues, in the midst of the Great Depression, with millions of workers pounding the streets looking for jobs, insisted that unemployment couldn't happen, and if it did it was the fault of workers for not taking pay cuts and adjusting to market conditions. Sooner or later they had to adjust. There was nothing useful for government to do. Left to its own resources, the economy would return to equilibrium at full employment.

It didn't happen. Prosperity wasn't just around the corner.

The system was not, as advertised, an automatic, self-adjusting mechanism.

It still is not. Real-world economic systems operate on such principles as these:

- People, acting as individuals, in organizations or governments, make things happen; wages, prices and other variables are shadows of what people do.
- But economic events sometimes ride humankind.
- Ignorance is widespread among people, but it is not total; rationality and irrationality coexist.
- Self-interest is a powerful motivating force, but it comes in many shapes: short-term and long-term, narrow and broad, individual and social, intelligent and stupid; and altruism may emerge when all else fails.
- The market exists in both democratic and totalitarian countries, whether on the surface, underground, or as a phantom which planners cannot escape; but all markets are imperfect.
- The real world is never in equilibrium.
- The real world is a place where people, especially economists, do not often listen to those with whom they disagree nor confront each other's arguments; people have very strong vested interests in ideas which they have already mastered and have written articles and books about.
- Economists theorize, but politicians make the decisions, usually on politically expedient grounds.

Sir John Hicks, a winner of the Nobel Memorial Prize in Economic Science, says a few economic problems are *static,* and the prestige of scientific method has led economists to attach importance to them, for this is the field where economics appears to be most "scientific." But the more characteristic problems, he adds, are problems of *change,* of growth and retrogression, and of fluctuation; the extent to which these things can be reduced to scientific terms is limited, for at every stage, new things are happening, "things which have not happened before." And Professor Hicks concludes: "As economics pushes on beyond 'statics,' it becomes less like science, and more like history."

In this book I have tried to use some recent history to show how our economy changes, grows, retrogresses, and fluctuates in the real world—and why. I have also sought to show why it works as well as it does. I end with some thoughts on how to make our system work better.

Chapter

2

HIGHMINDEDNESS
AND DUPLICITY

On November 2, 1963, President Ngo Dinh Diem of South
Vietnam and his brother Nhu were shot to death in an armored
car in Saigon by officers of the South Vietnam army. On November 22, President John Fitzgerald Kennedy was killed by
Lee Harvey Oswald in Dallas, and Lyndon Baines Johnson
became President. And on November 26, President Johnson
issued National Security Action Memorandum 273, reaffirm-
ing the Kennedy Administration's policy on Vietnam. The
order confirmed United States support for the new regime in
Saigon and called for the drawing up of plans for "clandestine
operations by the Government of South Vietnam against the

North, and also for operations up to 50 kilometers into Laos."[1]
And the fate of the Johnson Administration was sealed.

Vietnam was not what the Johnson Administration was supposed to be all about. Lyndon Johnson thought his great contribution to United States history would be a strengthening of
the American economic and social structure, a war against
poverty, a completion of the New Deal reforms begun by his
hero Franklin D. Roosevelt, the building of a Great Society.
Lest it interfere with such mighty goals, the cost of the Vietnam
war was kept secret from Congress and the American people.

JOHNSONIAN FRUGALITY

While his Administration was not unique among governments
in combining highmindedness and duplicity, President Johnson was an unusually gifted and passionate exemplar of both
those attributes.

In late January 1964, when he was putting the finishing
touches on his first budget message, I had my first interview
with Johnson. He said he wanted to "build confidence" in his
Administration among business executives and on Wall Street.
Kennedy had shaken business confidence by his battle with the
steel industry in 1962. When U.S. Steel raised prices after
Kennedy had used his influence with the United Steel Workers
union to get a moderate wage settlement, he felt betrayed by
steel management and said his father had warned him that
"businessmen were a bunch of bastards." Most business leaders had seen nothing subsequently to convince them that the
Kennedy Administration was "on their side" or concerned
about their needs.

Johnson told me he intended to put "his own brand" on the
existing economic policy. His first goal would be to put
through the big tax cut that Kennedy had proposed. The Ken-

[1] *The Pentagon Papers, The New York Times* (New York: Bantam
Books, 1971), p. 232.

nedy tax cut, $11 billion as originally proposed, had been stalled in Congress, and Johnson meant to push it through right away, when Congress, after the assassination, would be responsive to a Presidential plea for prompt actions to unite and strengthen the nation.

Johnson said he did not intend to use government spending as a solution to national economic problems. Government spending, in and of itself, was neither good nor bad. If expenditures were wasteful, or went for programs worth less than they cost, they should be cut.

"But if programs are needed, for their own sake," he said, "you should spend the money—but even then you should be careful how much you spend. If you cut spending but the economy still needed more of a push, you should use tax cuts to make up the gap."

He said gaining business confidence was not just good politics but good economics because it would help to give business spending a boost, and help spur the economy. And he intended to continue to use his office to hold down excessive wage or price increases. The Federal Reserve, he said, "shouldn't get restrictive until it has to." Tight money would offset the effect of the tax cut. The Fed should be ready to tighten up if real inflation showed up, not before.

Once he had the tax cut, Johnson said, he would tackle other unsolved national problems, especially poverty, unemployment, and their root causes—poor education, poor health, racial discrimination. But his was going to be a "frugal" Administration. Secretary of Defense Robert S. McNamara would curb the appetites of the generals and admirals. Johnson said budget-cutting made good sense, economically and politically. Cabinet members were getting their biggest ovations, even from labor groups, Johnson said, by talking up his economy drive.

I asked him why he thought it was imperative to hold spending in his new fiscal 1965 budget below the current budget. "You want to know why I've quit beating my wife," he said sharply. "There was nothing 'imperative' about it. I just worked the budget over and I got it down half a billion lower than this year and at least $2 billion below what our budget people thought it would have to be a month ago."

He saw nothing "magical" in what he had done. The defense budget had gone up $17 billion since Kennedy had met with Khrushchev in Vienna. With a $1 billion cut in defense spending, he said, he still had more money to spend on defense than President Eisenhower had—"plus the benefit of all the spending that's taken place since 1961." He didn't see why he should be taken as a miracle worker for getting rid of what he considered "useless cavalry regiments." He had just used "friendly persuasion" to get his old buddies in the Senate and House to accept cuts in atomic energy and cuts in defense programs for their own districts.

THE SECRET BUILDUP

While Lyndon Johnson was espousing the economics of frugality, plans for the covert war in Vietnam were moving ahead. On December 21, 1963, after a two-day trip to Vietnam, Defense Secretary McNamara had informed the President that plans drawn up by the C.I.A. station and the military command in Saigon were "an excellent job." On January 2, 1964, Major General Victor H. Krulak of the Marine Corps told Johnson the plans would "result in substantial destruction, economic loss and harassment" of North Vietnam. The strikes against the North would rise in tempo and magnitude in three phases during 1964 against "targets identified with North Vietnam's economic and industrial well-being."[2]

On February 1, 1964, two weeks after President Johnson spoke to me about his plans for holding down military expenditures, what the Pentagon Papers described as "an elaborate program of covert military operations against the state of North Vietnam" was launched.

General Krulak regularly informed Secretary McNamara of

[2] Ibid., pp. 234–253.

planned and conducted raids. Secretary McNamara directed the operations for the President through a section of the Joint Chiefs of Staff called the Office of the Special Assistant for Counterinsurgency and Special Activities. The Joint Chiefs themselves periodically evaluated the operations for Secretary McNamara. Secretary of State Dean Rusk was also informed, though in less detail. The attacks were given "interagency clearance" in Washington by coordinating them with the State Department and the Central Intelligence Agency, with advance monthly schedules of the raids submitted for their approval.

The clandestine war was waged according to the best bureaucratic procedures.

FINE-TUNING AND TAX-CUTTING

In economic policy, it was the heyday of fine-tuning. Walter W. Heller, chairman of the Council of Economic Advisers, had been a bit surprised and disturbed when Johnson's budget for fiscal 1965, which the President had played close to his vest, came up with a spending total lower than fiscal 1964's. To Heller and the C.E.A., this meant that the pending $11 billion tax cut would have to carry a heavier burden than they had expected.

But Johnson was not disturbed. He regarded his spending cuts as important if he was to get the tax cut through the Senate. He wanted it particularly to gain the support of Senator Harry Byrd of Virginia, a conservative Democrat, who, the President told me, was "most cooperative when understood." Johnson said that any time he could get "11 for 1" (that is, an $11 billion tax cut for a $1 billion spending cut) he would regard it as "a good deal."

But Johnson was more than willing to go along if someone could show him how to put more zip in the economy to offset the drive to cut spending. Heller thought he could—by cutting the withholding rate on personal income, not to 15 percent as proposed in the House bill, but to 14 percent from 18 percent. That would keep the total fiscal package as stimulative as it was in the first place. Johnson bought Heller's proposal.

So Congress passed the $11 billion tax cut (it was later recalculated as amounting to a cut of $14 billion). It was an historic event in United States public policy—not only the biggest tax cut in history but one adopted when the budget was already running $10 billion in the red. To add to its singularity, the tax cut was not made during a recession; the economy in 1964 was moving up briskly, though unemployment was still, at 5.4 percent of the labor force, considered too high—4 percent was regarded as the "interim target." And the cut was made despite what Walter Heller called the nation's "Puritan ethic," which, in fiscal matters, meant: *Balance the budget, stay out of debt, live within your means.*

The tax cut marked a triumph for the Keynesian doctrine of increasing demand to stimulate economic growth and reduce unemployment. As Keynes had written, "The ideas of economists and political philosophers, both when they are right and when they are wrong, are more powerful than is commonly understood. Indeed, the world is ruled by little else." It was a quotation much beloved and often cited by economists at the time.

The Morgan Guaranty Bank, in its survey, noted the Keynesian theory behind the Kennedy-Johnson tax cut without turning a hair. It said the tax cut had been "tailored generously enough to achieve the goals at which it aims, including a significant whittling down of the unemployment rate," and suggested that it "could well lead to a longer and stronger expansion than even the optimistic consensus" of forecasts had implied. The bank worried a bit, however, about "oversuccess," and called for flexible fiscal and monetary policies should the expansion prove too strong. The Keynesian doctrine was supposed to be symmetrical: Cut taxes and ease money to spur an underemployed economy, but raise taxes and tighten money to curb inflation should the economy reach full employment and move ahead too fast.

The prestige of the economists who had made the case for the big tax cut hit an all-time high. For, as taxes went down, the economy went up, and the budget deficit shrank; theory had become reality. But Lyndon Johnson insisted he was no theorist, just a practical man. His aide Jack Valenti, later the president of the Motion Picture Association, told me, "He's like Abe Lincoln. Lincoln once said, 'My policy is to have no policy.' "

GUNS AND RANCID BUTTER

In June 1964, at a Vietnam war strategy session in Honolulu, Ambassador Henry Cabot Lodge urged "a selective bombing campaign against military targets in the North" to bolster shaky morale in the South. Lodge questioned the need for a Congressional resolution to support the bombing of North Vietnam. Rusk, McNamara, and John McCone of the C.I.A. supported the idea of asking for a Congressional resolution. A Canadian diplomat, J. Blair Seaborn, had met secretly in Hanoi with the North Vietnamese Premier, Pham Van Dong, to warn him that "the greatest devastation" would be inflicted on his country if it escalated the war.

But President Johnson resisted pressures from the Secretaries of State and Defense and the head of the C.I.A. to ask for a Congressional resolution immediately to back an American escalation of the war.

He was campaigning against Senator Barry Goldwater in 1964 for the White House and wanted to contrast his own prudent, cautious approach to Vietnam with the hawkishness of Goldwater, who had called for heavy bombing of the North.

Yet, on September 7, at a White House strategy session two months before the election, Johnson and his top officers reached agreement that air attacks against North Vietnam would probably have to be launched. They expected these attacks to start "early in the new year."

Johnson the dove buried Goldwater the hawk in a landslide in November.

When I next interviewed Johnson, it was January 24, 1965, budget time again. Gardner Ackley, who had succeeded Walter Heller as the President's chief economic adviser, brought me to the Oval Office. Johnson asked Ackley if he wanted to stay, and Ackley said pleasantly, "You don't need me." "Okay, so leave," said Johnson.

Ackley had given me an advance copy of the budget in preparation for the interview; this was normal practice, since the budget was "embargoed" until its release date three days later. The most noteworthy thing about the new budget, I thought, was that Johnson, still working his "frugality" theme, had kept the spending total under $100 billion. So I opened the interview by saying to the President, "Well, I see you were able to hold the budget below $100 billion again."

Johnson, suspecting a leak, exploded. "You see no such thing," he said. "How in hell would you know the budget was under $100 billion if I don't know it? Don't you come in here and try to pull that on me."

I didn't think it appropriate to tell the President of the United States I knew he was lying about the budget, which was right there in my briefcase, so I just went on with the interview. The next morning Gardner Ackley called me to say that the previous night, just before Johnson had been admitted to Bethesda Naval Hospital suffering from a bad cold, he had asked Ackley to call me to say he was sorry about what he had said to me on the budget total—he simply hadn't realized I had a copy of the budget.

Doubtless, worrying about the Vietnam buildup, which he was keeping secret, Johnson was trying to be cautious about the budget. He wanted his Great Society programs in the worst way and did not want to go to Congress to ask for a tax increase to pay for the war. It might have killed his domestic programs.

His economic advisers supported his program, accepting low Pentagon estimates of the rate of spending on the war and hoping to pay for it out of growing employment and output. Despite their nagging worries about the United States balance of payments, running persistently in deficit, and about rising prices and wages and the jolt to the wage-price structure that might follow the windup of the steel labor negotiations in the spring, the President's economic advisers insisted they were "moderately optimistic." They forecast that gross national product would rise to $660 billion in 1965, a gain of about $38 billion over 1964. Ackley said this gain would make a considerable dent in unemployment, which had been holding close to 5 percent. Johnson, the Old New Dealer, was highly sensitive about unemployment at that level; he said he would "examine every idea I can find, and do everything in my power, to reduce unemployment."

Yet he drew back from submitting a more stimulative budget, because he felt boxed in by other considerations, including, he said, holding prices stable, closing the external payments gap, and preserving the confidence of the business community. Hence he said he was holding Federal spending "within acceptable limits," moving toward a balanced budget—but "in a balanced economy"—and trying to avoid jarring business by too frontal an assault on industrial price increases, as Kennedy had done.

But he told me it had made him "mad" when he heard that the press assumed it would get copies of the report on steel wages and prices that his economists were preparing. He said, "I'll decide to release the report when I see it." Johnson was ferocious on the matter of leaks; he was known to change an important decision or reverse a high appointment if news of it leaked before he was ready to announce it.

As eager as he was for business support, he told me he would not "kowtow to business." He was annoyed by suggestions that he had been too mild in his response to automobile wage settlements that exceeded the Administration's 3.2 percent productivity guideline for noninflationary wage settlements.

Business, he said, often acted contrary to its own best interests, as when it let its timidity about the budget slow the economy down: "Some businessmen want to take me back to the 1880s—and some labor leaders want me to charge forward into the 1980s." He kept looking for "the consensus," but it was hard to find, and his economic advisers weren't very much help. "Some advisers," he said, "like blondes, some like brunettes, and some can't tell the difference." He was skeptical about the economists' ability to forecast, although his economists had virtually scored a bull's-eye the year before. Ackley said: "He thinks we were lucky."

Despite his political and emotional roots in the New Deal, Johnson knew he was living in a wholly different era. "We are producing in a month almost as much as we did then in a year," he remarked to me.

He sometimes would affect a country-boy ignorance or anti-intellectualism, but was certainly knowledgeable about the essentials of economic policy.

He followed the economic indicators ardently, week by week, especially retail sales. His preoccupation with the weekly figures reflected his anxiety lest the growth of the economy be interrupted. He considered economic growth crucial to his other goals—increasing education, reducing poverty, improving "the quality of life," a term that was then just coming into usage. "I do not believe recessions are inevitable," he said in his 1965 economic report; that was not standard economic wisdom at the time, but Johnson's continuous-growth doctrine did capture many Democratic economists. I remember the late Otto Eckstein, a Harvard professor and Johnson adviser, telling me: "Why be afraid of growth? If we can keep growing, maybe we can solve all our problems out of a growing GNP."

Johnson thought he could combine growth with restraint. He wanted the world to take note of his commitment to "defend the dollar at its present gold price" of $35 an ounce. He tried to reinforce that commitment by telling the world he regarded William McChesney Martin, the Federal Reserve chairman, as "an outstanding, dedicated public servant." Johnson said he would follow "a very prudent and responsible course," one that the world's financiers would understand and approve.

But that would be done within a pattern of growth. "We have had 48 months without a dip so far, and I mean to keep it going indefinitely," he said. Indeed, the Johnson years were recession-free. But not inflation-free.

HEATING UP THE WORLD

The economy moved up faster than President Johnson's economists had forecast. Instead of rising to $660 billion in 1965, as predicted, gross national product climbed to $681 billion. Unemployment, which was equal to 5 percent of the labor force at the start of 1965, fell to 4.1 percent by December of that year. Consumer prices, which had been rising by 1 to 2 percent per year through the 1950s and early 1960s, increased by 2.4 percent in 1965—seemingly a minuscule acceleration, but the start of something worse.

In 1966, driven by the tax cut, Great Society programs, and Vietnam buildup, the economy was racing toward full or overfull employment. By February 1966, the unemployment rate had fallen to 3.7 percent.

The Johnson Administration found itself caught in a cleft stick and couldn't get out in time. The President's basic strategy was to go for one more year of strong economic growth, push through a guns-and-butter budget, and impose only "modest restraints" on the economy. In March 1966, Johnson asked Congress for a $4.8 billion supplemental defense appropriation—all the extra money the Pentagon said it needed for the foreseeable future. Some of his closest political advisers told Johnson it would be stupid for him to rush back immediately to Congress for more taxes to pay for the war or to fight an inflation that the President and his aides had publicly insisted was not happening. Signs were multiplying that the inflation was indeed starting to happen. "The fine mist of incipient inflation may be turning into light rain," said Walter Heller, now back at the University of Minnesota. Among private economists (and covertly among Johnson's own economists) a consensus was forming in support of raising taxes to head off the inflation.

On Capitol Hill, the Joint Economic Committee said the evidence was increasing daily that the nation "will need a tax increase this year, and that it will be needed quickly." Most Congressmen, however, were averse to boosting taxes in 1966, an election year. The House of Representatives even declined to reinstate telephone excise charges, as the President had requested in his budget.

Pollsters provided data to show that most Congressmen and the President were correct in thinking that the public was not ready for a tax increase. Johnson decided to sweat it out. Not only was it an election year, and not only was the Vietnam buildup in full swing, but there was a new factor that made the President determined to press ahead with his social programs: racial unrest was rising. In mid-March 1966, blacks rioted in the Watts area of Los Angeles, the first of a wave of riots that was to hit Newark, Detroit, and other cities.

The President decided to let the economy continue in its long, strong expansion; that, he figured, would whittle unemployment down further among blacks and teenagers and help cool the situation. He elected to submit a budget that called for both more military and social expenditures but to bring the budget closer into balance "by any means available" to prove his "fiscal responsibility." And the Fed would provide moderate monetary restraint (that is, control the money supply) against tendencies for the fully employed economy to overheat. Yet he insisted the Fed must avoid "premature" anticyclical actions.

For public consumption, Johnson's advisers and policymakers strongly supported his strategy. Only Fed Chairman William McChesney Martin dissented. He broke out of the policy-making "quadriad"—the four-man group that also included Treasury Secretary Henry H. ("Joe") Fowler, C.E.A. Chairman Gardner Ackley and Budget Director Charles L. Schultze. Martin pressed the Federal Reserve Board to increase the discount rate to 4 percent, an increase of half a percentage point. It passed the board by a one-vote margin. By the Johnson Administration, Martin's move was regarded as treacherous.

The White House accused Martin of spoiling the President's plans for the right mix of fiscal and monetary actions. Treasury Secretary Fowler declared that the economy's ability to sustain the burdens of the fighting in Vietnam was "vastly greater" than at the time of Korea. He said it would be unnecessary and unwise to take strong fiscal action to prevent inflation and made speeches calling for "unrelenting vigilance," rather than immediate action.

Johnson held all his fiscal dissenters in line except Fed Chairman Martin, who was saying openly that monetary policy alone could not hold inflation down. He said he was afraid that, if fiscal policy stayed so stimulative, trying to keep money tight would send interest rates soaring and damage housing, the savings and loan companies, state and local governments, and many small businesses. The stock market took alarm and turned down.

Finally, in August 1967, Johnson turned around and asked for the tax increase some of his advisers had been urging upon him for more than a year. But Congress did not give it to him for another year. By then it was too late. The 10 percent surtax on personal and corporate income failed to check the inflationary trend and the public's inflationary expectations. Consumer prices rose 4.7 percent in 1968 and 6.1 percent in 1969. By weakening the dollar and speeding the outflow of gold from the United States, the Vietnam war exacerbated inflationary trends in the world economy.

Walt W. Rostow, a key adviser to President Johnson during the Vietnam war, has said that most economists, including himself, would have preferred "at the time and in retrospect to have seen President Johnson succeed in persuading Wilbur Mills to join forces in achieving a tax increase in 1966."[3] But he contends that two quite different and much more powerful inflationary forces began to operate in the mid-1960s throughout the world economy:

"First, the decline of world prices of crude materials, which had been going on since 1951, ended in 1964. It had dampened inflationary pressure both directly and by causing labor to modulate claims for wage increases. It gave way to the slow acceleration of inflation in the late 1960s which preceded the price explosion at the end of 1972.

"Second, productivity increases began to decelerate from the mid-1960s in all the advanced industrial countries. The average deterioration in rate of increase was about 20 percent between 1965 and 1970; for the United States about 30 percent. The reason for this phenomenon was the quite normal waning of potentialities for productivity increase in the leading sectors of the postwar boom: e.g., motor vehicles, steel, plastics, synthetic fibers, television, etc."

Rostow contends that the upsurge in world inflation in the late 1960s was "quite normal," the outcome of underlying historical trends. But I believe this understates the importance of deliberate policy actions, and inactions, by national governments, especially that of the United States.

Until the Vietnam war, the United States, whose currency was the linchpin of the world monetary system, had preserved price stability, recognizing its key role in the international economy. It was Lyndon Johnson, with his guns-plus-butter policy, that played the critical role in ending price stability.

A POLITICAL FAILURE

Gardner Ackley, President Johnson's chief economic adviser at the time, makes no bones of the policy failure of the Johnson

[3] Letter to *The New York Times*, Sunday, Feb. 12, 1984, Section 3, pp. 10–11.

Administration. In his Adams Lectures at the University of Michigan in the winter of 1983, Ackley said that by the end of 1965 it had become evident to the Council of Economic Advisers and Charles L. Schultze, director of the Bureau of the Budget, that the combination of tax cuts and swelling military expenditures threatened an end to the five-year period of expansion with essentially stable prices that had begun in 1961.[4] They concluded that avoiding inflation would soon require a major reduction of other Federal spending, an appreciable tax increase, and a tightening of monetary policy.

"The mere announcement of the expanded military activity, and knowledge of the new procurement contracts or orders that began to be discussed or executed," said Ackley, "began to affect the economy in 1965 even in advance of the actual further increase in Federal spending."

But Johnson would not act. In the absence of fiscal restraint, the Federal Reserve began to move toward tighter money in December 1965, to Johnson's vast annoyance. Finally in January 1967 he recommended a general tax increase to Congress, but Congress did not respond until mid-1968—as Ackley says, "at least a year and a half too late." He concludes: "This first major U.S. peacetime application of Keynesian policies may have been an analytical success: on balance, I believe that its predictions, and its advice, turned out to be basically correct. But the delay in enacting a tax increase to finance Viet Nam spending represented a clear political failure for stabilization policy."

Economics in the real world plays second fiddle to politics. It was no coincidence that the postwar era of steady growth without inflation came to an end during the Johnson Administration. Politicians and their advisers cannot find absolution for their duplicities and evasions of responsibility in the abstractions of economics and the inevitabilities of history.

[4] Gardner Ackley, "Some Uses of Economics," Henry Carter Adams Lecture No. 3, University of Michigan, Nov. 8, 1983. See also Angus Maddison, *Phases of Economic Development* (New York: Oxford University Press, 1982), pp. 133–136.

Chapter

3

"THERE AIN'T A VOTE
IN IT"

When Richard Nixon took over the Oval Office in January 1969, his main economic job was to check the inflation. But Nixon meant to do that without inducing a recession. He felt strongly that when he had first run for the Presidency against John F. Kennedy in 1960 the third Eisenhower recession had cost him the White House. Hoping to ease down the inflation he had inherited from Johnson without forcing the economy into a slump that would sharply increase unemployment, Nixon adopted a policy that came to be called "gradualism." That policy got its name from a statement of Nixon's first chairman of the Council of Economic Advisers, Professor Paul McCracken of the University of Michigan, who said that stopping the inflation "will have to be done easily. It will have to be done gradually."

The main tool of gradualism would be what McCracken called a "Friedmanesque" monetary policy. Nixon's advisers had pretty much bought the theory of Professor Milton Friedman that slow, steady growth of the money supply would check inflation without causing recessions.

Friedman's rule was this: "I would specify that the Reserve System shall see to it that the total stock of money ... rises month by month, and indeed, so far as possible, day by day, at an annual rate of X percent, where X is some number between 3 and 5."[1] The reason for choosing those numbers was that the underlying growth rate of the production of real goods and services in the United States was assumed to be between 3 and 5 percent per year, and hence, if money grew at the same rate, prices would be stable—and reasonably steady growth in real output could also be expected. But the real world proved not to be so smooth and manageable as the theory suggested it would be.

At the start of the Nixon Administration, William McChesney Martin was still chairman of the Federal Reserve Board. He and his staff were by no means enamored of their archcritic Professor Friedman; nevertheless, Martin, an experienced hand at working with Presidents, sought to accommodate the new Administration by trying to pursue the steady-growth rule favored by its economists, including Arthur F. Burns, who was in the White House as Counselor to the President.

During the first half of 1969, the money supply seemed to be growing at an annual rate of only 2 to 3 percent, and Professor Friedman sharply criticized the Fed for being too restrictive and for threatening to put the economy into a recession. However, the preliminary data on which Friedman had based his attack proved to be faulty; the money supply—defined as demand deposits plus currency in circulation (the most basic "M-1" definition)—actually was found on revised figures to

[1] Milton Friedman, *Capitalism and Freedom* (Chicago: University of Chicago Press, 1962).

have grown at a 4.4 percent rate from December 1968 to June 1969.

But instead of slowing down, the inflation rate had moved up to 5.8 percent, faster than in the last year of the Johnson Administration. Friedman had said monetary policy operated with a lag, which he thought would be about six months. Since the money supply had increased at a rate of 7 percent in the last half year of the Johnson Administration, the acceleration of inflation in the first half of 1969 could be blamed on the Fed under the influence of the Johnson people.

Martin, however, was disturbed about the speeding up of inflation; his main precept had always been "to lean against the wind," and he decided that monetary restraints had been too lax. In the second half of 1969, the Fed held the growth of the money supply down to 0.6 percent, practically no growth at all. And in the final quarter of the year a recession began; gross national product declined slightly and began to drop at an annual rate of 3 percent in the first quarter of 1970. Nevertheless, inflation still showed no sign of declining; on the contrary, during the first half of 1970, consumer prices rose at an annual rate of more than 6 percent. Unemployment, which had averaged 3.5 percent in 1969, climbed to 5 percent in May 1970.

Business confidence suffered a hard blow. The Federal budget was sliding into deficit, and interest rates climbed to levels not seen in a hundred years. The stock market went into the worst decline it had experienced since the Great Depression.

International developments worsened the problem. It was the worry that the Cambodian invasion by American troops would cause a massive increase in government spending, and hence in the Federal debt, aggravating strains on the money and capital markets, that put Wall Street into such a fright. Suddenly the specter of another 1929 loomed. Nixon sought to rally the market by declaring that if he had any money he would be buying stocks. He assured the nation that he meant to pull United States troops out of Cambodia shortly and would continue to withdraw them from Vietnam. And he sent Arthur Burns to replace Martin as chairman of the Federal Reserve.

A new fright broke out in June with the collapse of the Penn Central Railroad, the greatest business failure in history. It raised fears of a wider liquidity crisis. The Fed's tight money policies were blamed for the crunch. Burns, the new Fed chairman, fearing a panic, now threw Friedmanism to the winds and began to pour money into the economy. During the year after the near-panic following the Penn Central failure, the money supply defined as M-1 grew by 8.5 percent. And the money supply defined as M-2, to include not only money in circulation and checking accounts but also time and saving accounts, grew by 13 percent. These rates were double or triple the Friedman prescription.

Burns was famous as a pragmatist. During the Eisenhower Administration, his policy advice was essentially Keynesian, though he had earlier been known as a harsh critic of Keynes. And he had been a critic of the doctrinaire Friedman, his longtime associate at the National Bureau of Economic Research, where Friedman was much junior to Burns. Burns, however, felt that he could use a Friedman slow-growth money-supply rule when it suited the political and economic circumstances of the time, or set it aside when other circumstances required a more stimulative policy. It was the type of policy Paul A. Volcker was later to call "pragmatic" or "operational" monetarism.

At a White House dinner given by Nixon for 42 businessmen and stockbrokers on May 27, 1970, when he was striving to rebuild business confidence, Arthur Burns declared that no rigid rule on how rapidly the money supply should be allowed to grow would deter the Federal Reserve from supplying more money in case of a liquidity crisis. The Fed, he said, would discharge its obligations as a "lender of last resort," and business had no need to worry about the Fed's alertness or ability to supply the money needs of the country. The Fed, Burns said, "would not let the economy collapse."

But the President's hopes of avoiding a recession had already been shattered. There was a marked slowdown in output, and unemployment rose from 2.7 million at the end of 1969 to more than 5 million by the end of 1970. The slump and the continuing inflation resulted in a political setback for the Republicans in the Congressional and gubernatorial elections of November 1970. Nixon had no intention of risking his own defeat in 1972 with a continued experiment with "gradualism."

THE NEW ECONOMIC POLICY

With inflation continuing despite the rise in unemployment, Burns again demonstrated his pragmatism by coming out for an "incomes policy"—that is, a program to check inflationary wage and price actions by business and labor through Presidential pressures or persuasion. Burns had earlier been a critic of wage-price guidelines but had decided that, if the President was determined to regenerate the economy without kicking off inflation, an incomes policy was needed to curb wages and prices.

The President and some of his more conservative advisers did not agree. An incomes policy, which they regarded as a euphemism for price and wage controls, was ideologically and indeed morally repulsive to the noninterventionists, and besides, they contended, it would not work; it would only cloak for a while the buildup of inflation resulting from too expansive a monetary policy.

The White House was therefore eager to stop Burns from continuing his campaign for an incomes policy, and at the same time it wanted to warn him against choking back on the growth of the money supply as the threatened alternative to an incomes policy. So it struck at Burns in a curious way, apparently intended either to diminish his impact on public opinion, bring him to heel, or force him to resign to make room for a more docile head of the Federal Reserve. On June 28, 1971, a Presidental aide, DeVan L. Shumway, a member of the staff of Herbert Klein, Nixon's Director of Communications, leaked to *The Wall Street Journal* that the President was seriously considering making legislative recommendations to bring the Fed into the executive branch of the government. The Fed, a creature of Congress, is considered an independent entity—as William McChesney Martin used to say, "independent within the government but not independent of the government."

Further, said Shumway, Nixon was "furious" with Burns for continuing his public campaign for a wage-price review board. The "final straw," he added, was Burns's appearance before the Joint Economic Committee of Congress on July 23, 1971, at which Burns had said there had not been "any substantial progress" against inflation. The President was tired of hearing from bankers and businessmen that "the great Arthur" was contradicting Nixon's assertions that the economy was recovering satisfactorily, with considerable progress being made against inflation. Then the really dirty smear was applied: The White House aide said the chairman of the Federal Reserve Board was being "hypocritical" about inflation because he had been "trying to get his own salary raised from $42,500 to $62,500."

A Federal Reserve spokesman, when asked about this, said that Dr. Burns "hasn't requested any salary increase," but declined further comment. Presidental Press Secretary Ronald L. Ziegler passed up chances to disavow the personal assault on Burns in succeeding days.

But by the end of the week a White House official told *The New York Times* that the earlier "leaks" about Burns were "not a legitimate expression of Presidential opinion." Nixon himself then said that Burns had received an "unfair shot."

The assault on Burns and threat to the independence of the Fed had provoked an extremely worried and hostile reaction to the White House from the business and banking community, so Nixon backed off.

Then, hard on the heels of the effort to smear Burns for advocating an incomes policy, Nixon did a complete turnaround. A first hint of a coming change in his "game plan" came on August 4, when Nixon said his mind was open on the question of a wage-price board, but that he would make no move until Congressional hearings could be held sometime in September. On the weekend of August 15, he met at Camp David, the Maryland retreat named for Eisenhower's grandson, with his closest economic advisers, supposedly to discuss defense spending, but actually to put the final touches on his New Economic Policy. Not all members of the quadriad knew the big switch was coming. Treasury Secretary John B. Connally, Jr., knew; in fact he was the prime mover in the switch. Budget Director George Shultz certainly knew. But Arthur Burns and C.E.A. chairman Paul McCracken were left in the dark until the last minute.

That Sunday night, Nixon went on television to launch his new program, complete with a freeze on wages and prices, a stimulative fiscal policy, a 10 percent surcharge on imports designed to pry a dollar devaluation loose from the United States' trading partners, and a suspension of the convertibility of dollars into gold. Nixon, never given to understatement, called his program "the most comprehensive" since Roosevelt's New Deal.

Nixon said he was launching a simultaneous attack on three fronts—unemployment, inflation, and international speculation against the dollar. Calling the winding down of the Vietnam war the major cause of unemployment, he proposed a 10 percent "job development credit"—actually a revival of the tax credit to business for investment in new plants and equipment. After one year, he said, the 10 percent credit would drop to 5 percent. He also proposed to speed up personal income-tax exemptions by letting taxpayers deduct an extra $50 for each exemption a year earlier than planned. To stimulate auto sales and production, he called for repeal of the 7 percent excise tax on cars. These tax cuts were to be offset, he said, by a $4.7 billion cut in Federal spending, including a six-month postponement of pay raises for government employees, a 5 percent cut in government personnel, and a 10 percent cut in foreign economic aid. He also asked Congress to postpone any revenue-sharing program with the states for three months and to put off welfare reform for a year. Taken at its face value, a fiscal policy to cut taxes by $4.2 billion to create jobs combined with $4.7 billion in proposed cuts in Federal programs which would destroy jobs would be cross-sterilizing.

Charles Schultze, formerly President Johnson's budget director, who had gone to the Brookings Institution when he left office, calculated that in real terms the measures Nixon had proposed would effectively cut taxes by more than expenditures, because the expenditure cuts were largely on paper. "Despite the rhetoric about balancing tax cuts with expenditure cuts," Schultze told Congress, "the President's fiscal program quite appropriately provides a significant overall fiscal stimulus."

But the biggest stimulus to the economy was to come from monetary policy, although this did not and—given the President's decision not to raise the issue of the independence of the Federal Reserve—could not be made a part of his declaration of his New Economic Policy. However, Arthur Burns and the Fed, as it happened, came through for Nixon; the narrowly defined money supply, M-1, grew by 9.3 percent in 1972, the broader M-2 by 13 percent, and the still broader M-3 by 14.1 percent, building up inflationary pressures.

Immediately, however, those inflationary pressures were to be contained by controls. Nixon had announced a freeze on all prices, wages, and rents for 90 days. Corporations were asked to extend the freeze voluntarily to dividends (not a heavy sacrifice for corporate managers). Congress had already given Nixon the power to impose such a freeze—over his protests that he did not want that power—through the Economic Stabilization Act of 1970. Although he said the freeze would depend on voluntary compliance, the legislation provided for court injunctions and fines.

And to discourage "international speculators" who, said Nixon, "thrive on crisis," he slammed the gold window shut, declaring that convertibility of the dollar into gold and other reserve assets was suspended. But he assured Americans that the dollar would be worth as much as ever at home, and he told the nation not to fear what he called the "bugaboo" of devaluation.

THE BULLY BOY

President Nixon's field general for the New Economic Policy was Treasury Secretary John B. Connally, Jr., the former Texas Governor, who had ridden in the car with John F. Kennedy in Dallas the day he was killed. When Nixon picked Connally to replace David M. Kennedy, the inarticulate Chicago banker at the Treasury post after the Republican losses in the 1970 election, the first reaction of old Washington hands was that Nixon had made a clever but politically risky move. It was clever because Nixon needed a Treasury Secretary with political experience, a forceful and aggressive personality, and the ability to do a strong selling job on a Democratically controlled Congress. But the move was risky because Connally, with a strong political base of his own after his three terms as Governor of Texas, would have considerable leverage on the President. If Connally, a man lacking experience in the economic and monetary areas, should blunder, Nixon would find it hard to control or discipline him. The political costs of firing him might be great.

Connally had taken the Treasury post to serve not solely the President's aims but, obviously, his own as well. As a conservative Texas political leader, closely tied to oil and gas interests, he did not have much hope of gaining a place on the Democratic Party ticket as Presidential or Vice Presidential candidate. A brilliant performance on the economic front for Nixon would open up at least the second possibility for him on the Republican ticket—and perhaps eventually a shot at the top job.

In the possession of a tough and able man like Connally, the Treasury command post can be an extremely important one. Formally, the Treasury Secretary has three major jobs—adviser to the President, financial agent for the Government, and law enforcement officer; but beyond these the Treasury Secretary has a potential mystique and power, which is not all that difficult to explain: It derives from money.

Connally moved into the international financial sphere, as he said, like "a bully boy" onto the "smooth, well-kept playing" fields of the foreign central bankers and finance ministers. At the London meeting of the Group of Ten—the ten principal countries of the industrial world—Connally stressed that the key aim of the Administration's New Economic Policy was to achieve a surplus in the United States balance of payments. The thought within the Administration was that with a balance-of-payments surplus the United States would regain its international economic strength, which it considered critical to its international political power.

Connally said he saw no need for the United States to change the fixed ratio between the dollar and gold at $35 an ounce. This was disingenuous. A major aim of the import surtax that Nixon had imposed was to pry loose a dollar devaluation—although the Administration would have much preferred this to be achieved by an upward revaluation of other currencies, a step that would have had some cosmetic and political value for the United States. Connally said the United States was in no hurry, and in fact did not desire, to go back to buying and selling gold.

Foreign governments were sharply opposed to a resolution of the growing crisis that would leave the dollar with all of its old privileges, especially the privilege of the United States requiring other countries to accept dollars rather than gold in settlement of its debts, however huge. This was why the European countries insisted that the United States devalue the dollar in terms of gold as part of an overall settlement. In London, at the Group of Ten meeting, Pierre-Paul Schweitzer, a Frenchman who was then managing director of the International Monetary Fund, offered what he described as a compromise solution between the American and European positions, calling for:

1. A general realignment of exchange rates of the world's leading currencies, including an upward revaluation of the major European currencies and the Japanese yen, and the devaluation of the United States dollar.
2. A new monetary reserve system, in which created reserves, called Special Drawing Rights and nicknamed "paper gold," would assume some of the monetary reserve role held by gold and the dollar.
3. An effort to swing the United States balance of payments from its current deficit to surplus, with America's allies assuming a share of the burden.
4. After the achievement of these steps, removal of the 10 percent surcharge by the United States on imports.

West Germany's finance minister, Karl Schiller, welcomed the Schweitzer proposal as a good one, but the Nixon Administration remained strongly opposed to devaluing the dollar in terms of gold. Until the United States got the currency revaluation from other countries, it hinted, it was prepared to see the dollar float indefinitely. Many American economists, including such otherwise opposed thinkers as Yale's James Tobin and Chicago's Milton Friedman, said they would be glad to see the dollar float forever. They believed that a floating system would be the optimal monetary system to replace Bretton Woods. But they were opposed to the Administration's combination of a floating dollar with the retention of protectionist economic devices, believing that dollar devaluation alone would be enough to strengthen the United States trade position, whereas protectionism, provoking retaliation, would damage world trade and production.

As it floated, the dollar was starting to shrink. At a Rome

meeting of the Group of Ten in early December, Secretary Connally said the United States would consider a formal devaluation of the dollar. He asked foreign finance ministers how they would react to a 10 percent dollar devaluation.

On world currency markets, the dollar plunged to new lows. Foreign central banks, which earlier had insisted they were already holding too many dollars, were forced to buy up hundreds of millions of additional dollars, to keep their own currency values from rising too much, injuring their exports.

But the New York stock market rallied strongly on the news that the Nixon Administration was pushing for a devaluation of the dollar. Investors thought it would improve the marketability of American goods and spur the profits of American companies.

Connally, arriving at Andrews Air Force Base outside Washington, declared that the Rome meetings had been marked by "warm and good feelings." The stage was set for the Smithsonian Agreement.

At the old red-brick Smithsonian Institution building on the Mall in Washington on December 18, 1971, the world's ten leading non-Communist nations reached agreement on a new pattern of exchange rates, including devaluation of the dollar by 8.57 percent. Speaking to reporters at the end of the negotiations, President Nixon said, "It is my great privilege to announce, on behalf of the finance ministers and other representatives of the ten countries involved, the conclusion of the most significant monetary agreement in the history of the world." He was a fast man with the hyperbole.

Secretary Connally said that the realignment of currencies was tantamount to a 12 percent devaluation of the dollar, since other currencies were moved upward or held in place as the dollar went down. The Japanese yen would in effect be appreciated by 16.88 percent and the German mark by 12 percent. Since the British pound and the French franc did not change their value in terms of gold, they moved up 7.89 percent against the dollar.

The price of gold was lifted from $35 an ounce to $38. But dollars held by foreign central banks remained inconvertible into gold or other United States reserve assets.

In exchange, the United States agreed to lift the import surcharge and to end the "Buy American" clause in the new investment tax credit. And the bands within which currencies could fluctuate up or down around their par values were widened by the Smithsonian Agreement to 2.25 percent compared to 1 percent under the old rules.

All of this was intended to preserve the Bretton Woods monetary system. The strategy failed.

FAREWELL TO BRETTON WOODS

The "most significant monetary agreement in the history of the world" did not last long. Under the impact of ongoing inflation, at varying rates in different countries, and wild speculation in the foreign exchanges, the effort to set up a new structure of fixed exchange rates failed.

A rare insight into how the President of the United States was reacting to these complex international financial events is given by the Nixon tapes, as subsequently disclosed by the Watergate inquiry. On June 23, 1972, at about 10:20 in the morning, H. R. (Bob) Haldeman, the President's chief of staff, asked Nixon whether he had got the report that the British Government had decided to float the pound.

"No, I don't think so," said Nixon.

"They did," said Haldeman.

"That's devaluation?" asked the President.

"Yeah," said his chief of staff. "Flanigan's got a report on it here."

"I don't care about it," said Nixon. "Nothing we can do about it."

Haldeman then tried to get the President to hold still for a rundown of Peter Flanigan's report on the British pound, but

Nixon did not want to hear it. Haldeman told him that Flanigan argued that the British float showed the wisdom of the United States' refusal to consider convertibility of the dollar into gold "until we get a new monetary system."

The President said, "Good. I think he's right. It's too complicated for me to get into."

Haldeman, still determined to brief the President, told him, as the official transcript has it, that "Burns [Arthur Burns, chairman of the Federal Reserve Board] expects a 5-day percent devaluation against the dollar." This actually meant that Burns was expecting a 5-to-8 percent devaluation of the pound against the dollar. The pound, fixed at $2.6057 by the Smithsonian Agreement, had by then fallen to $2.38.

Nixon said, "Yeah. O.K. Fine."

Haldeman, pressing to keep the President involved, said, "Burns is concerned about speculation about the lira."

And Nixon replied, in one of the more celebrated remarks of his administration, "I don't give a shit about the lira."

The President then asked how "the House guys" were reacting to some [unintelligible] development, and Haldeman told him, "All our people are, they think it's a great—a great ah—."

"There ain't a vote in it," Nixon interrupted. "Only George Shultz [who had become Secretary of the Treasury when John Connally decided to leave the Administration, having been nixed for the Vice Presidential slot in the 1972 campaign] and people like that think it's great [unintelligible]. There ain't a vote in it, Bob."

Thus the President ended the morning's economic discussion.

President Nixon had not bothered to struggle to correct the weak United States payments position by the conventional methods of deflation (that is, decreasing the amount of money and credit available) and slowing the growth of the economy. Rather, with the 1972 election bearing down on him, he had instead pushed for faster domestic growth, allowing a huge accumulation of dollars by other countries, thereby swelling world monetary reserves and exacerbating world inflation. Speculators were pouring hundreds of millions of dollars into Europe, especially into West Germany, in anticipation of further dollar devaluation. As the flood of dollars rose, Karl Klasen, the head of the German Bundesbank, was asked how much longer the Germans could go on taking in dollars. Sounding more like a riverboat gambler than a German central banker, Klasen said, "The sky's the limit—it's our paper for theirs."

For the moment, the German gamble worked; the tide of inflowing dollars receded. Yet Klasen knew perfectly well that the sky was not the limit on how many extra dollars the Germans could take in. For an excessive Bundesbank issue of paper money—with marks flowing out of the central bank as dollars flowed in—would unleash inflation if continued long enough.

The world's monetary reserves were being swollen not only by the outflow of dollars but by the run-up in the price of gold as it became increasingly clear to speculators that the fixed-rate Bretton Woods system was breaking down, with severe inflationary results. The Smithsonian revaluation of the official gold price to $38 looked like a joke. By May of 1972, the price of gold in the free market was up to $60, but American officials insisted that this did not mean a thing; Arthur Burns told a Montreal audience, "I would expect the monetary role of gold to continue to diminish in the years ahead while the role of Special Drawing Rights increases. . . . In the future, as the SDR's assume increasing importance, they may ultimately become the major international reserve asset."

But the gold speculators noted that, however much United States officials might affect to talk gold down and insist that it was finished, they were hanging on to their last $11 billion worth (figured at the official $38 rate) as though the nation's fate depended on it. The gold producers and the gold speculators continued to believe that, despite solemn pledges to the contrary, governments all over the world would go on inflating and marking up the price of gold. The strength of gold, they insisted, was living proof of man's distrust of man and of the vulnerability of governments to the pressures of vested interest groups.

By the end of July 1972, the price of gold was up to $70 an ounce and still going.

THE SINKING DOLLAR

The world monetary system, as reconstructed after the Second World War, had been founded on the strength of the American economy, on the strength of the dollar, on a fixed gold price, and on the deficits in the United States balance of payments that were required to put other countries back on their feet.

But that system was built on a fundamental contradiction: A strong dollar and a fixed dollar-gold rate of exchange would in time prove to be incompatible. Either the dollar would weaken or the American deficits would have to be ended. But the American deficits went on and on.

America's persistent payments deficits were not due solely to its military actions and economic aid programs. Of growing importance as the years went by was the overvaluation of the dollar in relation to both gold and other currencies. This hurt United States exports and made its imports, as well as travel and foreign investment, cheaper for Americans. So the migration of American business overseas went on apace, with corporations using abundant and overvalued dollars to buy up foreign assets, start branches and subsidiaries abroad, hire foreign labor, and use foreign resources to increase their worldwide profits.

Foreigners, in the midst of the postwar prosperity, were schizoid about the trend. Many, especially those in close partnership with the Americans, welcomed the growth that United States capital, technology, and managerial know-how helped bring. But there was increasing concern in Europe about the inflation that the dollar inflow was also helping to breed.

President Nixon had inherited the inflation from President Johnson, but had wound up making it worse. Finding rising unemployment politically intolerable, he had announced, "I am now a Keynesian," and had switched to a policy aimed at producing high employment in time for the 1972 election. Under Nixonian management, the United States balance-of-payments deficit had worsened, and the dollar had weakened even further.

The object of the Smithsonian Agreement from the American standpoint was, as we have seen, to devalue the dollar enough to produce equilibrium or, if possible, a big surplus in the balance of payments. This would, it was hoped, restore American economic power and prestige in the world, and hence political leadership as well. For this reason the Nixon Administration was originally unwilling to "devalue the dollar" rather than have other countries revalue their currencies upward; logically, mathematically, there would seem to have been no difference. However, there was a symbolic difference. The dollar had been regarded as the fixed star of the world monetary system, the star around which all the other national currencies revolved. For the dollar to change its own value in relation to gold and other currencies would symbolize a radical change in the conception of the world monetary order, like the Copernican revolution in astronomy, in which the earth was no longer seen as the unchanging center of the universe.

After the Smithsonian devaluation of the dollar, no matter how much the Americans might insist that the dollar was still the fixed center of the world monetary system, the skeptics would go on saying, like Galileo, "But it does move." In fact, after the Smithsonian Agreement, United States officials themselves gradually accepted the new concept of a movable dollar.

For Nixon, the "benign neglect" of the value of the dollar meant that the United States could pursue as stimulative a policy as it chose to push the economy toward full employment. And if other countries could not demand gold in settlement of United States deficits, they would have to accept dollars in unlimited amounts in settlement of their claims against the United States.

But the Nixon Administration underestimated the effect of the outflow of dollars and the deteriorating value of the dollar on world inflation and the world economic order. By so aggressive an approach to the solution of its own problems, the United States hurt the world economy—and itself.

If the United States does not provide the leadership for maintaining world stability, no other nation or group of nations can provide it.

There is always a strong temptation for an American President to prove how tough and "realistic" he is in pursuit of national self-interest, not soft-headed and do-goodish like his predecessors. But the powerful politician's personal interest is easily confused with his nation's self-interest.

Adam Smith celebrated self-interest, recognizing its force as a motivator of human actions which, when disciplined and guided by the invisible hand of the market, would work for the common good. In politics, the self-interest of a leader in power, even in a democracy, lacks a constantly competitive market to discipline and guide it. Party opposition, public opinion, the press, the threat of being turned out at a future election—all these are wavering and uncertain forces, capable of being blocked or manipulated by a clever leader.

In the political realm, principles, ethics, a genuine sense of the common good are vitally needed as a substitute for the invisible, restraining hand of the market.

Chapter

4

THE OIL SHOCK

The impact of devaluation on inflation caught Washington and most economists by surprise. American economists tend to minimize the importance of foreign trade to the United States, perhaps because of a kind of cultural insularity or because, in their conventional way of analyzing the national economy, net exports are seen as a very small proportion of the gross national product.

But the dollar devaluation, combined with the expansive monetary and fiscal policies of the Nixon Administration, intensified inflationary pressures, which its price and wage controls could barely suppress. Those controls gradually eroded, through phases of decontrol, and soon after Nixon was reelected by a landslide vote over Senator George McGovern they were dropped altogether. And the suppressed inflation burst forth.

Devaluation aggravated that domestic inflation by raising the dollar prices of internationally traded goods, not only those of imports entering the United States but also, and more important, those of all exportable American goods as well. Many American products suddenly looked like terrific bargains to foreigners, and they rushed to buy—beef in Chicago, oil in Baton Rouge, and paintings at Sotheby Parke Bernet Galleries in New York. The impact on prices was dramatic. Randall Hinshaw of Claremont Graduate School in California found that the effect of dollar devaluation was immediate on primary products, such as food and raw materials, but more gradual on the prices of manufactured goods, especially under then existing price controls. However, as the prices of such basic internationally traded raw materials as iron and steel, copper, aluminum, zinc, lead, and plastics rose, so did the prices of autos, tractors, and other manufactured goods. And when price controls were lifted in 1973, the prices of industrial goods, like the prices of raw materials, soared.

Ironically, the devaluation of the dollar initially had a perverse effect on the United States balance of trade and payments. Economists had expected some lag, due to the so-called J-curve, in which lower prices of exports initially yield lower returns from abroad, until the volume of sales increases. But the lag was longer than expected. The reason was that the devaluation increased the dollar price of imports more than it reduced the volume of imports, especially as the American economy was expanding more rapidly and sucking in more imports. Simultaneously, devaluation cut the dollar price of American exports, causing foreign demand for cheaper American goods to boom; but the Nixon Administration imposed export controls on soybeans and other agricultural goods in short supply, thereby restricting the rise of United States earnings abroad. Even more important, booming demand at home restricted the growth of American exports. Hence the American trade position worsened, and dollars continued to flow overseas to cover the payments gap.

The basic United States blunder was to think it could run a devaluation of the dollar without first slowing the economy. It did just the reverse—coupling devaluation with strong fiscal and monetary stimulus.

THE DOLLAR HEMORRHAGE

So dollars continued to hemorrhage out of the country. On February 12, 1973, there was a second dollar devaluation, amounting to 10 percent, following a dramatic round-the-world flight by Under Secretary of the Treasury Paul A. Volcker to talk with government officials from Bonn to Tokyo. President Nixon cut short a stay in San Clemente, California, to return to the White House. At a late-night news conference, Treasury Secretary George Shultz said that "the proposed change in the par value of the dollar is acceptable" to "our leading trading partners in Europe." He said he did not expect any changes in their exchange rates except that the Japanese had decided to float the yen. The Canadian dollar, the British pound, and the Swiss franc were also afloat.

The purpose of the second devaluation was to halt the currency crisis, with flight from the dollar going on into gold and other currencies. But instead of calming the foreign exchange markets, it roiled them further. In late February and early March, dollars began to flood into West Germany because the mark looked like the safest port in the storm. The German central bank took in over $3 billion a day, paying out marks to all comers in a vain attempt to keep the mark's exchange value from rising.

After paying out billions of marks, German monetary officials finally grew alarmed over the prospects for inflation and threw in the sponge. They stopped defending the fixed exchange rate between the dollar and the mark; so the mark floated upward, and the dollar floated downward.

Otmar Emminger of the German Bundesbank later wrote: "As one who participated in (and was partly responsible for) the decision of West Germany to go over to floating in March 1973, I can testify that the main reason for this decision was the effort to shield the German monetary system against further inflationary foreign exchange inflows, after the central bank had to absorb a dollar inflow worth more than DM20 billions within five weeks, equivalent to more than double the amount of new central bank money required for a whole year."

Emminger noted that the breakdown of the fixed-rate system was also inflationary in the United States and other deficit countries. In Britain, as Angus Maddison notes, there was "an almost berserk feeling of liberation from the old constraints of stop-go which led to the adoption of a wildly expansionist policy." Control over the stock of money was virtually nonexistent. Bank credit to the private sector rose by 50 percent, most of it to finance consumer spending or real estate deals. Public borrowing to finance government debt climbed to 6 percent of gross national product.

The price of gold kept climbing. By early June 1973, it was above $125 an ounce, almost double where it had started the year and nearly four times its official price. The dollar kept sinking and in the foreign exchange markets had lost one-fifth of its value relative to the German mark. The United States was suffering from the worst inflation in half a century and, with the Watergate crisis coming to a boil, its most intense Presidential crisis in a century.

Was panic at hand? George Shultz, the softest-spoken of Nixon Administration voices, said no. He said he was puzzled by the weakness of the dollar and the stock market—there were "bargains galore," he said, adding that he would be buying good common stocks if the funds he managed did not belong to the United States Treasury.

So the Bretton Woods fixed-rate system ended, with a whimper and not a bang. The world monetary system was de facto a floating system.

But inflation was anything but dead. The loss of respect for the dollar brought on a flight from all currencies into anything precious and scarce that promised to hold its value in a time of monetary troubles—gold, silver, platinum, and many other commodities. Overnight it seemed as though the long-range forecasts of the so-called Club of Rome of the exhaustion of world resources were coming true in a rush, with soaring prices the fever gauge of commodity shortages.

The collapse of Bretton Woods exchange-rate discipline and the relaxation of monetary and fiscal constraints in many countries touched off a world boom in production in 1972–73, in the Communist and third world countries as well as in the industrial world. Prices of manufactured goods were climbing smartly, but prices of commodities were climbing even faster.

Accidents of nature fed the commodity inflation. One of the weirdest was the disappearance of anchovies off the coast of Peru. Why this happened was unclear; one theory was that the 1972–73 invasion of a warm-water current called El Niño had upset the ecology of the cold-water Humboldt Current, drastically reducing the supply of plankton and other nutrients on which the anchovies feed. Most marine biologists doubted this, pointing out that El Niño comes roughly every seven years—it had last arrived in 1957 and 1962—but had not earlier seriously damaged the anchovy stock. Did an influx of predators eat the spawn? Were the young fish blown into hostile waters? Nobody knew. Whatever the explanation, Peru's anchovy catch fell from more than 10 million tons to 2 million tons in 1973, wiping out a critical part of the world's fish-meal supply, which is used to feed livestock.

Bad growing weather for cereals, the failure of much of the Soviet crop, the massive Soviet-American wheat deal—the "Great Grain Robbery" that was a key element in Nixon's détente with the Russians—worsened the commodity inflation. The price of wheat, which had been only $1.48 a bushel in 1970 and $1.58 in 1971, climbed to $1.90 in 1972 and then soared to $3.81 in 1973 and $4.90 in 1974. All farm prices moved up in sympathy, and there was an almost immediate effect on the cost of living all over the world.

But, whatever the accidental factors, the overall inflationary trend was no fluke. All the industrial nations were in a simultaneous boom; world demand was outrunning world supply.

The widespread perception of rising prices suddenly was transformed, as happens when an inflation lasts long enough, into a perception that paper money was losing its value and was not worth holding. Speculators were rushing out of currencies into gold and into commodities. World commodity prices more than doubled from the start of 1973 until the month of October.

And then the Arabs launched the Yom Kippur war against Israel on October 6. As part of their strategy, they declared an embargo on oil shipments to the United States and the Netherlands, and threatened to extend the embargo to any other country that provided support for Israel.

THE CALLED BLUFF

The Arab oil embargo threw the Western world into a frantic scramble for oil, and the prices of crude oil and refined petroleum products began shooting up. Seizing the opportunity this presented for acquiring wealth beyond the wildest dreams of avarice, the Organization of Petroleum Exporting Countries, whose members included Saudi Arabia, Kuwait, Iran, Iraq, Libya, Venezuela, and Nigeria, raised the posted price of a barrel of crude oil, as measured by Saudi Arabia light, from $3.01 (its production cost was only about 25 cents) first to $3.65, then to $5.11, and then, by December 1973, to $11.65.

The oil embargo and the war in the Middle East dealt a severe shock to the NATO alliance. The Europeans blamed the United States for trying to bully them into backing the American position on Israel, for not consulting with them, for giving them no warning before putting American bombers and other forces on worldwide alert, and for expecting them to risk a cut-off of their oil from the Middle East and North Africa, on which Europe depended for more than 80 percent of its supply.

The United States in turn blamed the European members of NATO for acting like a collection of small creatures trying to hide in the woodwork, for not looking beyond the moment's problems, for putting oil above principle, and for refusing to work with the United States to draw up a common policy toward the war—and the strategic threat of the Soviet Union and its allies.

Within Europe itself, strains intensified as a result of the Arab cut-off of 15 percent of Western Europe's oil supply. The nine members of the European Common Market met in Brussels to discuss the sharing of oil, but the French and British, who regarded themselves as being in a specially favored position with the Arabs, were reluctant to pool their oil with the Dutch, who were facing the loss of 70 percent of their oil, and the West Germans, who got much of their fuel via the Dutch port of Rotterdam.

Secretary of State Henry Kissinger, in the midst of the Watergate crisis with a distracted President fighting for his political life, attempted to put together a common Western response to the Arab demands. There were hectic discussions of a contingency plan for stockpiling and sharing oil, developing new energy resources, and imposing a counterembargo of industrial goods, agricultural products, military equipment, technical know-how, shipping, and even money against the oil-producing countries. But nothing much came of it all, in the midst of Western disunity.

The West German Foreign Ministry called on the United States to stop loading American weapons for Israel aboard Israeli freighters at the United States forces port in Bremerhaven. Several NATO members issued "neutrality" declarations and advised the United States that it could not use their facilities or airspace for resupply of arms to Israel.

The United States chastised its allies lightly. Secretary of Defense James R. Schlesinger said of the German opposition to United States use of German territory for the resupply of Israel: "The reaction of the Foreign Ministry in Germany raises some questions about whether they view enhanced readiness in the same way we view enhanced readiness." State Department spokesman Robert J. McCloskey said: "Our view is that maintenance of the military balance and establishment of a durable peace in the Middle East—which in our view and in our actions is what the resupply of Israel is about—is just as much in the vital interest of West Germany and the other NATO allies as it is in our interest. . . . We found ourselves in a period of tension and we would have appreciated some unified support."

And on November 21, Kissinger threatened "countermeasures" if the Arab oil embargo continued "unreasonably and indefinitely." He indicated that there were limits to American patience, although Washington had a "full understanding" of the reasons for the embargo. "We still hope," said Kissinger, "that some of the steps that were taken when certain assumptions were made about the principal American objective in that area will be changed when it becomes apparent that we are attempting to bring about a just peace."

The Arabs were nothing daunted. Sheik Ahmed Zaki al-Yamani, the Saudi oil minister, promptly responded on November 22, warning that there would be an 80 percent cut in oil production if the United States, Europe, or Japan took measures to counter the oil embargo or production cuts already in effect. Speaking in Copenhagen, Denmark, Yamani threatened to blow up certain oil fields if the United States took any military action. "Obviously, the United States and Japan and Europe could take some countermeasures," he said. "I think what we have as an oil weapon is far greater. What we have done is nothing at all." Noting that the United States "have their own local supply," Yamani cautioned Europe and Japan against joining the United States in any kind of countermeasures, "because your whole economy will definitely collapse all of a sudden." He said American military action, "also a possibility," would be "suicide."

PANGLOSSIAN ECONOMICS

The Arabs played their cards well. By the end of December, in appreciation of the flaccid Western response, the Arab oil countries announced that they would increase production by 10 percent in January and would supply Britain, France, Japan, Spain, and other "friendly countries" with their "full oil needs." Speaking in Kuwait, the peripatetic Sheik Yamani said, "We do not wish the nations of the world to suffer."

The move suggested that the Arabs saw little prospect that Europe and Japan could induce the United States to force Israel to return to its 1967 borders or yield to other Arab demands. "We only intended to attract world attention to the injustice that befell the Arabs," said Yamani.

Nevertheless, the Arabs kept the heat on the United States and other countries, including the Netherlands, Portugal, Rhodesia (which had not yet become Zimbabwe), and South Africa, which they accused of sympathy or support for the Israelis. Their announcement of a 10 percent increase in output—which by some murky arithmetic they described as reducing the cutback from 30 to 25 percent—would still leave the world well short of its normal oil requirements, though it was hard to know how much, since surreptitious deliveries above quotas to some countries were going on.

Meeting in Tehran in late December, OPEC doubled the crude oil price to $11.65 a barrel. A British official, hearing the news from Tehran, said, "The last chicken of colonialism is coming home to roost." In announcing the price rise, Shah Mohammed Riza Pahlevi of Iran, whom the United States regarded as its greatest ally in the area, declared, "The industrial world will have to realize that the era of their terrific progress and even more terrific income and wealth based on cheap oil is finished."

The Shah made no bones in asserting that the West was too fat and that the Middle Eastern powers were moving to claim their rightful share of the world's wealth.

The OPEC oil ministers meeting in Tehran collectively warned the Western countries against trying to hang on to their wealth by increasing prices of their exports, on penalty of an even faster increase in the price of oil.

The implications of the soaring oil price for the flow of dollars to the OPEC countries were almost inconceivable. Early estimates, based on an assumed $5 price for a barrel of crude oil, were that OPEC revenues would total $350 billion for the period 1973 to 1980; but the climb in price to $11.65 by the end of 1973 meant that the total through the rest of the decade might approach $1 trillion—and even that assumed that oil prices would rise no higher.

The most anxious economists, politicians, businessmen, and novelists began to conceive horror stories based on that flood of wealth to the oil-producing states—the devastation of the balance of payments of the industrial economies, the collapse of the dollar as an international currency, the unleashing of global inflation, the breakup of the Western alliance, a breakdown in world production and trade. Some saw a massive shift of political and military power looming, with the rich oil-producing countries acquiring a huge stake in Western industries and banks and greatly increasing their military (and nuclear) capabilities.

Such scenarios were exaggerated and far too simple. The money the oil producers earned in the capitalist world had to be spent or invested somewhere or it would be nothing but useless paper.

Too rapid an escalation of oil prices would bring not just a shift of wealth to the oil-exporting countries but a worsening of world inflation; if they went too far too fast, the oil countries could find themselves in the position of those classic traders who wound up exchanging million-dollar cats for million-dollar dogs—or, still worse, destroying their customers' and their own fortunes. But if they played it right, they would be able to go on milking the rich nations of the industrial world—and, for that matter, the poor, developing nations of the third world—indefinitely. The power of the oil producers to extract monopoly prices and payments would still cause enormous transfers of income and wealth to themselves.

If one could not break OPEC's power, some Western financiers and oilmen began to reason, why not join them and get some of the loot which would be transferred by the billions and billions out of the pockets of consumers and businesses all over the world in payment for the oil?

So, in opposition to the doomsday school of economic worriers, a school of Panglossian economists emerged to argue the case for relaxing and enjoying the rape of the West by the oil producers. Following the principles of divine automaticity of adjustment enunciated by Voltaire's Dr. Pangloss (whom he titled "Professor of Metaphysico-Theologo Cosmolonigology") these economic optimists contributed two new doctrines:

1. It does not matter how much money the oil-importing countries pay out to the oil-exporting countries, because the money will flow back to the oil-importing countries as investments or to pay for their goods.

2. It does not matter if the outflow of money to pay for oil causes a temporary cut in consumption in the oil-importing countries, because this will be a form of saving, and the "petrodollars" in the hands of the Arabs and other oil producers will then increase the world's stock of capital, furthering growth and damping down inflation.

These were principles that appealed strongly to United States and other Western banks who saw magnificent opportunities for profit in helping to "recycle" the dollars earned by the OPEC nations. By keeping the money game going, the banks could earn enormous revenues by accepting the deposits of the oil producers and relending them, at high interest rates, to oil importers everywhere, including the poor countries of the third world. Thus they sowed the seeds of an international debt crisis in the third world—and endangered their own liquidity.

The Western oil companies also saw great opportunities in facilitating the price increases and transfer of wealth to the OPEC nations. Climbing oil prices might spell bad news for the auto industry and auto drivers; for the airlines and air travelers; for electric companies and homeowners confronting oil, gas, and electric bills; for the unemployed; and for the deficit-ridden third world countries—but amid the general wailing and gnashing of teeth, the multinational and domestic oil companies were able to maintain their composure. As the eighteenth century French writer François de La Rochefoucauld observed, "It is remarkable with what fortitude we are able to bear the misfortunes of others."

RECONCILIATION WITH OPEC

Soaring prices of crude oil forced on the world by OPEC did not hurt the international oil companies, such as Exxon, Shell, Gulf, Texaco, Mobil, Socal, or the others who bought their crude from OPEC producers. On the contrary, the OPEC price increases caused the profits of the oil majors and indeed all the oil companies to increase enormously.

Avram Kisselgoff, formerly the chief economist of Allied Chemical, did a study for the National Bureau of Economic Research that demonstrated just how the huge increases in OPEC crude oil prices were translated into higher prices and profits by American oil companies.[1] The study found that at all three stages of operation—production, refining, and marketing—the oil companies were able to increase their margins substantially.

[1] Avram Kisselgoff, *The Propagation of Prices in the Oil Industry,* Working Paper No. 245 R, National Bureau of Economic Research, July 1980.

For instance, refiners' gross margins—the difference between the composite price of a barrel of foreign and domestic crude and the price of a barrel of refined petroleum products—rose from $1.36 in 1972 to $1.78 in 1973 and to $2.72 in 1974. These increases in margins meant additional gross receipts for refiners of about $1.9 billion in 1974.

Dr. Kisselgoff stressed that what counts in the oil industry is the absolute size of the margin and not the percentage markup. The oil industry itself has historically used the concept of margin in absolute terms. While prices rose sharply in 1974 and actual margins increased, margins in percentage terms declined at the refining and marketing levels. With the explosion of crude oil prices and the imposition of stricter price controls on gasoline, the oil companies increased their profits by raising the prices of other products faster than that of gasoline.

Using data from the Chase Manhattan Bank on 29 United States–based oil companies, Dr. Kisselgoff found that annual gains in net income after taxes, which had not exceeded 10 percent in the 1967–72 period, jumped by 70 percent, to $11.7 billion, in 1973, and by a further 40 percent, to $16.4 billion, in 1974.

The companies held on to a much larger share of that rising income: Retained net income of the 29 oil companies rose to 65 percent in 1973 and to 71 percent in 1974, from 45 percent in 1972. As a result, the net worth of the group of 29 rose by 11 percent in 1973 and by 15 percent in 1974.

This rise in net worth helped to make the oil companies' profits lower in percentage terms. While their reported profits declined to 12.8 percent in 1975, from 15.5 percent in 1973, their actual net income after taxes remained about the same.

Dr. Kisselgoff contended that a "meaningful evaluation of the profitability of the oil industry" should take into account not only the behavior of changes in net worth over time but also many other factors, including the extent to which the oil industry is investing in reserves of fuel other than oil, such as coal, uranium, oil shale, and timberland. As a result, he observed, the oil industry had come into possession of assets "whose potential profit increases inexorably with the rising value of the reserves."

Thus the self-interest of the oil companies, as well as of the big international banks, dictated a gentle response to the OPEC assault, the greatest financial coup by far in history. As the cynical La Rochefoucauld put it: "Being reconciled with our enemies is only a desire to improve our position, a weariness of the conflict, and a fear of disaster."

MACHIAVELLI AND PARETO

By early February 1974, Washington had decided to settle down and live peaceably with OPEC. Secretary of State Kissinger, whose critics had accused him of not knowing much economics, prepared what looked like a sophisticated brief for the Washington energy conference of the second week of February. Kissinger had generally been hailed as a disciple of such masters of political expediency as Machiavelli, Metternich, and Bismarck. But he went before the energy congress of wary and apprehensive ministers from major oil-consuming countries as a student of the Italian economist Vilfredo Pareto (1848–1923), author of the concept that the summum bonum is attained when no one can be made better off without making someone else worse off. Kissinger aimed for "Pareto-optimality" on a worldwide basis: taking technology, management, capital, and oil from areas where these are abundant to those areas where they are scarce. Kissinger's argument was couched in terms of "interdependence," suggesting that nations which sought to promote their self-interest at the expense of others would wind up injuring themselves—by weakening the entire world system of production, trade, and investment for decades to come.

This long-range American strategy was intended to counter suspicions and charges, coming particularly from the French, that Washington had summoned the energy conference as a move to re-establish its hegemony over the European nations and Japan. The French, represented in Washington by Foreign Minister Michel Jobert, had taken the lead in warning against collective action by the Western nations, or what he called "confrontation tactics," which they feared would only anger the Arabs and provoke them into new price raising or production cutbacks or expropriations of oil companies. Indeed, the submissiveness of the oil companies had a rational basis. As the energy conference in Washington was getting under way, Libya, as though to hammer home the point, nationalized operations of three American oil companies, terming this "a fresh slap in America's face" and announcing it just as the consuming-country conference began.

For its part, France adopted a "sauve qui peut" line, and Britain, Japan, West Germany, and others followed suit, each negotiating their own bilateral deals with the Persian Gulf producers, offering armaments and industrial goods for their oil. The principal United States goal was to start to build a common approach among the Western powers as an alternative to risky, costly bilateral deals that could rip the West apart. The United States also had some self-interest going, of course: It would gain an important competitive advantage over the other industrial countries if it could avoid getting locked into an inflated oil price for years to come. The American strategy was based on the assumption that in the long run the price of oil would be lower, not higher, than it was in early 1974—at least in relation to the prices of other goods.

The first four planks in Kissinger's program were designed to ensure that result. His first plank was conservation—"the new energy ethic." He stressed that the United States, the world's most profligate energy consumer, had already demonstrated that it could curb its appetite for oil and gasoline. His second and third planks—alternative energy sources such as coal, shale, and offshore oil, plus more money to be spent on research and development of new energy technologies—would encourage an increase in energy supply. His fourth plank—emergency sharing of oil—was pointed primarily at helping nations over periods of acute shortage; but a mutual program for sharing oil could also prevent disorderly markets and wild run-ups in price, he argued, like the one that had just occurred. There was skepticism about how much oil the United States could or would share, although Kissinger could point to American willingness to help the embargoed Dutch. More significantly, he argued, America's ability to help others would grow year by year—"as we move toward self-sufficiency."

In his final three points, Kissinger came out strongly for policies to nurture and safeguard global interdependence, lest rampant inflation, worldwide depression, and balance-of-payments breakdowns result from the energy crisis. His fifth plank called for international financial cooperation, including new mechanisms to recycle the enormous flows of money going to the oil-producing countries back to the rest of the world in the form of capital investment. Such recycling, both Kissinger and William E. Simon, then the energy administrator and a former Wall Street bond salesman, contended, would be very much in the interests of the oil producers as well as of the nations receiving the backflow of capital. Simon held that money invested now would be worth considerably more than oil in the ground a decade from now. In his sixth plank Kissinger also stated that "the wealth of the producer nations opens up a potential new source of large-scale capital assistance for development," almost as though they were the new Robin Hoods for the poor. Seventh and finally, Kissinger declared that the ultimate goal of all should be to create a framework within which producers and consumers could accommodate their differences and reconcile their "needs and aspirations."

He did not forbear to combine this pitch for producer-consumer cooperation with a warning that "excessively high prices are already calling forth massive investments in alternative energy sources, which raises the prospect of lower prices and shrunken export markets for the producers of the future."

Enlightened self-interest, Kissinger held, should imply a

"just price," which sounded like a rather unfamiliar moral or even medieval concept. However, Kissinger's concept of justice was not intended to call for sacrifice by the oil producers or oil companies, because "stable oil earnings, at just prices, wisely invested and increasing by the principle of compound interest, will be available as a long-term source of income."

The oil producers, on hearing Kissinger, faced a difficult intellectual and financial problem. Should they listen to Kissinger's siren song of producer-consumer cooperation? Or should they take the money and run?

They decided to take the money and run.

INFLATION AND CONTRACTION

The fantastic transfer of hundreds of billions of dollars to the oil-producing countries created an unprecedented shock for the world economy. That shock was, paradoxically, both inflationary and contractionary. The huge increase in oil prices and payments worsened inflation in the industrial world by increasing both living costs and costs of production. It put powerful pressure, both direct and indirect, upon the industrial and developing countries to increase their export prices in order to cover their oil deficits. To be sure, high and rising *prices* would gradually bring out more oil supplies and curb demand, eventually putting downward pressure on oil prices.

But there would be intense strains in the West before that time arrived. The enormous transfer of funds to the oil producers threatened to choke off consumption and productive investment in the industrial countries, and to cause even more devastating economic and financial hardships in the developing countries. The buildup of oil-producer holdings, and the huge deficits in importing countries that were their counterpart, could cause a collapse of the world monetary system.

It was as though the King of Saudi Arabia, the Shah of Iran, Colonel Qaddafi of Libya, and the others had levied an annual tax of $100 billion a year upon the rest of the world. Such a tax increase, as modern economic theory teaches us, would have a contractionary effect on national economies unless the money collected was put back into the economies from which it was taken in the form of expenditures on consumer goods or capital goods. If the major share of the "oil taxes" was not respent or reinvested in production, it would choke off output and income in the oil-importing countries. Some nations—those that were the best investment bets—would receive substantial shares of the oil money back; that would be true for the United States, West Germany, and Japan. But others, those with the weakest payments positions and the worst inflations, would have to borrow massively to stay afloat; and that would be true for Mexico, Brazil, Argentina, and the other ambitious developing countries.

The nations of the West could fall, as world markets contracted, into economic warfare, each struggling to reduce its own deficit by excluding foreign-made goods or depreciating its own currency. For those nations caught with the worst deficits, there would be a severe risk of defaults on their foreign borrowings. Once again, as in 1929–31, the world appeared to be facing the danger of an international liquidity crisis—the inability of nations to pay their bills. Such a crisis, if it hit a few countries simultaneously, could race like greased lightning through the entire world financial system and bring on a global collapse.

But the current situation was vastly different from that which followed the collapse of the world monetary system in 1931, which turned the 1929–31 recession into the worst depression in history. That depression was intensified by a massive deflation. This time massive inflation loomed. For, with the breakdown of Bretton Woods, a monetary system pegged to the dollar at $35 for an ounce of gold, an enormous increase in national monetary reserves resulted from the soaring price of gold and the accumulation of huge amounts of dollars.

So inflation and contraction occurred simultaneously.

Chapter

5

THE QUIET CRASH

As monetary discipline eroded in the early 1970s, fear of inflation created a foul mood of apprehension in the business and financial world. Ashby Bladen, the senior vice president for investments of the Guardian Life Insurance Company of America, observed during the last days of the Nixon Administration: "We have now reached a point at which our economy could not support the existing debt structure if its real burden were not being steadily reduced by accelerating inflation. In hard, practical terms, this means that any significant reduction in the availability of credit is likely to produce massive bankruptcies of overextended people and businesses, leading to a deflationary collapse."

Bladen thought the crash was bound to come, because, given

the existing rate of inflation and the enormous accumulation of debt to finance it, a return to either price stability or financial stability without an intervening crash "appears to me to be practically impossible." The longer the crash was postponed by continuing the inflationary process of excessive credit expansion, he said, the worse it would be when it did come.

In the post-Watergate mood of national disillusion, some members of the financial community were speaking out with unwonted candor. "We might as well be realistic," said A. W. Clausen, president of the largest bank in the country, the Bank of America. "We're dealing with double-digit inflation. No government anywhere is going to clamp down on fiscal and monetary policy to the degree necessary to root inflation of that order out of the economy. And the inflation problem is now so pervasive that no nation can hope to overcome it alone."

Clausen suggested that was the reason why Milton Friedman "is talking up the Brazilian indexing system" of linking wages, bond yields, and other forms of income to the rate of inflation. "He is saying: If we can't cure inflation, we'll have to learn to live with it."

But Clausen himself proposed something else: measures to increase production to catch up with and get ahead of demand—an early declaration of "supply-side" economics. And since he appeared to distrust the conventional economists, he proposed a national economic commission to be composed of the "national leadership," broadly conceived. His commission would "mobilize the leadership of government, business, labor, consumers, the financial community, and other interests and bring them together in a sort of supra-government council—a summit commission representing all the interests that would have to agree in order to put a new economic policy into effect."

The President of the United States would be on the economic commission, together with members of Congress, so that it would "accept political responsibility for putting its findings into practice." But what sort of findings those would be Clausen declined to say. All he seemed sure of was that "we have reached a critical juncture. We must either stop inflation or reconcile ourselves to living with its consequences, which include the ever-present threat of a serious recession."

Should the nation continue to ride the tiger of inflation? Clausen seemed to be saying: Go on riding him, but try to slow him down. Bladen seemed to be saying: Jump off now before he grows hungrier and uncontrollable.

The Federal Reserve under Arthur F. Burns spoke in dolorous tones. It talked about the need to stop inflation now, no matter what the shock, while continuing to supply ample reserves to the banking system. The Fed appeared to be pursuing the doctrine of Walter Bagehot, the great nineteenth-century editor of *The Economist,* who warned in his book *Lombard Street* that a financial panic was sure to be caused if the banks' reserves were allowed to fall too low. "At every moment there is a certain minimum," Bagehot wrote, "which I call the 'apprehension minimum,' below which the reserve cannot fall without great risk of diffused fear; and by this I do not mean absolute panic, but only a vague fright and timorousness which spreads itself instantly, and as if by magic, over the public mind. Such seasons of incipient alarm are exceedingly dangerous because they beget the calamities they dread. What is most feared at such moments of susceptibility is the destruction of credit; and if any grave failure or bad event happens at such moments the public fancy seizes on it."

Therefore, banks' reserves should never be allowed to fall below or even get too close to the "apprehension minimum" lest some accident bring on the evil that is feared.

The Federal Reserve also followed the Bagehotian principle that in times of incipient crisis the central bank should lend without limit to American banking institutions in serious trouble. Internationally, however, it was far from clear that governments and central banks were willing and able to lend without limit to endangered institutions or nations.

AN ATTENDANT LORD

A rising star of the Nixon Administration little noticed by the general public was Paul A. Volcker, the Under Secretary of the Treasury for Monetary Affairs, who by the spring of 1974 was growing increasingly uncomfortable about staying on in an Administration he found morally reprehensible.

Volcker had carried the working responsibility for managing the United States' badly strained monetary relations with other countries and striving to patch up and then reform the tottering world monetary system under President Nixon's three Secretaries of the Treasury—David M. Kennedy, John B. Connally, and George P. Shultz. A less homogeneous trio could scarcely be imagined: a wary white-haired Mormon banker and former Federal bureaucrat; a tough, charismatic Texas politician with an eye on the White House; and a quiet, stubborn academic of conservative Friedmanian views.

Serving under those chiefs, Volcker could say, with T. S. Eliot's J. Alfred Prufrock,

> No! I am not Prince Hamlet, nor was meant to be;
> Am an attendant lord, one that will do
> To swell a progress, start a scene or two,
> Advise the prince; no doubt, an easy tool,
> Deferential, glad to be of use,
> Politic, cautious, and meticulous.

Volcker, a very experienced, hardheaded economist, operator, and negotiator, always shrank from extremes of ideology—or even of economic logic—as a skeptic about all theory who would use a theory only as it served his pragmatic purpose. In a valedictory address he delivered in late May 1974 at Pepperdine University in Malibu, California, shortly before he left government, Volcker characteristically rejected two sharply contrasting views about the world monetary system, which he held to be in serious danger.

The first extreme view, he said, is that "we have in fact achieved nothing since the breakup of the Bretton Woods monetary system. Monetary reform is a failure and should be politely buried. Let's wait awhile and start again." This view, he said, is held by those who associate monetary order only with fixed exchange rates and was "somewhat inaccurately" labeled the "Continental European view."

The other extreme, he said, "is a school which says the problem has been solved. Despite the best (or worst) efforts of the finance ministers and central bankers, we are happily floating. That's the way the world should be organized, and we only need a little dressing up around the edges." He suggested that this represented the "American academic view."

What the two views have in common, said Volcker, is that the "reform efforts upon which I have been engaged have been irrelevant." Dropping the public vagueness and confusing rhetoric, of which he is one of the greatest masters since Dwight D. Eisenhower, Volcker said: "Both views are wrong. Both lead to a dead end. The first is a counsel of despair. If we can't have it all, we have nothing, and each is free to go his own way. The second fails to recognize the problems of the present system—the tendency toward less cohesion, rather than more." What he was most concerned about as he left office was "the problem of the world-fragmenting tendencies, political and economic."

He insisted that the International Monetary Fund, severely shaken when the Nixon Administration suspended the convertibility of the dollar into gold in 1971, needed to be significantly strengthened. He said plans for such a strengthening were well under way and would soon be approved by the "Committee of Twenty" leading financial nations. That committee, he said, would be replaced by a Council of Ministers of national governments that would supervise the functioning of the system and give the I.M.F. "more political clout."

The Committee of Twenty had moved a long way, he disclosed, toward agreeing on rules for changing exchange rates;

the system would be neither rigidly fixed nor freely floating but would depend on managed, flexible exchange rates through international cooperation. "It's an illusion that we can build a monetary system that insulates us from the need to cooperate with the rest of the world," he said. "We need rules—rules for floating and rules for an open trading system."

Volcker also thought it an illusion to think the United States alone could run the show; there needed to be a more equal relationship between the United States and others in the monetary system. "Europe collectively," he said, "is now almost equal to the United States, and Japan is a great financial power, too. The developing countries need to be respected."

The pressing problems of the system, greatly intensified by the Arab oil-price squeeze, could not be solved "by a new gadget here and there." He repeated the United States view that the monetary system should move away from both gold and national currencies, and made a plea for a redefined Special Drawing Right as the key form of international money.

He warned that the oil crisis could have "severe repercussions on a group of countries who have no way to pay for oil without facing starvation and the wreckage of their economic development programs." The West could not ignore their plight; the time had passed when the developing countries could be regarded as "way out in left or right field" from the standpoint of their importance to world monetary and economic stability.

"We are caught in midstream by vast new problems—oil and inflation—before some important issues have been resolved," he said. Anything like the present rate of rapid world inflation could not be handled within a "well-ordered" system. That was why new rules were needed, rules that "ordinary" government ministers and their agents could follow. The rules would have to make economic sense by respecting market realities and promoting competition and make political sense by being even-handed and treating countries equally. They would need to be simple and workable.

Volcker was calling for rejection of both the "benign neglect" that had captivated the free floaters of the Nixon Administration and also of the rough, abrasive nationalism that had marked the Connally era at the United States Treasury.

THE DISMAL, GUILTY SCIENTISTS

But nothing came of Volcker's and the Committee of Twenty's efforts to reform the international monetary system. Chaos persisted in the financial markets, and some skeptics now felt that there was no hope for reforming the monetary system in the existing state of inflationary turbulence and diminished confidence in the dollar. Nicholas L. Deak, president of Deak & Company, the nation's oldest and largest currency-exchange firm, said: "Fixed rates are an illusion when there is no confidence in world monetary markets. Striving for fixed rates, under present conditions, only tends to focus even more attention on the problem. And this, in the past, has produced even wider fluctuations, due to panic." Deak thought it "obvious" that "we are going to have a floating currency system until such time as we find one currency with solid backing to act as an anchor."

The economists, never the jolliest of people, were more dismal than usual, and guilt-ridden to boot. They were certainly in the White House doghouse. Nixon had boxed the compass of contemporary economic theory. He had successively been a disciple of Milton Friedman's monetarism, as a means of checking inflation; of John Maynard Keynes's fiscalism, proclaiming "I am now a Keynesian" when the cost in unemployment of slowing down inflation had proved too high to suit his political goals; of John Kenneth Galbraith's wage-price controls as a means of coupling growth stimulus with anti-inflation restraint; of Paul A. Samuelson's dollar devaluation as a spur to exports; of Friedman's and Samuelson's floating exchange rates as the key to balance-of-payments equilibrium;

and eventually back to Adam Smith's laissez-faire and the pre-Keynesian Republican old-time religion of cutting government spending and balancing budgets.

Had the fault been in the execution of national policy or in the economic theories on which policy was based? At every turn different economists—depending on which theory was receiving a workout at the White House—put the blame on the politicians for not holding to a line long enough to test it, but dropping it as soon as the going got rough. That was the argument of Friedman's disciples, who contended that slow growth of the money supply was well on the way to stopping inflation when Nixon switched to his New Economic Policy of August 1971, mixing price controls, fiscal stimulus, and dollar devaluation.

But economic theories could operate only through the political process, and it appeared that, with the advance of economic knowledge on how to fight depression and mass unemployment, the industrial societies had all acquired an inflationary bias that could not be extirpated without more pain than those societies were willing to endure. "We live in the Age After Keynes," said Paul Samuelson, America's first Nobel laureate in economics. "Electorates all over the world have eaten of the fruit of the tree of modern economic knowledge, and there is no going back to an earlier age." He himself did not want to go back, because he regarded unemployment and depression as worse evils than inflation. But he recognized that "for anyone nostalgic for an era in which prices are reasonably stable and in which the purchasing power of money might even rise under the impact of cost-reducing technical change, the present general diagnosis may be profoundly pessimistic."

Monetarism, the would-be antidote to the inflationary bias of Keynesian policy, appeared to be faring little better in the real world: Either the growth of the money supply had to be held so tight to stop inflation that it would dump the economy into recession or depression, or it would be too loose to prevent inflation. Henry Kaufman, the seer of Salomon Brothers, contended at a monetary conference in London in June 1974 that monetarism, like Keynesianism, had an inflationary bias, leading to an overextension of credit, soaring interest rates, and the draining of funds from thrift institutions into commercial banks. He held that "attempts at monetarism were a convenient vehicle for our central bank to shift to a technical approach as a way of escaping some of its basic responsibilities as the inflation took hold in recent years."

Kaufman himself favored intervention by the Federal Reserve to keep credit expansion reasonable. He wanted the Fed to use moral suasion, issue open letters of warning of disciplinary action to the banks if they overlent at home or abroad, impose interest-rate ceilings and limits on housing and consumer finance, together with other forms of credit rationing, as the central bank once did. He thought the removal of ceilings on commercial banks' negotiated certificates of deposit, which the monetarists had favored, had helped to push interest rates sky high.

Nor had floating exchange rates yet displayed the symmetrical effect advertised by many economists of checking both inflation and deflation. Conceivably, one day they would arrest world inflation by checking the outflow of dollars from the United States to the reserves of central banks all over the world. Immediately, however, as the dollar floated downward, the world inflation problem had not lessened and American inflation had intensified. One could see this not only in the soaring gold price but in many specific products; for instance, as the dollar depreciated, United States beef was a terrific bargain for foreigners. Meat brokers rushed in and bought American beef until the price rose to the level of beef prices in other countries. But when higher beef prices resulted in greater supplies, and beef prices began falling, the Nixon Administration moved to buy up surplus beef to help the American cattle industry. That is how the modern "ratchet" of government works to keep prices from falling but not from rising.

THE NEW STEADINESS

With the securities markets in a state of desperation over the problems of the American and world economies, President Nixon's ability to conduct economic policy had been thrown into doubt. At the end of July 1974, the action by the House Judiciary Committee in voting articles of impeachment against the President, charging violation of his Constitutional oath, misuse of government agencies, obstruction of justice, and refusal to honor the committee's subpoenas, appeared to assure that the crisis of the Presidency would last for months—unless Nixon decided to resign or step aside. Senator William Proxmire of Wisconsin indeed suggested that, under the 25th Amendment to the Constitution, Nixon ought to take a leave of absence to concentrate on his impeachment defense, thereby permitting Vice President Gerald Ford to deal with the nation's problems as acting President.

But Nixon's new White House economic counselor, Kenneth Rush, a former president of Union Carbide whom Nixon had known as a Duke University law professor, rejected the idea, saying that Nixon was spending "a vast amount of time" on economic matters and that anybody else stepping into the job would only bring on uncertainty. Actually, the President's new economic line—a "steady as you go" policy, which took its name from Treasury Secretary George Shultz's dictum—was designed to minimize Nixon's policy-making activities.

The primary emphasis in checking inflation would be on monetary policy—the province of Arthur Burns and the Federal Reserve System. To the extent that there was an acting President for economic policy, it looked more likely to be Burns than Ford. Burns had become the prime exponent of the "old-time religion" of slow monetary growth and balanced budgets, to be achieved mainly by budget-cutting rather than tax-raising. Burns, now a stern foe of excessive growth of the money supply, declared that an annual growth rate of even 6 percent was too high if inflation was to be stopped.

But consumer prices were climbing at an annual rate of more than 12 percent—the first double-digit rate of inflation in the United States since the First World War. And if monetary growth were held below 6 percent—actually it was running at a rate of 5.2 percent—then either inflation would have to be cut drastically or real output would have to fall sharply, or there would be some combination of both.

The Administration was counting on keeping any rise of unemployment in 1974 below 6 percent; at midyear the jobless rate was running at 5.2 percent, but Nixon knew the rate was likely to rise a bit as the Fed tried to slow the inflation. In a television address Nixon said, "Chairman Burns has assured me of the Federal Reserve's intention to avoid extremes of restriction in the effort to conduct an effective anti-inflationary monetary policy—an effort which every American should endorse." Nixon gave his assurance that there would be "no credit crunch in which the money for essential economic activity becomes unavailable." But building-trades workers were gathering to protest high interest rates, which they saw as depriving them of their jobs. And their protests were reinforced by those of building contractors and thrift institutions, alarmed about the slump in housing construction, which was declining from more than 2 million new units started in 1973 to 1.3 million in 1974.

President Nixon showed no sign of bringing pressure on Burns and the Fed to force down interest rates. He had accepted the now conventional view of the monetarists that "the best way to reduce interest rates is to reduce inflation," as Walter B. Wriston, chairman of Citicorp, a confirmed monetarist, put it. Wriston said he wanted to allow thrift institutions to diversify their portfolios to compete for deposit funds more effectively against the commercial banks; he would also remove legal ceilings on mortgage rates to encourage more financial institutions to enter the housing market. He felt that the market could take far better care of meeting social priorities than could government. He contended that, in a time of high and variable inflation, variable-rate mortgages "more in tune with market rates" would relieve many of the cyclical problems of builders, home buyers, and institutions with large mortgage portfolios.

Such thinking appeared to be more in line with President Nixon's own renewed dedication to reducing the role of government. He wanted "the trade-offs between industrial production and government requirements for environmental protection and safety to be re-evaluated." Nixon made clear that he had no intention of adopting price and wage controls again. However, he had decided to do a certain amount of "jawboning" of business and labor, and was urging them to "act responsibly." That was a shift from his original position of January 1969, when on taking office he had explicitly said he would not urge them to restrain prices or wages, because "much as these men might personally want to do what is in the best interest of the nation, they have to be guided by the interests of the organizations that they represent."

Nixon also decided to jawbone consumers, urging them to save more by reducing their personal consumption by 1.5 percent. Since the savings rate had got up to more than 8 percent, some economists feared that if consumers did what Nixon was asking, it would only deepen the steep 1974 slump.

The President had now surrounded himself with extremely conservative and noninterventionist economists and businessmen. Alan Greenspan, president of the economic advisory firm Townsend-Greenspan and Nixon's choice to succeed Herbert Stein as chairman of his Council of Economic Advisers, was known as a disciple of the libertarian philosopher Ayn Rand. And William E. Simon, an impassioned right-winger and former partner of Salomon Brothers, succeeded George Shultz as Secretary of the Treasury.

A kind of caretaker government of businessmen appeared to be in place to deal with economic policy during the impeachment ordeal. However, a Congress absorbed in the impeachment crisis was unwilling to accept leadership from Nixon on economic policy—or anything else. And despite the heavy conservative cast of the beleaguered Nixon Administration, much of the business and financial community appeared to have decided that it had more to lose than to gain from Nixon's continuation in office. Its mood as the summer wore on, and as the inflation worsened, was to wish the ordeal would end quickly.

On August 9, 1974, Richard Milhous Nixon resigned, saying he hoped his departure would "start a process of healing that is so desperately needed in America." On August 10, Gerald Rudolph Ford became the 38th President of the United States, declaring that "our long national nightmare is over."

A Bleak Dawn

But on the financial front, Wall Street was not convinced. In the first dozen trading sessions after Ford took over the White House, the Dow Jones industrial average of prices on the New York Stock Exchange fell almost 100 points. In only one session—the day Ford chose Nelson Rockefeller as his Vice President—did the market manage to post a slight gain. The Dow had fallen below 700, having lost over a third of its value since soon after Nixon's landslide victory over George McGovern in 1972, and was at its lowest level in four years.

This was the Quiet Crash. And a long Quasi-Depression followed it. History never repeats, but it has its analogues.

Chapter
6

"WHIP INFLATION NOW!"

"We are all soldiers in a war against brutal inflation," said President Ford shortly after taking office. He promptly called for a "summit" conference of American leaders and economists to help him map strategy on how to win that war. On the way to the summit there would be various "foothill" conferences with assorted experts—on business and manufacturing, natural resources and recreation, health and welfare, banking and finance, housing, transportation, state and local government, and on the science of economics, a discipline whose members had grown more lugubrious than ever in the midst of roaring inflation and slumping output and employment.

Was this "summit" concept a peculiarly American brand of nonsense? The Ford Administration's first grand venture in news management? A rally to lift the spirits of the people?

Would it produce the greatest confusion of voices and instructions—the President said he would be there "to listen"—since the Tower of Babel? Would the new Administration do just what it intended to do anyhow? The answer to all those questions was yes.

President Ford and his aides did not wait for the summit to proclaim their own doctrines. Their basic line was that money should be held tight and the Federal budget cut to stop inflation. Further, the people should be rallied to the cause. The Administration's great new slogan was "Whip Inflation Now!" or "WIN!"

But this would be a voluntary campaign. The President advised Congress "emphatically" that he did not intend to ask for either standby or mandatory wage and price controls, although he did indulge in some mild coaxing of business and labor not to increase their prices or wages too much. He told General Motors he was "disappointed" over its nearly 10 percent increase in prices of cars and trucks, in the face of slumping sales and rising competition from abroad; G.M. decided to increase its prices only 8.6 percent in response to the President's disappointment.

Though the economy was suffering from both unemployment and inflation, the President, like the good conservative that he was, decided that inflation was "public enemy number one." There were strong grounds for his stress. Consumer prices had risen at an annual rate of 12 percent and wholesale prices at 20 percent during the first half of 1974. In the three months just before Ford entered the White House, wholesale prices had soared at an annual rate of 37 percent, led by skyrocketing oil prices.

But as grave as the inflation problem was, it was not the only worry. Unemployment was moving up. Nationally, the rate of unemployment in August was still only 5.4 percent, but in Detroit it was 9.3 percent, in Buffalo 9.4 percent, in Jersey City 9.5 percent. Tight money, the Ford Administration's chosen weapon against inflation, seemed sure to drive the jobless rate higher all over the country.

Whether unemployment was regarded (especially by conservatives) as the necessary consequence of moving to sound monetary policies for checking inflation or (especially by liberals) as the unfair or cruel result of taking too narrow an approach to solving the problem of "stagflation," rising unemployment seemed sure to intensify the feelings of lower-income groups and minorities that they were getting the dirty end of the stick.

Some conservatives—such as Professor Martin Feldstein of Harvard—thought there simply was no way to root inflation out of the system except by holding the economy well below its full-employment level for a string of years, perhaps half a dozen, perhaps longer.

Reducing inflation by squeezing down the growth rate might take several years. On "optimistic" assumptions of how quickly slow growth would pull down the rate of wage and price gains, Professor James Tobin of Yale estimated that unemployment would rise to a level of about 7 percent by the spring of 1978. On more pessimistic assumptions, Tobin estimated in the fall of 1974 that unemployment would crawl upward for the next eight years, reaching a level of 9 percent in 1983 before turning down. (The jobless rate actually reached a peak of 10.8 percent in December 1982.)

Attempts to fight inflation by cutting the Federal budget would also worsen social inequities if those members of the Ford Administration who favored cuts in social expenditures had their way. Trimming payments for health, education, manpower training, low-income housing, local transportation, food stamps, and so on might help to balance the budget but only by transferring the burden of slowing inflation to lower-income groups.

But the burden of inflation did not fall on the poor alone. The securities markets had taken a terrible beating from the combination of inflation and climbing interest rates. Indeed, the highest interest rates in this century had caused a precipitous fall in the stock market; the shares of just eight of the nation's leading companies—I.B.M., General Motors, General

Electric, A.T.&T., Avon Products, Polaroid, Xerox, and Sears Roebuck—had lost $80 billion of their value from their highs of 1973. Many lesser stocks had lost 80 to 90 percent of their value. The assets of many pension funds, foundations, banks, and individual investors had plummeted. The cash position of many corporations was severely strained.

The most ominous aspect of the economic crisis as it emerged in 1974 was that it was worldwide. Lester R. Brown of the Overseas Development Council warned: "The need to develop global approaches to the new worldwide problems arising from scarcity in the marketplace is now urgent. The shift from traditional buyers' market to global sellers' market for a lengthening list of commodities is bringing a host of far-reaching changes, many of which are still only remotely sensed. This new phenomenon will have profound implications for global politics of the last quarter of this century." The most tragic of those shortages was food, with a worldwide drought threatening millions in Africa and Asia with starvation. And the most economically and financially dangerous was the contrived scarcity of oil, which simultaneously intensified the pressures of inflation and depression, an unprecedented phenomenon.

THE OLD-TIME RELIGION

Facing these complexities, President Ford reverted to the simplicities of the old-time Republican religion: Cut government spending, balance the budget, and don't interfere in the private economy.

In taking that course, he had the strong encouragement of his principal economic advisers—Secretary of the Treasury William E. Simon; Arthur F. Burns, chairman of the Federal Reserve Board; and Alan Greenspan, chairman of the Council of Economic Advisers. All three had been appointed by President Nixon.

Ford took a special liking to Greenspan, who knew how to

talk as confidentially to the President as though he were a corporate client and who, in his polysyllabic way, could make the most familiar articles of the conservative faith sound sophisticated, full of market savvy, and brand-new. "I think we have got to the point where our major problem is the total impact on credit markets of Federal Government direct and indirect borrowings," he said, stressing his view that the answer to the credit squeeze was to cut the Federal budget.

But Greenspan was no Pollyanna. He made no secret of his worries about the financial dangers facing both the United States and the world economy. One danger, he said, was of a "world financial crisis following the failures of one or more of the major Eurocurrency banks as a result of borrowers in oil-importing countries defaulting on their loans." A second danger, he warned, was that the oil-importing countries would "attempt to avert the consequences of the shift in real income implied by the dramatic change in oil prices and in the process exacerbate their already very difficult inflation problem."

On domestic policy, Greenspan was a devoted noninterventionist on wages and prices. He denied the power of large corporations or labor unions to cause inflation, holding that "market power" might affect the distribution of income but not the rate of inflation. He saw no evidence that labor or business monopoly power was growing.

Greenspan credited Arthur Burns with having been most instrumental in persuading him to come to Washington, despite what he called his "aversion to the political environment." As a conservative completely dedicated to free enterprise, Greenspan said he was against raising taxes to fight inflation; he did not wish to provide extra revenues that could ultimately be used by Congress to swell the size of the Federal Government.

However, he said he would also oppose liberals who called for tax cuts under existing circumstances to prevent recession and rising unemployment, because he regarded inflation as the more serious menace. Though worried about what he considered an inadequate flow of funds to business for capital investment, he felt that tax cuts on business would be unwise "in the context of budget-balancing."

His right-wing libertarian philosophy seemed balanced by political pragmatism, economic realism, and personal reasonableness, and even charm that won him a number of friends among the influential liberals, such as Arthur Okun, Charles Schultze, and Joseph Pechman at the Brookings Institution on Massachusetts Avenue in Washington—headquarters of the so-called government-in-exile of Democratic economists. Greenspan gained the liberals' respect by treating their ideas seriously whether he agreed with them or not; he later said that the most important thing he learned in Washington was that all important changes in government policy originated in academia. He displayed a grave respect for economic statistics, and never seemed to play fast and loose with them, however sad the message they conveyed. He was determined to rebuild public and professional respect for the Council of Economic Advisers, which he felt had run down during the Nixon years.

While he reveled in his professional friendships with the liberal economists and vowed that he would maintain them for the sake of his own enlightenment and professional integrity, he made friends on the right with Nixonians, Goldwaterites, gold bugs (Greenspan said he wanted gold ownership by Americans to be legalized immediately), and even with the Eastern Establishment Republicans.

But most of all he made a close friend and admirer of President Ford, and he helped to reinforce Ford's tendency to pursue a policy of laissez-faire, a free translation of which is "Leave the economy alone."

WASHINGTON VERSUS NEW YORK

When Ford succeeded Nixon, the political scene briefly brightened, but the economic scene darkened. Washington, the political capital, staged a joyous celebration, hailing Ford's simplicity, decency, honesty, and determination to unify his own party, to be kind to the Democrats, and to treat inflation as public enemy number one. But New York City, the nation's financial capital, sank into despondency, with the stock market the clearest indicator of despair.

What accounted for the difference? One explanation was that beauty or ugliness, hope or despair, is in the eye of the beholder, and that Washington and New York are two very different beholders. Washington is a one-industry town. Its business is government, and nothing makes its spirits rise like a new President. It can then speculate on who goes up, who goes down, who comes in, who goes out; and there are fresh opportunities for all who were in the doghouse with the past Administration—not just politicians but lawyers, journalists, hostesses, lobbyists—to make a new beginning. There is also fresh excitement over what will happen to policy, ideology, and the state of the nation, or at least of Georgetown, Wesley Heights, and environs.

But the business of New York is business. While Washington was wallowing in Watergate, New York was sloshing around in the economic mess. Inflation and high interest rates agonized Wall Street and raised fear of a major slump and huge financial losses. Washington's financial worries are always more remote and abstract. It can afford to be calm about the economy, because Washington plays with Other People's Money. New York tends to be more manic-depressive, because it plays with Its Own Money, with "real" money.

Washington thinks big, and vaguely, about gross national product, national income, employment, revenues, expenditures; but its own work goes on through depression and prosperity. New York not only thinks concretely about money, production, and jobs—it can sink concretely.

From the start of the Nixon Administration to the start of the Ford Administration, the nation added 5.3 million jobs, but New York City lost 247,000 jobs. The jobless rate in Washington, D.C., when Ford took office, was 4.3 percent—"full employment" by the economists' yardstick—but in New York the jobless rate was 7 percent. No matter how big the national debt, Washington would prosper; but New York City, awash in debt, could literally go bankrupt and have to lay off tens of thousands of workers and cut back heavily on police, fire, education, hospital, and other services.

Washington's economists never lose their jobs. This gives them a high degree of composure as they recommend policies for tightening up the money supply and cutting the national budget, although they realize full well this will increase the national unemployment rate; they may express sympathy mournfully over this outcome, but they can bravely endure it. In New York, by contrast, the stockbrokers, securities salesmen, clerks, and stenographers who labor in Wall Street lose their very own jobs when hard times come. From 1969 to the spring of 1974, employment in the New York securities industry dropped 28 percent—from 105,200 to 75,700. A small decline in the global perspective, but a painful one for those involved, and their friends and relations.

It was difficult for Wall Street to take a calm, high-minded, and philosophical attitude under the circumstances, especially in the face of billions of dollars of losses for partners and customers. Wall Street knew it was in a depression (when you lose your own job or money), but Washington was not even sure whether there was a recession (when somebody else loses his job or money).

New York is coarse and earthy. Washington is fond of rhetoric, particularly upbeat rhetoric. It likes slogans—New Deals, Fair Deals, New Frontiers, Great Societies, New American Revolutions, "Fords not Lincolns." New York lives on the bottom line.

Washington is provincial (despite the presence of Embassy Row); New York is cosmopolitan and international (even leaving the United Nations aside). New York directly feels the winds and storms that blow in from the Atlantic—or the Mediterranean and the Middle East. Washington looks westward and southward and northward to the 50 states that supply representatives, senators, politicians, bureaucrats, lobbyists, fixers, and the rest.

New York counts costs, knowing it must. Washington counts votes, translates these into appropriations or tax cuts, and then back into votes.

Washington is a small town; it sees and reacts to the big shots who live and work there. New York is a metropolis; it reacts to shadows on the wall—the mass media create the shadows. So Washington can be immediately bucked up by a new personality or an old friend—and Gerry Ford, an old friend, cheered it up. New York waited and wondered. It saw the economic fundamentals unchanged, the inflation continuing, profits slipping, recession developing, no matter what new political style or rhetoric was emerging. Washington was convinced the new mood mattered. New York was from Missouri and wanted to be shown.

THE PARDONER'S TALE

On September 8, President Ford granted former President Nixon an unconditional pardon for all Federal crimes that he had "committed or may have committed or taken part in" while in office. At his home in San Clemente, California, Nixon accepted the pardon, saying only that he could now see that he was "wrong in not acting more decisively and more forthrightly in dealing with Watergate."

Ford must have known his decision to grant Nixon a "full, free, and absolute" pardon would provoke some opposition and criticism. But he failed to anticipate what a great shock it would be, even to the business and financial community.

The pardon stirred cynicism about the Ford Presidency. When the familiar conservative Michigan politician succeeded Nixon, he had moved to put Watergate behind the nation—by his simple and modest style, his seeming openness to outside advice, by his homespun gravity and unaffectedness. There was hope that the Nixon "bombs" would be a thing of the past now that the White House was in the care of plain old Gerry Ford. The pardon was another Nixon bomb, and Ford never entirely recovered from it.

THE HIGH-OIL-PRICE STRATEGY

The Ford Administration developed a new plan for dealing with OPEC: to accept the high oil price the cartel had established. The plan was disclosed on November 24, 1974, in a forum at Yale University by Thomas O. Enders, Assistant Secretary of State for Economic and Business Affairs. Enders had earlier been the chief architect of Secretary of State Kissinger's energy policy for establishing the International Energy Agency and setting up a $25 billion fund of the industrial nations for recycling Petrodollars.

The new plan for energy was based on a report titled "Project Independence" of the Federal Energy Agency. That report set forth two basic patterns that would result from either (a) accepting the then existing $11 price in the world market or (b) pressing for an early reduction in the world oil price to $7 a barrel. The F.E.A. data indicated that the growth of domestic production would be much faster at $11 than $7 and that there would be a far greater drag on the growth of oil consumption. By 1985, at the $11 price, the study forecast, the expanded supply of oil plus the expanded output of coal and nuclear energy could eliminate the need for imported oil in the United States.

But at the $7 price, it said, the gap could widen to about 13 million barrels a day, or more than half of all of the United States' petroleum needs. The American dependence, and probably foreign dependence, would thus increase at the lower price.

The Enders speech at Yale was startling against the background of repeated declarations of high American officials that OPEC nations must reduce their exorbitantly high prices; it meant that the United States was now founding its policy on the $11 "real" price—which it assumed would continue to rise step by step with other goods if world inflation continued.

Without following the Project Independence report slavishly, Enders said the high oil prices had started a world boom in oil production. "Substantial finds of oil have been reported from Mexico, Peru, China, Indonesia," he said, "and the wave of exploration is just beginning." He estimated that the finds already made represented the possibility of new production a few years from now of more than 10 million barrels a day— "and more will follow."

OPEC members would try to sustain the high price by cutting their production as more world output came on stream. OPEC by 1974 was producing at less than three-quarters of capacity, said Enders, and how long they could sustain the existing price would depend on how fast the world market for oil developed. Cuts in consumption by the United States and other major users in response to the high price would be crucial to breaking the oil cartel, if it were to be broken.

Enders thought the cartel could fall apart if demand was restrained and new production from non-OPEC producers was brought to market. Negotiation of the required cutbacks in production by OPEC would become more and more difficult. "First clandestine, then open violation of production quotas would occur," he said. "Ultimately all efforts to sustain the artificial price would collapse."

Paradoxically, the United States was worried that such a downward break in world oil prices could come too soon and would be devastating for American and other Western investment in the development of alternative energy sources, which were being launched on the assumption that the "real" $11 oil price would continue.

What was important, Enders argued, was that all major oil companies adopt policies having the effect of creating stable investment expectations at a level of return roughly equivalent to present oil prices. He wanted an international agreement "to embody this fundamental decision."

In informal conversation with me, Enders said there was a catch-22 in the American position: It was designed to reduce Western dependence on foreign oil and ultimately break the OPEC oil price, but when the oil price finally came down, the United States and its partners would hold up their own oil prices to protect high-cost domestic production.

In other words—for the sake of illustration—if the world oil price dropped to $5 a barrel before the Western oil coalition (which might be called anti-OPEC) was ready, the United States and its partners would continue to pay $11 to their domestic producers. Foreign oil would then enter the United States only at about the $11 price, with the United States collecting the $6 difference, whether through a tariff, a government oil-importing agency, or some other device.

As the price for foreign oil declined—and Enders made clear that he expected it to come down substantially by 1985—the United States and its partners would move toward a two-tier structure for energy: "One assures the consuming countries their desired degree of independence; the other balances a constant demand and growing supply for imported oil at prices that diminished, or even reversed, the accumulation of assets by producers."

And when this happened, much of the investment now undertaken in energy in the United States and elsewhere would no longer be viable; it would either have to be protected against low prices elsewhere, said Enders, or the United States and others would have to "succumb again to the comforts and vulnerabilities of reliance on cheap imported oil."

Did this plan make sense? Or was it a brutally expensive plan for first stimulating and then protecting domestic oil and other energy producers?

J. K. Jamieson, chairman of the board of Exxon, found the Kissinger-Enders plan "overoptimistic." He said Enders and

the Federal Energy Agency had overestimated future oil production in this country on several counts. For instance, he said,
the F.E.A. had expected far too much from secondary and tertiary oil recovery. "All fields are already under secondary recovery," he said, "and there is no current technology for
tertiary recovery that would not require energy inputs in excess
of the energy output." Jamieson also thought the United States
Government had been overoptimistic on nuclear power and
other energy sources.

Professor James Tobin of Yale raised questions about the
cost of the program and whether it was the most economic way
either to protect United States oil supplies or to deal with the
problem of the transfer of so much wealth to the OPEC countries. He contended that there might be cheaper ways to "buy
insurance," such as through increased storage or standby production capacity.

The political feasibility of the Kissinger-Enders plan was
also questionable. Other Western nations might refuse to go
along, and if the United States did succeed in driving down the
world oil price, those who stayed outside the oil-price-fixing
deal would have a clear cost advantage in production and
competition in world trade—in effect, a free ride resulting from
the sacrifices of "anti-OPEC."

The steadily mounting flow of arms to the Middle East—
from the United States, France, Britain, and others—to pay for
oil imports was one aspect of the problem to which Enders did
not address himself. Nor did he address the dangers to the
Western nations of another oil-price explosion that might result from political instability or revolution in a country like
Iran.

Political and military troubles were to exacerbate the world's
economic troubles for years to come and drive the oil price
higher than anyone, including Kissinger and Enders, expected.
Soaring oil prices did eventually produce a glut in the world oil
market, pushing the price down. But for the longer run,
America's failure to develop a stronger energy policy left it
vulnerable to future threats from the Middle East.

Ford asked little of the country, and seemed to realize it. "I think the American people are ready to make more sacrifices than maybe the Congress and even the executive branch including the President, believe they will," he told reporters. Yet moments later he was citing a public-opinion poll showing a huge majority agreeing with his opposition to a 20-cent-per-gallon gasoline tax. "If 81 percent of the people agree with me and don't agree with the various people who are advocating this," he said, "I think I'm on pretty solid ground."

When the country needed leadership, Ford offered followership.

Chapter
7

FEARS OF COLLAPSE

Economists were in a state of acute anxiety over the strange mixture of inflation and economic stagnation, for which a new term was coined: "stagflation." Robert Triffin of Yale preferred his own term, "infession"—inflation-cum-recession—and I introduced "slumpflation." But "stagflation" prevailed.

Economists of the left put their major stress on the disease on the first part of it, the stagnation and rising unemployment; economists of the right stressed the second part, inflation. Henry Wallich, a conservative member of the Federal Reserve Board, said he feared an inflationary climax. Rates of inflation, he said, had been spiraling upward from cycle to cycle, and if monetary policy did not put a stop to the cycle, it would swirl out of control. The danger, he thought, was greater than most people realized: The capitalist system was being undermined by inflationary measures meant to cure slumps. "The end," said Wallich, "is illiquidity and insolvency, as we have already seen in the case of utilities and real estate trusts." Inflation was making the entire society dependent on government; this would lead to "state capitalism."

In the spring of 1975 I went to Europe to take soundings. Lionel Robbins—Lord Robbins, chancellor of Stirling University and a celebrated economist of the older generation—said he grieved for Britain, "once so stable, now dominated by ideas that have gone soft and silly." He said the world was already in a depression, but of a quite different kind from the last great one. The Keynesian Revolution, in breeding inflation, had augmented the power of the labor unions. Robbins feared a worsening political crisis not only in Britain but throughout the world. He thought it was already being acted out. One aspect of it, he said, was the shift of wealth and power to the Middle East. Another was the rising strength of the Communists. The two trends, he said, were coming together; the Soviet Union was playing on the Arabs' anti-Israeli animosity to strengthen their own power in the Middle East.

THE THREAT FROM THE RIGHT

I went to Austria to interview Bruno Kreisky, Austria's Jewish chancellor and leader of his country's Socialist Party. Kreisky was trying to play the role of mediator between the Arabs and the Europeans. He told me, as we talked in a tavern in Lech in the Austrian Alps, that his greatest worry was of a huge political shift to the right in Europe—a shift that would be brought on by the combination of inflation and unemployment. He said both problems needed to be attacked, not one or the other. Political leaders in the West, he contended, were yielding to heavy pressures of the conservative press and business leaders to make inflation the dominant worry. As they always did, the conservatives feared inflation as the real threat to the political and social order, and to their own position and power.

By this time, Kreisky said, they were using the double weapons of inflation and unemployment to beat the left. They could claim, with some plausibility, that it was the conservatives, the business interests, who were the providers of jobs, not the Socialists or the trade unions. The real danger today, as in the 1930s, he thought, was that the world economy, weakened first by inflation and then by the rising unemployment, had entered the downphase of a "long cycle," one of those deep 50-year cycles described by the Russian economist Nikolai Kondratieff.[1] Weak economic policies could never cure such a cycle in the West, he said. His own continent had entered a phase where basic structural change was needed to create conditions for economic growth, the only solvent for worsening political tensions.

Expanding on that theme, Hannes Androsch, then Austria's Finance Minister and Vice Chancellor, said Europe needed to reorient its production away from construction, autos, textiles, and other industries suffering from overcapacity. He wanted greater investment in mass transportation, education, energy, and other "post-industrial" fields.

Both Kreisky and Androsch[2] also believed that Europe would have to reorient its trade policies toward third world and OPEC countries. He said OPEC countries were more will-

[1] See Nikolai Kondratieff, *The Long Wage Cycle* (New York: Richardson & Snyder, 1984). Kondratieff, who died in one of Stalin's prison camps, held that there were long waves of economic fluctuations in prices, production, and trade, lasting 50 to 60 years. He believed these cycles were inherent in the nature of capitalism and that wars and revolutions, the opening of new markets, major technological innovations, were not random events but part of the rhythm of capitalism.

[2] On December 11, 1980, Androsch, in the midst of public criticism of his private business activities while Austrian Finance Minister, resigned from the Kreisky Government to become a director of Creditanstalt-Bankverein. In 1982, he became director general and board chairman of Creditanstalt, the bank whose failure in 1931 triggered the collapse of the international banking system.

ing to enter into long-range investment and trade deals than Western countries, who were afraid of a shift in the balance of power—and a shift of wealth—to the oil-producing countries. He thought there ought to be a triangular pattern of trade among the industrial countries, the oil producers, and the developing countries as a basis for global economic equilibrium.

To promote such a balance, Kreisky had been cultivating close relations with the leaders of the oil-producing states, especially in North Africa. He had just returned from a visit to President Houari Boumediène of Algeria.

Later, in Vienna, a spokesman at OPEC headquarters, Hamid Zaheri, told me that "we have been on very good terms with the Austrian Government. Kreisky is trying to make Vienna the third great city for international organizations, along with New York and Geneva." Boosterism can be a socialist as well as a capitalist phenomenon.

Vienna was already a regional center for the United Nations and the headquarters of the International Atomic Energy Association, as well as of OPEC. Whatever the direct advantages to Austria, which is formally a "nonaligned state" under the Four Party agreement of the United States, Britain, France, and the Soviet Union, however, Kreisky seemed to be engaged in much more than an Austrian promotional campaign. He was hoping to play a peacemaking role in the Middle East, since he regarded the danger of war in that area as a threat to Europe and the entire world.

But he was far from confident that fighting could be avoided. The Arabs, he told me, could not publicly concede Israel's right to exist. He thought Israel, without demanding full public acknowledgment from the Arabs as a state, should give ground to both Egypt and Syria, and should permit the establishment of a Palestinian state on the West Bank of the Jordan River.

Kreisky recognized that any settlement between Israel and a new Palestinian state would be extremely difficult to achieve, and that the road toward accommodation would be mined with violence. But he said he believed that not only other Arab states but also the Soviet Union would not interfere. Indeed, he thought the Russians, in combination with the United States, might be willing to underwrite a settlement between Israel and its neighbors.

He was wrong as hell.

OPEC DIGS IN

OPEC, meanwhile, was talking peace and friendship with the West. Its official rhetoric, adopted by "solemn declaration" in Algiers in the spring of 1975, called for "a new economic order founded on justice and fraternity."

This rhetoric looked anything but meaningless. OPEC members were trying to do several things: nail down the gains they had made in incomes and wealth since the Arab oil embargo that began during the Yom Kippur war and the quintupling of oil prices; stave off a confrontation with the West, whether this should include countermeasures on prices, trade barriers, or even military actions; secure the allegiance of the oil-poor developing countries to OPEC's cause; and avoid a worsening of world depression that would further damage the market for their oil and possibly tear OPEC apart.

The slump in the economies of the United States, Western Europe, and Japan, in combination with the impact of high oil prices and such conservation measures as some importing countries had taken, had already produced a glut of oil in the world and weakened OPEC's bargaining power.

It had also produced a conciliatory tone on the part of OPEC's chief spokesman, Secretary General Meshach Otokiti Feyide, a Nigerian chief whose formal title was the Obania of Ipele. The chief, a petroleum and mining engineer who had been educated at the Camborne School of Mines and the Imperial College of Science and Technology in England, told me, in an interview at OPEC's headquarters at 10 Dr. Karl Lueger-Ring in Vienna, that there had been "a lot of misinformation and distortion of the actions, proposals, and objectives of OPEC." He particularly objected to calling OPEC a cartel. "As a body," he said, "we don't sell anything."

But, I asked, did OPEC not promote a common price policy among its members?

"It depends," said Chief Feyide, "on what you call a common price policy. The price of crude oil is not the same everywhere."

He insisted that crude oil prices and production levels were set by sovereign governments in response to market forces; admittedly, however, OPEC was interested in stabilizing oil prices to avoid undue fluctuations. "Last year," he noted, "we made a small price correction for inflation to the tune of 3.5 percent, where the actual correction for inflation should have been 40 percent."

OPEC's price correction and freezing of prices until the end of September 1975, he said, were intended to help the Western industrialized nations overcome their economic difficulties.

"I look at a cartel," he said, "as a group able to hold others to ransom because they have a monopoly." But OPEC, he said, "has not ordered one single cut in production in its fifteen years of existence. It has not even advised on reductions. You will not find such a recommendation anywhere in our records." When I expressed skepticism about that, he said softly, "It is true."

He turned aside suggestions that the United States might undertake military action against OPEC nations if faced with the threat of "some strangulation," as Secretary of State Kissinger had once put it. "We maintain friendly relations with all people," the chief said. "I believe that basically the United States will not be hostile to us. We have nothing to hide."

He said OPEC members were eager to find greater security for their investments in industrial countries. "Anybody who is investing in another country would like to have some confidence that he is making a worthwhile investment both in terms of security of investment and the returns on it."

But, I asked, what about the reverse—security for investment by Westerners in OPEC and other developing countries?

"We cannot lay down hard and fast rules," he said. "There are many factors to consider—national interests, national security. Different policies may apply, according to national interests. It is easy to say one is opposed to expropriation. Everyone will say, 'Oh, no!' But everything depends on what is the nature of the investment, its strategic importance, its political importance. This applies to everybody."

The time had come, the chief said, for a common assault on all the interlocked problems of resources, trade, development, and monetary issues: "Let us set our house—our house being the world—in order. Everything should be looked at. The problems that now exist will not be solved by trying to resolve the oil problem alone. We must look at the whole structure."

THE NERVOUS RECOVERY

By the beginning of May 1975, it looked as though the worst recession of the postwar period was coming to an end. But if the slump was over, could another be far behind? Many American business people were worried about just such a cycle of aborted recoveries and recurrent recessions. Alan Greenspan, President Ford's chief economic adviser, told them they were worrying about the right thing. He warned a conference of institutional investors in New York that if the Government were to heed the advice of alarmists and pour money into the economy, this would resurrect inflation and set the economy up for another big cyclical downswing.

But Arthur Okun, who had been President Johnson's chief economic adviser, was telling business people that he suspected that the greater danger was that the recovery would run out of gas rather than going too fast.

The national mood in the United States, despite signs of imminent recovery, remained anxious. Working people, still fearful of losing their jobs as unemployment approached 9 percent, were not rushing out to buy expensive goods, such as homes or autos. The unemployment rate had reached 11.5 percent in New York City and 14.5 in Buffalo—rates not seen since the Depression of the 1930s.

Other blows hurt the nation's sense of self-confidence. The fall of Cambodia to the Communists and the imminent collapse of South Vietnam, following President Thieu's resignation and bitter denunciation of the United States as "untrustworthy," darkened the national mood.

The economists were agreed about little except that something was rotten and that policymakers were doing the wrong things. There had never been a time when the Federal Reserve had been subjected to such withering criticism from all sides— monetarists and Keynesians, business and labor leaders, farmers and home builders, bankers and congressmen.

A leading monetarist, Karl Brunner of the University of Rochester, denounced the Fed for contradicting its own instructions to the Open Market Committee and replacing net purchases of securities in the open market (which would have increased bank reserves and presumably the money supply) with net sales of securities (which would contract the money supply). The failure of the Fed to make the money supply grow at an adequate rate, said Professor Brunner, was "serious and regrettable. It prolongs and amplifies an already substantial economic downswing quite unnecessarily."

A leading Keynesian, James Tobin of Yale, took much the same position. He contended that the Fed was "not pushing hard—and could be pushing harder" without danger of rekindling inflation. With interest rates still high by historical standards, Professor Tobin denied that the economy was in a "liquidity trap." He said the banks would not, as some feared, sit on additional reserves if the Fed made them available, but would step up their loans and investments to regenerate economic expansion.

But the Fed chairman, Arthur Burns, insisted that he had

been doing quite enough to get the expansion rolling. He re-proved his critics for believing that there was a more automatic relationship between Federal Reserve actions, bank lending, the growth of the money supply, and the response of real economic activity than actually exists.

Could the deep problems of the economy be solved if the Fed would just put a bit more reserves into the banking system? To some that looked like wishful—and mechanistic—thinking.

Hyman P. Minsky, of Washington University in St. Louis, attributed the economy's underlying weakness to the "fragility" of the financial environment; many businesses were still relatively illiquid, straining to meet heavy payment commitments out of diminished cash flows from operations. This had forced them to cut back on investments and other outlays.

The way such a fragile financial condition had been remedied in the past was through a depression, but that was a costly and hazardous route. Businesses in time of depression are compelled to "liquidate"—turn their fixed assets, such as spare industrial capacity and excess inventories, into cash to restore a better balance between their current payment obligations and their income. Although some businesses were bound to founder in the process of liquidating assets, and many workers were thrown out of jobs, the deep depressions of history had accomplished three necessary results:

1. The financial system was made "robust" again by creating a healthier relationship between debt and income than existed before the depression by wiping out much of existing debt.
2. Businesses, banks, and individuals were cured of some of their proclivity to engage in speculative finance.
3. The low investment levels of the depression, as well as the bankruptcy of many companies, meant that the investments of the preceding period were partly used up and the unwarranted capital-boom spending in mistaken projects was written down.

However, modern societies are unwilling to take the cold-turkey cure of depression. The businesses facing the threat of bankruptcy (and the bigger the business, the greater its political clout), the unions of workers facing job losses, the farmers facing collapsing prices and the loss of their farms, and all other threatened groups would join in insisting that the fiscal and monetary authorities pump in enough money to float the economy off the rocks.

Thus there was danger that the slump would give way to inflation. The economists differed on how to deal with that danger. Alan Greenspan inveighed against turning on "the faucets of direct Federal outlays," which "down the road would not be expansionary but contractionary." So he gave support to President Ford's campaign to stop Congress from adding to antirecession outlays. Arthur Okun, uncommitted to a definite forecast a couple of years away, wanted to keep economic policy flexible, saying he didn't know whether the problem, after the initial recovery from the 1974–75 slump, would be rapid inflation or a relapse.

But Professor Minsky reached a radically different conclusion from either Greenspan or Okun. He contended that current policies, whether a bit more stimulative or a bit less so, would, whether with a shorter or longer lag, lead to the resumption of an inflationary expansion that would create an even more fragile financial structure than existed in 1973–74. This would indeed lead to threats of financial crises and a "replay of the scenario we have gone through three times in the past decade"—in 1966, 1970, and 1974–75.

DEPRESSION WITHOUT A DEPRESSION

What Minsky called for to break this dismal cycle was "a depression without a depression." By that he meant a period that would achieve the desirable effects of a depression—a more robust and liquid economy, less speculative activity, and the wiping out or writing down of unwarranted investments—but without the waste and suffering of mass unemployment.

How could this be done? Minsky argued that what was needed was a long stretch, perhaps a full decade, of low investment and high consumption in which employment would be maintained by public works, as during the New Deal period, rather than by increased inducements to the private sector to invest speculatively.

Some conservatives—such as Alan Greenspan, Arthur Burns, and Martin Feldstein—also favored a "depression without a depression"—that is, a long spell of underemployment that would sweat inflation out of the system, get rid of the overhang of heavy corporate and personal debt, and make the financial system robust again. They hoped to do this with less unemployment than that of the Great Depression, putting their faith that this could be done partly in the belief that welfare and military programs would provide a higher floor under employment and partly in the hope that private industry would adjust more readily to noninflationry policies and, with stronger balance sheets, would begin to invest again.

But the political process in America may not be compatible with "depression without depression." Some pessimistic economists in the midst of the sad '70s decided that capitalism was dying and would, like it or not, give way to a system of state control.

THE END OF THE ROAD?

One of these was Robert Heilbroner, the Norman Thomas Professor of Economics at the New School for Social Research. Heilbroner appreciated, as did Karl Marx, the fecundity of capitalism. "It has been the first to show what man's activity can bring about. It has accomplished wonders far surpassing Egyptian pyramids, Roman aqueducts, and Gothic cathedrals," said the *Communist Manifesto of 1848*. And Heilbroner wrote: "Much as we now inspect Chichén Itzá, the Great Wall, the pyramids, Machu Picchu, so we may someday visit and marvel at the ruins of the great steel works at Sparrows Point, the atomic complex at Hanford, the computer centers at Houston."[3] But worst of all, he warned in Orwellian style, we may one day long for the time when liberties were accorded to "artistic statements, social or sexual habits, political utterances."

Yet he could not bring himself to lament the passing of capitalism. No other civilization had ever permitted the calculus of self-interest so to dominate its culture. It had transmogrified greed and philistinism into social virtues, and subordinated all values to commercial values. The business civilization, he argued, combines liberty and selfishness, egalitarianism and extremes of wealth and poverty, democracy and vulgarity, creativity and waste, respect for the unique and autonomous individual and wage slavery, the conquest of space and the destruction of the environment.

This business civilization could not last beyond the lives of our grandchildren or great-grandchildren at the outside, he said, like the members of the Club of Rome, because nature sets the limits. Capitalism is dying, Heilbroner thought, not as Marx predicted, because of the growth of the proletariat and its progressive impoverishment, or because the downswings of the business cycle could not be controlled, but rather because of capitalism's very successes, as Joseph Schumpeter had argued near the end of World War II.

Capitalist affluence creates an anticapitalist mentality among the intellectuals and among the children of the well-to-do. Affluence liberates the workers from desperate immediate need and increases their power, thereby breeding chronic inflation. Advanced industrial technology requires the hierarchical organization of work—and hence, hierarchical control—both within corporations and outside them, via the government. But in the end this mighty industrial machine spews

[3] Robert L. Heilbroner, *Business Civilization in Decline* (New York: W. W. Norton & Co., 1976).

forth so much output that it depletes the earth's resources and pollutes its environment, jeopardizing human life.

So economic growth must cease. But growth was the daemon of capitalism, and capitalism cannot survive in a no-growth world. Without continuously increasing real income with which to buy off and pacify the lower classes, the struggle over distribution of income and wealth will intensify, nationally and internationally.

Even if disastrous conflicts could be avoided, Heilbroner thought, the cessation of growth would fatally undermine the spirit of capitalism. The driving capitalist entrepreneurs would give way to the carefully calculating state planners, who would forcibly suppress the populace's appetite for material growth. Private property and the market mechanism would then lose both their legitimacy and their functional purposes.

What would succeed capitalism? Here Heilbroner grew vague. He contended that terms like "fascism" and "socialism" would have little applicability to a society struggling to adapt to a stringent and demanding environment, in which the main goal would be survival. He resorted to analogy with the decline and fall of Rome to suggest that the business civilization would not suddenly die as the result of a single dramatic event; as Roman institutions lingered long after Rome was sacked in A.D. 410, capitalist forms and variant social orders would persist for many years. But finally the capitalist institutions and the capitalist spirit would expire, as did the "classical" spirit of Rome.

A crucial element in the transformation of the business system would be the rise of a new religion that would play the role that Christianity did in first undermining the old Roman order and later providing the spirit and shaping the institutional forms of the new order in the Western world. What sort of religion would transform capitalism? A "statist" religion, said Heilbroner, that would elevate mankind's "collective and communal destiny" and would absolutely subordinate private interests to public requirements.

In principle, freedom of expression might survive in such a "survival-minded" society, but in practice, he feared, the centralization and intensification of political authority made this doubtful. Perhaps on the more distant horizon there might be dissolution of centralized power and a turn to self-sufficient and "ecologically safe" small-scale communities. But such a world could not be reached until the massive structures of industrial civilization had been disassembled, the threat of nuclear obliteration removed, and the administration of economic life internalized and divorced from the need for external sanction. Such a world was not on the agenda for the coming century.

But was this grim vision founded on a correct reading of trends—or did it ignore potentialities that could lead to a less alarming and dictatorial outcome?

Are the capitalist societies less productive than the totalitarian societies? Are they more pollution-prone? Are they more disliked by their citizens or subjects? Are they less capable of developing and exploiting science and technology to deal with emerging problems? What could centralized power do that decentralized power could not do better?

In the United States in the mid-1970s the public mood had turned against big business; but it was also turning against big government, a possibly more important shift to which the politicians were responding. Why should a society shifting from the production of goods to services become a more centralized system rather than the reverse? Even within the corporate world, as the communications revolution demonstrated, new technology was undermining monopoly. The new technology, linked to spirited individual enterprise, was making smaller enterprises more efficient—even in politically powerful old-line mass-production industries like steel. Expanding fields like medicine and the arts and sciences had little to gain and much to lose from central control.

Capitalism, somewhat astonishingly in the midst of its stagflationist troubles, had actually gained a new lease on life.

Chapter

8

THE ROAD FROM
SERFDOM

Friedrich August von Hayek, born in Vienna, Austria, in 1899, who fled Nazism and became a British subject and a professor of economics at the London School of Economics and the University of Chicago, is probably the most distinguished conservative economist of his time. He prefers to call himself a "liberal," in the classical European sense—that is, a foe of government intervention in the economy, a believer in laissez-faire. He is famous for two prophecies, one wrong and the other right. The wrong one was that Franklin D. Roosevelt's New Deal, and similar efforts by Western governments to rescue their market economies from collapse, represented "the

road to serfdom."[1] Hayek himself now concedes that if his
view that the welfare state would lead to totalitarianism is
taken to have been a prediction he was wrong; but he chooses
to think of his early work as a warning rather than a forecast.
A personal friend but harsh economic critic of Keynes's advo-
cacy of government spending to cure unemployment, Hayek
also prophesied that Keynesian economic policy would breed
inflation, and inflation would in turn breed unemployment.
Most economists would give Hayek high marks for that prediction.

INFLATION AS THE CAUSE OF UNEMPLOYMENT

When I met Hayek, a small, dapper, and exquisitely polite
man, at his suite at the Waldorf-Astoria Hotel in New York on
June 29, 1975, I asked him whether he blamed the economics
profession for the stagflation we were experiencing. "Very definitely," he said. "There is no question about it at all. The present unemployment is the unintended but inevitable effect of
what was meant to be a full-employment policy, because this
attempt to create the maximum of employment, which in the
short run you can create by monetary pressure, leads to extensive misdirection of labor. When you draw labor into jobs
where the workers can be kept employed only so long as inflation continues, perhaps only so long as inflation accelerates,
you will get full employment at the end of every period of inflation. But at the end you will have on hand large numbers of
workers who have been drawn into employment which will not
continue after the inflation stops."

Was this statement based simply on logical reasoning, I
asked, or could he give me concrete examples of misplaced
workers?

In the traditional business cycle, he said, there was a regular

[1] Friedrich A. von Hayek, *The Road to Serfdom* (Chicago: University
of Chicago Press, 1944).

overexpansion of industries producing capital equipment and buildings, which became overextended, so unemployment occurred there. But he thought the present inflation was a little different from the typical business cycle, because the surplus jobs were largely financed by government spending, and "it's not easy to point your finger at the particular spots where the overdevelopment occurred."

But he had a good example from the inflation in Austria in the old days: "All the coffee houses made room for bank offices, and when the inflation ended, all the banks disappeared again and the coffee houses reappeared. Of course, all the bank employees who had been hired during the inflation lost their jobs."

In the United States, I said, it would be hard to blame the Great Depression of the 1930s on inflation; if you looked at price indexes, they hadn't risen much during the 1920s. Nor had there been in the United States big spending by government; it was the era of Harding, Coolidge, and Hoover—and laissez-faire policies on the part of all three.

"Well," said Hayek, "you had two things that were important. You had a very great increase of productivity, which normally would have led to a fall in the prices of manufactured goods. But that was prevented by a deliberate policy of maintaining prices constant in spite of increasing productivity and falling costs. Then you had the final episode, from 1927 to 1929. In the normal course of events the crisis would have come in 1927. But the Federal Reserve System tried successfully to prolong the boom for another two years, quite deliberately, by credit expansion. And that, I think, became the cause of the severity of the crash in 1929. You had, even then, substantial if short-lived inflation."

Did all that explain so deep and long and disastrous a depression?

"That the Great Depression lasted so long is a different story," he said. "I am only speaking about the collapse and the inevitable depression of a year or two. The later mistakes of policy, such as Roosevelt going off gold in 1933 just at the time when the international monetary conference in London promised some degree of stability, renewed the depression just when the first signs of recovery were appearing. There were also deliberate attempts to keep wages up at a time when there was a necessity for readjusting relative wages. All these were particular factors which prolonged the depression, once it had come."

Was our present position at all comparable to what we faced at the start of the Great Depression?

"Well, the reaction is certainly not as great as 1932–33," he said. "If you ask me about 1930, the position is not so very different. We are after the collapse of an inflationary boom. A mistaken policy which allowed a deflationary process to get under way might well drag us into a long-lasting depression."

HAYEK'S ANTI-INFLATION POLICY

What would he do to prevent another depression without reviving inflation?

"I would make a public announcement that I was not going to resume inflation," said Hayek, "but that as soon as any signs of an actual deflation set in, I would take every measure in my power to combat such deflation."

How much unemployment would he be willing to accept during the period of readjustment from the past inflation? I reminded him that he had said in the past that the unemployment rate might get up as high as 13 or 14 percent.

"But if it does," he broke in, "I don't think we could possibly prevent it. It is not in our choice. I think we could postpone it at the price of having even worse unemployment later. The manner of combating a rise of unemployment now would be to resume inflation, and the price of that would be worse unemployment later."

But was it politically feasible for any Administration to accept an unemployment rate of 13 or 14 percent without acting, through monetary and fiscal policies, to create jobs for the un-employed?

"I can only say I hope so," Hayek answered.

THE EVILS OF POLITICS

Did he really think a return to laissez-faire was possible?

"I certainly hope that dissatisfaction with government inter-ference and policy will so increase that we will ultimately re-turn to a system where coercion by government is limited to the enforcement of general laws. This does not preclude that the government render all kinds of services which are financed by taxation. We undoubtedly need certain services which at the present time perhaps only government can render. All I would object to is government's assuming a monopoly of these services. So long as other people are free to do better than gov-ernment, I have no objection against government providing various kinds of services."

Would a return to laissez-faire on the part of government require breaking up business monopolies and oligopolies? Would it not also require breaking up labor unions or abol-ishing them?

Hayek saw no need to do much about business monopolies, "because they are not based on any privileges that have been given by law." But, he said, "we have to remove certain privi-leges that the law has given to the labor unions. Their power, after all, is very largely based on the use or threat of force against people willing to work, and I think of that right they must be deprived. It doesn't mean abolishing labor unions, but it means depriving them of the power of coercion. And the coercion is largely the coercion of other workers."

Isn't there also close collusion between some business cor-porations and government? I asked. And isn't that an impor-tant source of heavy government expenditures and regulation?

"Oh, yes," said Hayek. "So long as government has the power of benefiting particular groups, there is no way of stopping it. You can only take the power from government. As long as the government has the power to interfere in economic lives, it will be forced to do so by the mere need of buying the support of particular groups. You cannot, with a potentially omnipotent government, obtain a majority to support it unless you buy the support of particular interests. To make government independent of economic pressures requires that the government be deprived of the power of conceding privileges to particular groups. As long as it has the power to do so, it will be forced to do so."

I asked him what his "second-best solution" would be on the assumption that for political reasons it would be impossible to reduce the power of big corporations, big unions, and big government. On that assumption, what sort of economic policies should government follow to reduce unemployment and achieve price stability?

"I am afraid that with our present political institutions we will be driven into more and more government control unless the situation becomes so impossible that people are willing to contemplate very severe restrictions on the powers of government," Hayek said. "And sometimes—maybe this is a perverse feeling—I almost wish that things should go bad very rapidly so that people are forced to reconsider that problem. The present danger is that people will consider this development an inevitable effect of democracy. There is at present a tendency to get disgusted with democracy which greatly alarms me. I do not regard democracy as an ultimate goal, but as an indispensable defense against dictatorship, against totalitarian government. And so I am very anxious to preserve and protect democracy against a blame which it does not deserve. But I must admit that I feel that the present form of democracy which confers unlimited power on the majority must be got rid of. I believe that what is failing is not democracy as such but the particular form of democracy which we have developed because of the superstition that a democratic government must be omnipotent."

How would he cure democracy of its ills?

"We must rediscover means of limiting the power of even a democracy, a problem which people have long regarded as insoluble. They even regarded it as a self-contradiction, because they believe you can limit the powers of democracy only by putting some other will above the will of the majority. But that is not so. You can limit the powers of democracy by embodying certain agreed principles into the constitution and design a constitutional system by which government is strictly limited by law—in the old sense of law, that is, not an authorization of government to do what it likes, but limiting its powers to the enforcement of general rules. That would mean restructuring the governmental organization. I am actually working on this problem because I am very anxious that if, as I expect, our present form of democracy will be seen to have failed, people do not believe that the experiment in freedom was a mistake, but to realize that we have made mistakes and ought to try in another way."

POLITICAL REFORMS

What reforms did he have in mind?

"I think the main thing is that we ought to use our bicameral system for a purpose different from that for which we use it now. We ought to have a government assembly which conducts current government but which is bound by the general rules laid down by another and independent assembly. And I believe that only the governmental assembly ought to be organized on party lines. I think it is recognized, and proved by experience, that you cannot conduct government except on party principles, with one party conducting government under the law and the other watching it as opposition. But I do not think this party organization is appropriate for a true legislature which lays down the general principles and which ought not to represent particular interests but ought to represent the state of general opinion on moral issues.[2]

[2] See Hayek's *The Constitution of Liberty* (Chicago: University of Chicago Press, 1960).

"I think for that reason we need an assembly not organized on party lines, and the main device needed to secure this would be to make the elected representatives to the legislating body not re-eligible, but elect them for long terms. They would be independent of party discipline, because they could not look for re-election.

"It is very curious that the great thinkers, particularly the founders of the American system of government, were all opponents of party governments. So far as the government functions of elected assemblies were concerned, they were evidently mistaken; governments cannot be conducted except on party lines. But proper legislation could be written without regard to party allegiance.

"To take it a little further," said Hayek, "the theory of democratic liberal constitutions is based on the idea of a division of powers between government and legislation. But for some reason the people did not feel that they could deprive the legislature of governmental powers. Of course we want government conducted democratically, but it must not be done by the same democratically elected body which legislates."

He was hitting at a major problem of democracies: how to convert interest-group politics into public-interest politics. Unlike so many economists who are criticized for merely moving the deck chairs around on a sinking *Titanic,* Hayek was seeking radically to transform the political-economic institutions of democratic society.

But a deep pessimism seemed to color his thinking. I asked him whether he thought our kind of interest-group democracy was ultimately headed for totalitarianism as the means of imposing "the public interest" on the conflicting special interests. I brought up the book that had made him famous—*The Road to Serfdom*—and asked whether we were several decades further down that road. Or, rather, had we not, by using the powers of government, economic and military, rescued our Western democracies from the threats of depression and mass unemployment, and from threats of fascism and Communism?

"Oh, yes," he said, accepting my second proposition. "But

let me say first that in one respect my book has been misunderstood. I have never argued that this development [totalitarianism] is inevitable. The book was meant to be a warning of the kind, 'Unless you mend your principles, you will go to the devil.' And to some extent the principles have been mended. I had then been arguing against the idea of socialism in the strict sense, that is, nationalization of the means of production and central planning. Now even the socialists have largely given up this aim. They have discovered that they can achieve the redistribution through taxation and no longer need to nationalize industry.

"Recently, a new danger has arisen. It now looks as if we may be driven into central planning in an unexpected way. The people are getting so alarmed about inflation that they demand price controls. Once you have price controls, the market no longer operates; we may well be driven that way, through price controls and direction of industry, into central planning and an authoritarian system. I am not so afraid for the American people, because you have the capacity of changing your opinions very rapidly, and if a system proves unsatisfactory, you throw it over again.

"I think we have more reason to be alarmed about the extreme left of my adopted country, Great Britain. I am a British subject, and I am very much concerned because there the extreme left is going back to the orthodox Marxist ideas of nationalization of industry. That, of course, would lead straight to a totalitarian system. Things are touch and go there. The danger is acute."

Hayek was saying this a few years before the Conservative Party under Margaret Thatcher took power in Britain—and the Republican Party under Ronald Reagan took power in the United States. Hayekian ideologies were on the ascendancy in both countries, with the combination of inflation and unemployment pushing electorates to the right.

CAPITALISM AND DEMOCRACY

I asked him whether he thought capitalism and democracy depended upon each other. After all, I noted, some countries, such as Latin American dictatorships, were essentially capitalist, while some democratic countries, such as the Scandinavian democracies, had important elements of socialism.

"It is a very paradoxical situation," said Hayek. "I am convinced that democracy can exist only under capitalism, that under any other system the nominal influence of the people is wholly fictitious. But I have to admit that, with their present dominant opinions, democracies are not likely to tolerate capitalism. They are likely to destroy the system which is the basis of their existence. You mentioned the Scandinavian governments. They are regarded as socialist, but they have almost completely abandoned the original socialist ideal of taking over industry and directing it. They have discovered that it is much easier to let the capitalist earn the profits and then take them from him. So they are preserving a sort of capitalism very carefully. They have been moving not to socialism but to a sort of welfare state, which is a rather unstable system. How long it will last I do not know."

Did Hayek think capitalism is dying?

"No, I don't think so. There is no alternative that is workable. Capitalism may be made very inefficient by all kinds of ill-advised controls and legislation. It probably will in any foreseeable future be much less efficient than it might be. But I think any attempt effectively to replace it by something else would so rapidly lead to extensive starvation in the world that people would very soon return to capitalism."

Did free markets, the basic condition of capitalism, ensure equality for the citizens of a democracy? Did he accept equality as a proper goal for a society?

"It depends on what you mean by equality. Equality before

the law, certainly. Equality in material position is wholly impossible, because that would require a completely directed system. In any free-market system you are bound to get great inequality of material conditions, and inequalities which have no direct connection with recognizable merit, because they are very largely due to accident of one kind or another. The market system is a discovery procedure in which those profit who make discoveries of new possibilities. You can never foresee this, and discoveries are not always a matter of merit but very frequently a matter of accident."

What about inherited inequalities and injustices? Would he have government make restitution for the fact that some people, such as poor blacks, do not start the race every generation at the same starting point as more fortunate groups?

"Well, you experience some frustration in this because you were rather slow in effectively conceding equality before the law, and you then suddenly decided to go to the other extreme, and to some extent actually granted privileges to people who now have chances which they have only because they are black, or female, and which they probably wouldn't have on their own merits," said Hayek. "I think we will gradually have to discover what is required by genuine equality before the law, where everybody has to take his chances and where the external conditions provided by government are the same for all. Freedom always produces inequality, and equality of a material kind can only be achieved by the abolition of freedom." Hayek seemed content with the proposition that nothing is fair in this world.

THE LEAKY BUCKET

But is capitalism necessarily a safeguard of human dignity and human rights? Money can buy some things that should not be for sale, including justice and political power. As the late Arthur Okun, chairman of the Council of Economic Advisers under President Johnson, observed, "The market is even permitted to legislate life and death, as evidenced, for example, by infant mortality rates for the poor that are more than one and one-half times those for middle-income Americans." The market does provide strong incentives for work effort and productive contributions, and in their absence society would thrash about for alternative incentives—some unreliable, like altruism, others intolerable, like coercion and oppression.[3]

The problem of modern democracies is somehow to combine economic efficiency with greater equality, even, if necessary, at some cost to efficiency. Okun scoffed at those contemporary intellectuals who forget the Declaration of Independence, ignore the Bill of Rights, and investigate the goal of achieving greater equality "as though it were an idiosyncrasy, perhaps even a type of neurosis."

To crystallize the issue, Okun invited people to participate in what he called the leaky-bucket experiment. Imagine that you could transfer $4,000 from each of the 5 percent of families at the top of the income ladder to the 20 percent of families at the bottom. Each family at the bottom would then get $1,000. But there was a hitch: The bucket in which you would transfer this income leaks.[4] Some of the money carried from rich to poor would leak out of the bucket and never reach the poor; it would be lost through resulting inefficiency in the system.

What if it leaked out so that the 5 percent of families at the top would each lose $4,000 but the 20 percent of families at the bottom would each gain only $900? What if half the money to be transferred leaked out? What if three-quarters of it were lost?

Okun said that John Rawls, the Harvard philosopher, would give a clear, crisp answer: Make the switch to increase equality unless an unequal distribution of income would definitely be to the advantage of everyone, both rich and poor.

[3] See Arthur M. Okun, *Equality and Efficiency: The Big Trade-Off* (Washington, D.C.: The Brookings Institution, 1975).
[4] Ibid., pp. 91–95.

Hayek would give a different clear and crisp answer: Let the market function, whatever the effects on material equality.

Okun's answer was not neat: He fell between the Rawlsian and Hayekian poles. Picking a subjective number, he said he would go on transferring income from rich to poor up to the point where about 60 percent of the income being transferred leaked out of the bucket.

There is no "right" answer. This is a matter for the broad society, not economists, most of whom are narrowly focused on economic efficiency, to decide on the basis of its social values.[5]

We must somehow resolve the conflict between the domain of money and the domain of human rights if we are to be a good and growing society. Perhaps we can never lastingly resolve that conflict because capitalism and democracy are, in some ways, an odd couple. "Maybe that is why they need each other," said Okun, "to put some rationality into equality and some humanity into efficiency."

But equality and efficiency are not always and necessarily in conflict. Improving human abilities, through education and through the abolition of stultifying and degrading poverty, is to improve the effective functioning and growth of the economy. The output that is lost from the neglect and waste of human potentials is almost certainly greater than the social costs needed to rescue and develop human talents and minds. Society's real leaky bucket is the one that wastes lives— through unemployment and underemployment, through poor health and ignorance.

[5] I would conclude that Republicans tend to accord a higher value to efficiency, Democrats to equality, in the efficiency-equality trade-off.

Chapter

9

THE POLITICAL-BUSINESS CYCLE

Gerry Ford's contentment with the underlying health and strength of the American economy, despite the steep 1974–75 recession, was shaken by the prospect of running for the Presidency in 1976 with unemployment so high. In 1975 the jobless rate of all civilian workers averaged 8.5 percent, the highest of the postwar period, and the rate wasn't coming down fast enough. So Ford set out to rev up the economy to support his election campaign.

Is the business cycle in America really political, a creature of the four-year Presidential electoral cycle? President Ford's proposal in the fall of 1975 for a $28 billion tax cut, to take effect January 1, 1976, to be followed nine months later by a $28

billion cut in government expenditures, looked like a deliberate effort to speed up the economy until the November election
and then to slow it down in an effort to head off the inflation.
Ford's proposal was criticized not only by his Democratic opponents but even by some of his conservative Republican supporters as cynical political economics. Senator Henry Bellmon
of Oklahoma, the ranking Republican on the Senate Budget
Committee, said, "If I had an evil political mind—and I
have—I might think there was some political motive in this
timing."

But Ford maintained that the linked $28 billion tax and
spending cuts would not have any particular short-term effects
on the economy. He sought to legitimate his policy by declaring his respect for the role of public opinion in a democracy.
Ford's press secretary, Ron Nessen, told reporters: "The President is convinced the American people want a bigger tax out."

The House Ways and Means Committee had written a bill
proposing only $12.7 billion in individual-income-tax cuts.
That was "too small," in Ford's judgment. He was confident,
said Nessen, that "the American people will let the full Congress know that they *do* want a bigger tax cut."

Was this a proper appeal to democratic public opinion? A
political philosopher, Robert Nisbet of Columbia University,
distinguishes between public opinion and popular opinion.
"Public opinion," he says, "is given its character by genuine
consensus, by unifying tradition, and by what Edmund Burke
called 'constitutional spirit.'" By contrast, says Professor Nisbet, popular opinion is "shallow of root, a creature of the mere
aggregate or crowd." Popular opinion could easily, if ten-
uously, be formed around a single issue or personage, he said,
but lacked the cement that only time, tradition, and convention
could provide.

Ford's critics could charge him with simply following in the
footsteps not only of President Nixon in 1972 but also of President Johnson in 1964, and other Presidential incumbents before them.

POLITICAL CYCLES

The economic scholars have belatedly been giving the political-business cycle the attention it deserves. Professor William Nordhaus of Yale[1] has postulated that democratic (small d) politicians behave as short-run vote maximizers. Whether their politics are of the left or the right, incumbents seek to maximize the votes they get by stimulating the economy in election years.

But Professor Douglas A. Hibbs, Jr., of Harvard University,[2] finds Professor Nordhaus's thesis a good deal too simple. To be sure, Professor Hibbs does not deny that there is an oscillation of monetary and fiscal stimulus in election years and restraint in off years, whether the Administration in office is Republican or Democratic. However, he contends (and offers statistical evidence to prove it) that the two parties oscillate, swinging from stimulus to restraint and back again, around different "equilibria"—different balance points in each party's preferred trade-off between inflation and unemployment. The Republicans shoot for a lower rate of inflation, the Democrats for a lower rate of unemployment.

The econometric evidence is that, by and large, each party has got about what it wanted. The reason is that each party tends to serve the economic interests of its own constituency.

Thus the Democrats, with much heavier labor support, aim to satisfy their constituents by achieving lower unemployment rates while accepting higher rates of inflation, because this combination exerts strong equalizing effects on the distribution of income, improves the well-being of those at the bottom of

[1] William D. Nordhaus, "The Political Business Cycle," *Review of Economic Studies*, 42 (April 1975), pp. 169–190.

[2] Douglas Hibbs, Jr., "Political Parties and Macroeconomic Policy," *American Political Science Review*, 71 (December 1977), pp. 1467–1487; and Hibbs, "Economic Interest and the Politics of Macroeconomic Policy," Center for International Studies, M.I.T., January 1976.

the income ladder, and shifts a larger share of national income away from business profits to wages and salaries.

The Republicans, with a constituency much more heavily weighted by upper-income people and business managers, who perceive inflation as a greater threat to their interests than unemployment, attach higher values to reducing inflation than unemployment in the trade-off between them. But since the parties compete for voters in the middle and within the constituency of the other party, the differences between the parties are not black and white but relative. Both Republicans and Democrats seek the balance point that will give them the largest slice of the electorate while minimizing electoral risks.

CLASH OF CLASS INTERESTS

Hibbs finds that not only the politicians but also the "elite" spokesmen for capital and labor recognize how their conflicting class or group interests are affected by fiscal and monetary policy. This is true not only in the United States but also in all other advanced industrial nations. He assigns the following scale of preferences to the principal political parties of the advanced democratic countries, with the criteria listed in decreasing order of importance:

- Socialist-labor: Full employment (highest value), equalization of income, economic expansion, price stability, and balance of payments equilibrium (lowest value).
- Conservatives: Price stability (highest value), balance of payments equilibrium, economic expansion, full employment, and equalization of income distribution (of little or no value to conservatives).
- Center parties: Price stability (highest value, but not so high as for the conservatives), economic expansion, full employment, equalization of income, and balance of payments equilibrium.

After examining the national experience of a dozen Western democracies, Hibbs finds that countries regularly governed by labor-oriented, working-class-based Social Democratic parties have typically experienced below-average unemployment levels and above-average rates of inflation. Countries regularly governed by Social Democrats, such as Denmark, Sweden, Finland, and the Netherlands, have had higher rates of inflation and lower rates of unemployment than the European-American average. But countries politically led predominantly by business-oriented, middle-class-based parties of the right and center, such as Belgium and Canada, have had higher rates of unemployment than the average.

In individual countries, where control oscillates from left to right and back again, as in the United States and Britain, the balance point between inflation and unemployment changes, depending on which party takes office and which problem, inflation or unemployment, is regarded as uppermost at the time a party takes office; the competition between the two parties, particularly in election years, also causes shifts in the balance point for each of the two parties.

RESULTANT OF FORCES

National economic policy is thus the resultant of two distinct forces: first, changes in the location of the balance point in the trade-off between inflation and unemployment, depending on whether parties of the right, center, or left are dominant; and, second, changes in the political-business cycle, with economic policies shifting toward the lower-unemployment, higher-inflation range of the scale in election years, and back toward the lower-inflation, higher-unemployment range in nonelection years.

If you were a politician seeking to maximize votes and still produce something resembling economic stability, the optimal political-economic strategy would be to arrange for the bottom of a recession to occur a few months before the election year begins, and have most of that year for recovery. This would simultaneously benefit the largest number of voters in all classes:

The unemployed workers will get jobs, the real income of the employed labor force will rise, the profits of employers and stockholders will rise, and inflation, in the wake of the recession, will not yet revive—provided you play it right and don't so overdo the economic stimulus as to let inflation out of the bag before Election Day.

Once the election is passed, and with it the midpoint of the political-business cycle, wages will rise and inflation will start to race ahead. Income will be shifted away from profits. Investment will slacken. The economy is then likely to slow down and may even fall into recession. Employment will slow down and unemployment will rise. A growing number of people will be disaffected, even cynical, in the year or two after the election. In the United States the problem of the political-business cycle has been complicated by the need of parties to wage election fights every two years. Presidents cannot always turn the economy around so fast, and losses of the incumbent party are common in the by-election two years after a Presidential election. Presidents primarily interested in their own and their party's victory in the Presidential election year focus their strategy on maximizing votes in that year.

Presidents do not have as much control over the political-economic cycle as they would like. The growth of international economic interdependence aggravates the problem of control for a national leader.

Nevertheless, though control is uncertain, there is a high correlation between economic expansion and national election years in the United States and other countries, as shown in Table 1, constructed by Professor Edward R. Tufte of Yale.[3]

In 19 of 27 democracies during the years 1961 through 1972, the growth of real disposable income—the take-home pay of individuals, adjusted for inflation—accelerated more in election years than in years without inflation. Combining all 27 countries, real income growth after taxes accelerated in 64 per-

[3] Edward R. Tufte, *Political Control of the Economy* (Princeton University Press, Princeton, N.J., 1978), p. 12.

TABLE 1

ELECTIONS AND ECONOMIC ACCELERATION, 27 DEMOCRACIES, 1961-72

	Percentage of years in which rate of growth of real disposable income increased		Did acceleration occur more often in election years than in years without elections?
	Election years	Years without elections	
Australia	75%	29%	yes
Austria	25	86	no
Belgium	67	63	yes
Canada	100	57	yes
Chile	50	44	yes
Costa Rica	100	50	yes
Denmark	25	43	no
Finland	67	50	yes
France	60	33	yes
West Germany	33	38	no
Iceland	33	75	no
India	50	43	yes
Ireland	67	63	yes
Israel	67	50	yes
Italy	33	50	no
Jamaica	100	44	yes
Japan	100	29	yes
Luxembourg	100	56	yes
Netherlands	50	57	no
New Zealand	75	43	yes
Norway	100	33	yes
Philippines	60	67	no
Sweden	67	50	yes
Switzerland	67	50	yes
United Kingdom	67	38	yes
United States	83	40	yes
Uruguay	33	50	no

Source: Tufte, *op. cit.*

cent of all election years compared to 49 percent of all years without elections. And for those 19 countries whose economies expanded faster in election years, real income after taxes sped up in 77 percent of the years when voters went to the polls compared to 46 percent when they did not.

In the United States, the growth of real income after taxes accelerated in 83 percent of the election years, both Presidential and midterm Congressional elections, compared to 40 percent in the years without elections between 1961 and 1972.

Starting in 1947, in five administrations—those of Truman, Kennedy, Johnson, Nixon, and Ford—there was a close tie between elections and economic expansion. In those five administrations, real income growth sped up in eight of 11 election years (73 percent) compared to only two of ten (20 percent) nonelection years. Only the Eisenhower Administration was an exception to the rule of faster growth in election years:

TABLE 2

NUMBER OF ELECTION YEARS, 1948–1976, IN WHICH GROWTH IN REAL DISPOSABLE INCOME

	Accelerated	Decelerated
Eisenhower Administration	0	4
Other administrations	8	3

The reason for the big difference is that the dominant political-economic goals of the Eisenhower Administration were to reduce inflation and balance the budget, especially by cutting spending, where the chief political-economic goal of other administrations in election years was to reduce unemployment, even if the budget was unbalanced.

Eisenhower thought his goals of shrinking inflation and budget deficits not only served the cause of free enterprise but were more popular with the electorate, and, as Tufte observes, "These goals were initially reinforced by the election returns: Eisenhower read his landslide victory in 1952 as the voters' express approval of these goals and as the rejection of the

Democratic focus on governmental intervention to reduce un-employment."[4]

This approach worked again for Eisenhower in 1956. But it failed in 1960, with Richard Nixon as the Republican standard-bearer. With the economy in the doldrums, Nixon lost to Kennedy. An embittered Nixon blamed his defeat on the conservative Eisenhower's refusal to stimulate the economy in time for the election, as Nixon had urged.

Tufte finds that, for all postwar administrations from Truman to Carter, omitting only Eisenhower, the annual growth of real disposable income in Presidential election years, with an incumbent President seeking re-election, averaged 3.4 percent; in midterm elections, it averaged 2.8 percent; in election years when incumbent Presidents were not seeking re-election, it averaged 2 percent; and in odd-numbered years when there was no election, real income growth averaged only 1.5 percent.[5] These data are set forth in Table 3.

The unemployment rate averaged one percentage point lower just before Presidential elections than the rate a year to a year and a half *before* the election, and nearly two points lower than the jobless rate a year to a year and a half *after* the election.

Tufte concludes that there is indeed a political-business cycle in the United States, consisting of

- a two-year cycle in the growth of real disposable income per capita, with acceleration in even-numbered years and deceleration in odd-numbered years,
- and a four-year cycle in unemployment, with downturns in the jobless rate during the months before the Presidential election and rises in unemployment starting a year to a year and a half after the election.

[4] Ibid., pp. 15–17.
[5] Ibid., p. 24.

TABLE 3

ANNUAL CHANGE IN REAL DISPOSABLE INCOME PER CAPITA IN RELATION TO THE POLITICAL NATURE OF THE YEARS, ALL POSTWAR ADMINISTRATIONS, 1946–1976, EXCEPT EISENHOWER'S

	No election (%)	On-year, incumbent President not seeking re-election (%)	Midterm election (%)	On-year, incumbent President seeking reelection (%)
1946			−2.6	
1947	−5.9			
1948				3.4
1949	−1.5			
1950			5.9	
1951	0.9			
1952		1.1		
1961	1.0			
1962			2.6	
1963	1.9			
1964				5.6
1965	4.8			
1966			3.9	
1967	3.0			
1968		2.8		
1969	1.5			
1970			3.0	
1971	2.6			
1972				3.3
1973	5.9			
1974			−2.3	
1975	1.0			
1976				3.3
Median Amount	1.5	2.0	2.8	3.4

Source: Tufte, *op. cit.*

THE ELECTORAL RHYTHM

But it is not a simple thing for an incumbent President to time the stimulus for his re-election and at the same time maintain the preferred balance point between inflation and unemployment. Gerry Ford wavered between goals, and his timing was off.

In his State of the Union address at the start of 1976, Ford acknowledged that unemployment, at 8.3 pecent, was much too high. But he said conditions were improving, as "people were being hired much faster than they were being laid off." His advisers assured him the jobless rate would keep coming down during the election year, and Ford was willing to take a chance that a majority of voters would react more to the decline of the unemployment rate than to its still high level compared to earlier postwar years.

The conservative Ford's main goal was to bring down inflation. He said he would veto any tax cut if Congress did not uphold his $395 billion spending ceiling. He said he would give the nation an extra $10 billion in tax reductions—but only if expenditures were cut dollar for dollar to match the tax cut. At the same time, he insisted on an increase in Social Security payroll taxes.

The Democrats attacked Ford's tax program as regressive, with its greatest impact hitting the poor, especially the aged poor. They warned that Ford could not expect to hold down social outlays and still get the big increase in military spending that he sought. Democratic liberals argued that the President's policies were bad economics and would impose needlessly sluggish growth and unemployment on the nation. Arthur Okun said the public was not impressed by Ford's call for spending cuts, citing a Gallup poll which found that a representative sample, by a four-to-one majority, thought the Democrats would do a better job than the Republicans in reducing unemployment. The same poll showed a two-to-one majority believing that Democrats would do better than Republicans in holding down the cost of living.

Okun urged Democrats not to be timid but to offer a strong program for bringing down both unemployment and inflation. "After eight years of Republican rule and high inflation and unemployment," he said, "it will be hard to blame it on the Democrats." But many Democrats still worried about what they saw as the antispending, antitax, anti-inflation mood of the country.

Ford decided to build his re-election campaign on the same perception of the nation's conservative mood. Besides, he had to stave off a threat to his right from ex-Governor Ronald Reagan of California, who had made Ford look like a middle-of-the-road moderate.

On the Democratic side, the liberal consensus of the 1960s—which dated from Roosevelt's New Deal of the 1930s—was breaking up. To be sure, Senator Hubert Humphrey of Minnesota, Representative Morris Udall of Arizona, and Senator Edward M. Kennedy of Massachusetts held to the old liberal line.

But Governor Edmund ("Jerry") Brown of California was groping for something new to suit the mood of a people entering the "post-industrial" society. He thought he had found it in the "small is beautiful" approach of the British economist E. S. Schumacher, but he was wrong.

Jimmy Carter, the former Governor of Georgia, offered a somewhat baffling mixture of conservatism, liberalism, populism—and piety. He supported the Humphrey-Hawkins full-employment bill but would not commit himself to its 3 percent unemployment target. He assailed Arthur Burns, chairman of the Federal Reserve, for creating tight money and high interest rates that were hurting farmers, workers, and other common folk. But donning a conservative hat, Carter called for checking the growth of Federal spending. Switching to a populist hat, he called for breaking up the big oil companies and keeping them from acquiring coal reserves. Then, pragmatically, he opposed breaking up General Motors. He also made a strong anti-inflation pitch and was the only Democratic candidate to call for standby wage and price controls, and for using Presidential power to restrain wages and prices; that stand did not sit well with organized labor, and he later dropped it.

Carter, the Outsider, won the Democratic nomination apparently by capitalizing on the nation's distrust of its familiar national leaders and by its worries about unemployment. Ford, the veteran Insider, ensured his defeat by his pardon of Nixon—and by his flaccid conduct of economic policy, allowing unemployment to hang high just before the election.

When Americans went to the polls in November 1976, too many felt frayed at the cuffs and down at the heels. In the beauty contest that is American politics, voters took a good last look at Ford and said, "We award the prize to the next one." And with Carter's election, the balance point in the trade-off between unemployment and inflation took another shift toward the lower-unemployment, higher-inflation end of the spectrum. That shifting balance point had also become part of the electoral rhythm of the American economy.

Chapter

10

IN SEARCH OF A PAINLESS POLICY

"Once upon a time there lived in the little village of Schlumpberg the good Burgomaster von Pleasemall. He was in truth the
very model of an agreeable man. That is, he loved to have
'round him only men who agreed with him, while he, on his
part, set an excellent example of this virtue by agreeing with all
who came to him with advice."

Those lines were written by John T. Flynn in *The New Republic* of July 10, 1935, and von Pleasemall of Schlumpberg
was Franklin D. Roosevelt. Jimmy Carter at the start of his
Administration in 1977 appeared to be in the process of
launching a mini–New Deal—*mini* because tightly constrained
by fears of large budget deficits and by his objective of achieving a balanced budget by fiscal 1981. Carter had committed

himself during the campaign to a balanced budget by the last year of his term; so, incidentally, had Roosevelt in the campaign of 1932.

Carter's worries about deficit financing and his efforts to appear fiscally responsible were evident from the start. In Plains, Georgia, just before taking over the White House, Carter asked his budget director–designate, Bert Lance, to lift the veil on their fiscal plan. Lance said he "hoped" the fiscal-stimulus package could be held to $15 billion, because it was "very, very important" that the budget deficit be restrained as much as possible. The next day Carter gave a highly confusing briefing to the press in which he said that "the total amount we are talking about is a little less than $15 billion in fiscal year 1977 and a little less than $15 billion in fiscal 1978."

This package was apparently designed to be low enough to satisfy conservatives—at least all those but the monetarists, who opposed any fiscal stimulus whatsoever. Since, however, the Business Roundtable, led by Reginald Jones, the chairman of the General Electric Company, had called for a $23 billion stimulus for the coming year, Carter's proposal looked moderate. But to make his program more pleasant to liberals, who wanted greater stimulus, he described the fiscal program as a $30 billion package for two years.

After Carter had succeeded in confusing the press with his own version of the program, using numbers that did not add up and were garbled in their details, Charles L. Schultze, the chairman-designate of the Council of Economic Advisers, took his turn at clarifying the numbers. This took some doing, because there was still considerable political and technical elasticity in the program. For fiscal 1977, the program appeared to have four main elements: direct expenditures for jobs, totaling $2 billion; tax cuts resulting from simplification of the standard deduction, $2 billion; tax cuts for business, probably by reducing its share of payroll taxes but possibly by raising the investment tax credit, $1 billion; and a one-shot income-tax rebate for individual taxpayers, ranging from $7 billion to $11 billion, depending on how the details were worked out. The total stimulus would be $12 billion to $16 billion. For fiscal 1978, the total remained roughly the same, but the composition of the package of stimulants changed. The tax rebate dropped out altogether. Direct spending on public works and public-works jobs would go up to $5 billion to $8 billion. Tax cuts for business might go up to $2 billion, and tax cuts from simplification to $6 billion, to make up for a retroactive shortfall of $2 billion the preceding year; therafter tax cuts from simplification would run on indefinitely at $4 billion a year, stated in terms of 1977 prices. Got it?

To be sure, those measures did not represent the whole of Carter's coming budget and tax program. He was still committed to initiatives in energy, health, welfare reform, housing, transportation, and other areas. Such programs might constitute net increases in expenditures, even beyond what inflation would cause, or they might represent substitutions for existing programs under the concept of "zero-base budgeting"—reexamining all existing programs from scratch—to which Carter had pledged his allegiance.

Further tax cuts might also lie ahead, since Carter would be pressed for relief by various groups ranging from the working poor to business interests. Business was insisting, in a mounting campaign, that it could not invest adequately to sustain a growing national economy that would employ a growing labor force unless it had bigger earnings after taxes as its share of national income. It would be difficult to satisfy any one group of tax petitioners without satisfying others; that was the source of the basic please-'em-all syndrome. But Carter tried to do much with little, scattering his limited seed money in as many directions as possible.

BALKY GERMAN LOCOMOTIVE

There was an international dimension to the Carter stimulus program that soon emerged: pressures on West Germany to act as a "locomotive" to help pull the industrial world out of the slump. But Chancellor Helmut Schmidt would have none of it.

In late January 1977, shortly before Vice President Walter F. Mondale and his economic advisers were to arrive in Bonn, despatched by Carter to put the heat on the Germans, I went to Bonn myself and, together with Craig Whitney, then *The Times*'s Bonn bureau chief, interviewed Schmidt in an anteroom of the German Parliament.

Schmidt was prickly and feisty when we raised the question of the Carter Administration's locomotive theory. Firing one across the United States' bow through *The New York Times*, Schmidt said Carter would be making a big mistake to put pressure on him to stimulate the German economy. "The German economy is in good shape," he said. Schmidt was opposed to *any* tax cuts—even to spur business investment. He voiced his disbelief that cutting taxes was a way to cure unemployment. "When we cut taxes here in 1975," he said, "we found that people just saved more money." The German Chancellor declared that "the time for Keynesian ideas is past, because the main problem is inflation."

West Germany's rate of inflation had come down to less than 4 percent, one of the lowest in the world. But this, said Schmidt, "is precisely because we have maintained strict policies." He advised the Carter Administration to do the same.

He said his Government needed no economic lectures from the United States ("or the Brookings Institution") because the German economic performance had been better than the American. "Not only is your inflation higher than ours," he said, "but also your unemployment rate is twice as high as ours." The German unemployment rate at that time was 4.6 percent, with one million workers jobless, compared to an American rate of 7.9 percent. However, about half a million registered foreign workers had left West Germany, and some observers in Bonn contended that a large additional number of unregistered foreign workers, perhaps as many as half a million, had also departed. If the foreign workers who had left

West Germany had been counted among the unemployed, the German jobless rate would probably have been about as high as the American. Nevertheless, Schmidt, in common with most German conservatives and probably the German electorate generally, felt that the best way to cure unemployment was to keep inflation down and the mark solid.

Schmidt's position was indistinguishable from that of the Bundesbank, Germany's central bank, whose independence from the German Government is considered even greater than the independence of the Federal Reserve Board from the United States Government. Karl Klasen, president of the Bundesbank, said, "It is no accident that Switzerland is not only the country with the stablest currency in the world but also the one with the lowest unemployment rate, namely four-tenths of 1 percent." The Swiss jobless rate was also held down by the departure of "guest" workers.

The German Chancellor was under pressure from his own country's trade unions to combat unemployment, as well as from the United States and his European partners. Heinz Oskar Vetter, the leader of the German unions, had urged Schmidt to launch a big public investment program. Schmidt was resisting. "Even if we have an investment program," he said, "it will not be financed by printing money. We will borrow the money, but not from the central bank—from the public, to keep it from causing inflation."

He warned that it would be unwise for President Carter's advisers to suppose that he could make the Bundesbank increase the money supply faster than the cautious rate of 6 to 7 percent it was pursuing. "Our central bank is autonomous," Schmidt told us. Chancellors, like Presidents, never lean on central banks except when they want to.

Schmidt said President Carter's Inaugural Address was eloquent but "lacking in clear direction." He said he thought it would be a mistake for Carter to go to an economic summit conference until he was thoroughly prepared.

Schmidt's hard-mark policy had wide support from German

industry, even with its strong orientation toward foreign trade. The appreciation of the mark had made its goods dearer abroad but, the industrialists felt, had kept them on their toes. Thanks to their heavy investment in modernization of equipment, vigorous sales and service efforts, and high productivity of their workers, German industries had been forging ahead in foreign markets even through the recessions in many of the countries to which they sold. It would not be easy for Mondale, when he arrived, to convince the Germans that they did not know their own best interests; the issue, however, was whether the Germans' hypercautious policies were in the best interests of the wider community of nations.

Conversely, Carter was facing the problem of how to stimulate the growth of the American economy to reduce unemployment without regenerating inflation and weakening the dollar. He blew his chance of resolving that problem by yielding to business and labor opposition to an effective wage and price policy.

CONFRONTATION WITH STEEL

During his campaign for the Presidency, Carter had called for an incomes policy to curb inflationary wage and price actions by business and labor; indeed, he had called for standby wage and price controls. But in December 1976, while he was still waiting to be sworn in as President, Carter's wage-price policy was challenged by the steel industry, which, in spite of weak demand for its products and high unemployment, put through a 6 to 7 percent price increase. Carter thus faced a confrontation with the steel industry—with wider implications for his relations with business in general—like that which confronted John F. Kennedy in 1961 when he took over the White House after eight years of Republican rule.

Actually, Kennedy's confrontation was more than a year in coming from the time he took office, although its seeds were sown early in his Administration. From Kennedy's first days in office, his top economic advisers had agreed that some special device would be required for putting restraints on prices and wages if full employment was to be regained without at the same time kicking off inflation. They argued that if that could be done there would be a genuine chance of breaking the business cycle and setting the economy on a course of long-term stable growth—a remarkable ambition but one that they considered attainable if Kennedy was willing to break new ground.

In the past, Presidents had often resorted to general entreaties to business and labor to show restraint. But the Kennedy Council of Economic Advisers—Walter Heller, Kermit Gordon, and Gardner Ackley—considered such pleas to have been ineffectual, because management and labor had interpreted restraint to mean doing what came naturally in particular market conditions.

The alternative approach of curbing inflationary wage and price actions by dumping the economy into a slump was considered unacceptable, since Kennedy, like Carter, had won an election on the pledge of getting the country moving again and reducing unemployment.

The fashioning of a new instrument for specific restraints on wages and prices came with the labor contract negotiations in the steel industry in 1961. That September, President Kennedy asked the United Steel Workers to hold their demands within what could be granted from productivity gains. And he made clear—or at least thought he had—to the steel industry that if labor held its demands down to a productivity guideline the steel companies would and should hold their prices stable.

But in April 1962, after signing a wage contract with the steel workers that was generally consistent with the productivity guideline, United States Steel, then headed by Roger M. Blough, followed by other steel companies, announced an increase in prices averaging $6 a ton.

Kennedy brought heavy pressure to bear on the steel producers—with the help of Inland Steel, which had refused to raise its prices—and U.S. Steel and the others announced a rescission of the price increase.

In one sense, Kennedy had gained an important victory. The wage and price guideposts became a widely accepted part of the apparatus of his Administration's economic policy—and got much of the credit for the years of noninflationary expansion that lasted well into the Johnson Administration, when the Vietnam war overheated an economy already close to full employment.

But in another sense, Kennedy's victory over steel came at a considerable price in terms of his relations with business, which remained hostile throughout the three years of his Administration. With business investment slow to gather force, the recovery was sluggish.

Presidents can't have it both ways; to govern, as Kennedy said, is to choose. Carter's pollster, Patrick H. Caddell, had suggested in the course of a 56-page memo to Carter in December that he consider, shortly after taking office, "an attack on Big Steel for its recent misbehavior."

But Carter did try to have it both ways: to curb business's price-raising proclivities but not to offend its sensibilities. While still President-elect, Carter said he was disappointed with the steel industry's decision to push through the 6 to 7 percent price increase in the face of weak demand—a criticism that went no further than President Ford's Council on Wage and Price Stability, which suggested that steel buyers should resist the price increases. Carter declined the overtures of some steel industry executives to meet with him to explain their action ex post facto. Instead, Carter announced his decision to drop his long-held support for standby price and wage controls. This decision, he thought, would remove the motivation of other industries to raise prices in advance of his entering the White House. He followed this up with another piece of appeasement for business and labor: He had changed his mind and would not require prenotification of major price and wage actions. The "incomes policy" to keep inflation down while he stimulated the economy into stronger growth to cure unemployment—the basic strategy on which he had campaigned for the White House—was dumped even before he took office.

VACILLATING RHYTHM

Carter kept shifting from position to position, searching for a political and economic consensus that was not there. The markets took alarm, sensing Presidential weakness. Carter contributed to public uncertainty not just by what he did but how he did it.

The perception of the President as an uncertain trumpet was heightened by his handling of the $30 billion package of fiscal stimulants he proposed—a package which had as its main feature a $50 tax rebate for individual taxpayers. But when this ran into political opposition—and even ridicule from the chairman of the Federal Reserve Board, Arthur Burns—Carter dropped it.

Carter's reputation as an economic policymaker had also been hurt by some of the people around him. The downfall of Budget Director Bert Lance, his closest and most trusted inside adviser, was the result of Lance's personal, not public, finances. Carter's obvious pain over the loss of his Georgia friend made the President seem all the more uncomfortable and uncertain with the advice he was getting from his other economic officers.

Carter kept vacillating in his relations with Arthur Burns, who continued to criticize the Carter Administration as severely as he liked from his redoubt at the Federal Reserve mansion on Constitution Avenue. Carter, turning the other cheek, routinely praised Burns and hailed the central bank's independence. But the President occasionally permitted his own economic advisers to criticize Burns for holding money too tight and pushing interest rates too high.

Carter had appointed five Ph.D.'s in economics to his Cabinet, but he appeared to trust none of them. I was traveling in the Middle East along with Treasury Secretary W. Michael Blumenthal in October 1977 when word reached us in Tehran from Washington that the White House had decided to delay the tax bill until some time in the coming year; Blumenthal knew nothing about this decision—and it was his bill. He hastily called a press conference in Tehran to say that the Administration had decided it wanted more time to "consult further with the business community" on existing tax proposals. "What we need is business investment and business confidence," said Blumenthal.

At the end of his first year in office, Carter's economic advisers were preparing what they called a "master agenda" for the coming year; they said the President had undergone a hard learning process during his first year, but now, with a surer grip on the essentials of economic policy, he was ready to wage a tougher fight against both unemployment and inflation.

But early in 1978, Carter's decision to replace Arthur Burns at the Fed with G. William Miller, the board chairman of Textron, Inc., rattled business confidence again. It was not that business or the markets regarded Burns as irreplaceable, but they were worried about the Miller appointment as a weak one. Miller had had no noticeable experience in domestic or international monetary affairs. The fear was that Burns had been reasonably tough on inflation but that Miller would not be.

Carter ran into immediate bad luck on the Miller appointment as the Senate Banking Committee held it up to look into charges that Miller had been responsible for a payment to an Iranian sale agency, Air Taxi, whose owner was General Mohammad Khatem, head of the Iranian Air Force, who had died in an accident in 1975. The payment was made by the Bell Helicopter Company, a Textron subsidiary, to obtain foreign contracts in Iran while Miller was Textron's chairman. The Administration (with backing from Arthur Burns) contended that Miller's prompt confirmation was crucial to provide leadership at the Fed in a period of extreme international financial stress related to the decline of the dollar. The committee did ultimately confirm him, but Miller never regained public confidence.

INFLATION 99, ADMINISTRATION 1

The dollar was sinking, inflation was rising, and the Carter Administration decided at the start of its second year in office that from now on inflation, not unemployment, would be its number-one target. The White House announced a "deceleration strategy" to clear up the trouble by enlisting the "voluntary cooperation" of business and labor.

This looked dubious. The real problem was that Carter himself had, with the help of Congress, exacerbated inflation during his first year in office by a whole series of governmental actions: the removal of larger portions of farm acreage from production to increase farm income; the forming of "orderly marketing agreements"—for instance, cutting the shipment of price-competitive Japanese goods to the United States; providing price protection for the American steel industry; benignly neglecting the dollar (Europeans saw it as "malign" efforts to talk the dollar down in order to cheapen the prices of U.S. exports and raise the prices of imports); increasing the minimum wage, which had not only helped to push up labor costs and prices but had helped shut those at the bottom—blacks and inner-city youth—out of jobs. There were other self-inflicted wounds, such as higher payroll taxes for Social Security that fed directly into prices and a federally promoted inflationary settlement to end a strike in the coal industry.

But now, presumably, all that was past. In the Economic Report of the President for 1978, a guideline was established for wages and prices: "Every effort should be made to reduce the rate of wage and price increase in 1978 to below the average rate of the past two years."

What did this mean? The Administration said it did not expect application of the guideline to be uniform; different industries were in different situations with respect to location, structure, profits, costs, etc. However, industry and labor would be asked to cooperate with the government, because "if a program for deceleration were to succeed, it will require strong efforts and cooperation at the level of individual industries." Early discussion between government and individual industry and labor groups with respect to specific inflation problems, the report said, "would be an important part of the deceleration effort."

The public regarded this anti-inflation program as nothing, or less than nothing, but the Carter Administration kept a stiff upper lip and insisted it was doing something. "The deceleration program is accelerating," Stuart E. Eizenstat, the 35-year-old Georgia lawyer who served as Carter's chief assistant for domestic policy, said in mid-June. Summarizing the Administration's position for me, Eizenstat said it consisted of four elements: openness, reorganization, targeting, and the pursuit of "a sustained and broad-based economic recovery." Sometimes Eizenstat sounded more like Carter than Carter.

Openness, he said, was crucial "after the years of unsupported war abroad and domestic crisis at home." Reorganization of government was vital to bring "incentives, rewards, and punishments" to the bureaucracy. Targeting was needed to "make better use of finite resources." Some critics of Carter had worried that he put too much emphasis on process, too little on substance; but Carter and his close aides seemed to think that process was substance. His chief domestic policy adviser talked of reducing Federal offices by 50 percent, Federal manpower by 25 percent, consolidating 25 civil rights functions into three, and various international cultural offices into one. He said the Administration would soon submit its Civil Service Reorganization Plan to Congress and that if it passed, the whole session would be a success. He hailed the Administration's use of zero-base budgeting, although a Brookings study had just shown that it had saved very little money and may have distracted the Administration from more meaningful budget savings and redirection of funds toward areas of more crucial need.

The fourth area of policy within Eizenstat's bailiwick was the national economy, which, he said, "overrides almost everything." A growing economy "provides funds to reduce the deficit" and "to reduce the unfinished agenda of public business," he said, defending the need for additional stimulus to keep the economy growing while citing the scaling down of the President's proposed tax cut of $25 billion to $20 billion because of "the dark cloud of inflation."

He worried about the resistance the Administration was encountering to its anti-inflation program, especially from organized labor. However, he felt the Administration had made an important breakthrough with the retail clerks' union, which he said had agreed to "abide" by the Administration's program. That looked like an overstatement to me; the retail clerks' president, William Wynn, had said he was against accepting the Administration's guideline for lowering wage settlements below the average of the last two years. However, he said, the union would "not go for that little extra something" in wages if it got protection through a cost-of-living clause against inflation. Paraphrasing Robert S. Strauss, the President's anti-inflation adviser, Eizenstat said the anti-inflation score was now inflation 99, Administration 1—counting the "victory" over the retail clerks as 1.

THE FULL BATHTUB

Where to go? What to do? The Keynesian Revolution appeared to have pinned the problem of chronic inflation on the American economy, since no downturn would be permitted in a democratic society to be deep enough, long enough, or catastrophic enough, as depressions had been in the past, to turn inflations into deflations, keeping the long-term price trend relatively stable.

It would be madness to bemoan the passage of the good old days of Depression, with their freight of human suffering and their common resolution in wars. I had never been able to forget Kenneth Boulding's bathtub theorem: the metaphor of the economy as a bathtub, filling up and up with capital goods until it began to slosh over—until war pulled the plug, drained the tub, and permitted the capital-accumulation process to start again. Not just the Keynesian Revolution but the coming of thermonuclear weapons had made a repetition of that horrible cycle of inflation-depression-war-expansion unthinkable.

But the new age of chronic inflation had brought painful problems in its wake, including the need to keep the economy under continuous fiscal and monetary pressure, lest the inflation get out of hand. And that combination of inflationary pressure and monetary counterpressure had produced stuttering growth and stagflation.

The number of possible cures was not infinite; the main choices seemed to be these:

- Three to four years of rigid price and wage controls. This might end inflationary expectations, if they remained intact and if no new disasters occurred, like a renewed world oil crisis. But price and wage controls are probably unworkable over time except under wartime circumstances, and even then, as we learned during World War II, they erode and generate black markets. In any event, during the Carter era they appeared out of the question, given the strong opposition of business, labor, agriculture, and other interest groups.
- Five to seven years of unemployment. It would probably take that long, with unemployment at 8 percent, to bring the inflation rate down below 3 percent. A deliberately induced long depression of that sort appeared politically out of the question; even Gerald Ford's much milder version was rejected at the ballot box.
- Nibbling policies. Chew fractions of decimal points off the price index by a long list of measures to reduce government subsidies and regulations; make private markets more competitive; free up labor markets; raise productivity; draw

down government stockpiles; reduce the minimum wage; etc. Some of these things could be done. But it looked as though, even if most of them were done, they would barely keep the dust down as new political demands for government help or regulation developed. The system was protection-prone, and the implications were inflationary.

- Supply-side moves. Give businesses tax breaks and investment tax credits to encourage them to invest more in more efficient equipment; raise output per unit of input; meet the rising tide of demand with a rising tide of goods and services. But in the short run, measures to spur investment might add to inflationary pressures and make the system less stable as inflation swung up and down. Alternatively, try to increase supply by putting the jobless to work and raising the productivity of labor by a variety of devices: public jobs programs, manpower training programs, incentives to business to hire the hard to employ, etc. Such steps might help to reduce the unemployment component of stagflation, but whether it would reduce the inflation component was dubious; it might even exacerbate it by requiring increased government spending and bigger deficits.
- Incomes policies. A variety of means of trying to restrain wages and prices. Liberal economists (and a few conservatives, such as Henry Wallich of the Federal Reserve Board) were pushing for a fundamental change in the tax system to provide incentives and disincentives to business and labor to hold down their price and wage actions. Proponents contended that such tax-based anti-inflation policies could be incorporated into the system and still leave decision makers free to make choices and hence not impair the efficiency of the system. But opponents argued that the policies would be horrendously complicated, difficult to administer, and would only constitute a new form of price and wage controls.

Carter didn't like any of the choices; indeed, there was not much to like.

But neither was there anything to like about the inflation, which was undermining his own position and, more importantly, the vitality of the American political and economic system.

When observed from day to day, inflation looks like a series of annoyances and accidents—an unexpected jump in food or oil prices, a steel strike or a coal strike, a drop in the dollar. But such episodic "accidents" reflect the underlying erosion of national will and purpose that threatens the dissolution of society into a game of threat and bluff among pressure groups. These continuously raise the ante of group against group. But the game is ruinous for the powerless, the poor, the unemployed, the ill, the aged, and, in the end, for the whole society.

That inflationary squeeze had to be ended, and President Carter knew it. He kept looking for a politically painless way to do it. But there was none.

Chapter
11

MIDDLE EAST ON MY MIND

The seventies were ending in a mood of despair.

The Carter Administration had grown fearful that the fall of the Shah of Iran and the coming to power of the Ayatollah Ruhollah Khomeini would be not the end but only the beginning of a time of acute troubles for oil-producing nations and for the industrial nations dependent on them. Ironically, it was oil wealth that had lifted the Shah and his regime toward vast military and industrial power, and oil wealth that destroyed him.

What had happened in Iran could happen elsewhere—in Saudi Arabia, Nigeria, Venezuela—who knew where? Rapid industrialization, explosive urban growth, galloping inflation, the widening gap between rich and poor, the rise of a new proletariat with religious fanatics or fanatical antireligious Marxists to lead it, the shock of new ways of living upon tradition-bound societies—none of that was unique to Iran.

Which country would be the next Iran? In February 1979, International Political Surveys, Inc., a company of political analysts, said the countries facing the highest risks of turmoil and revolution over the next 18 months were Rhodesia, Nigeria, Turkey, Lebanon, El Salvador, Libya, Portugal, Italy, Argentina, and Zaire.

The economists—respectable economists, not the professional scaremongers—were writing grim scenarios. Albert M. Wojnilower, of the First Boston Corporation, wrote: "Our ability to control inflation has been seriously undermined by policies to deregulate financial institutions and interest rates. . . . It is as though we lived in a city in which all the walls had been torn down because they injured drunks and speeders who crashed into them. . . . An early recession touched off by a debacle in the dollar—or any early recession, for that matter—would be extremely dangerous. . . . But policy makers have no safe options: A policy that refuses to risk recession is an invitation to runaway inflation, but a policy that allows a recession also courts disaster."

Robert H. Parks, chief economist of Advest, wrote: "Industry is now putting through price hikes out of fear of a greatly tightened wage and price control program. These price hikes will come on top of oil inflation, gasoline inflation, imported inflation (reflecting the lagged impact of dollar devaluation), unit cost inflation (reflecting the slide in productivity and rapidly climbing wage and benefit costs), tax inflation (reflecting the rise in the Social Security tax), indexed inflation (reflecting the link of private and government wage contracts to prices) and food inflation (reflecting soaring farm prices)."

Alan Greenspan, back at his post as president of Townsend-Greenspan, warned: "The effects of the political turmoil within Iran are soon likely to spread beyond its border. The impact on the United States is bound to be significant. . . . At best it appears that a significant part of the American losses in Iran, militarily, politically, and economically, are irreversible. The only issue which remains to be resolved is whether the loss is contained within Iran and kept to a moderate dimension, or whether the corrosive effects of the Iranian collapse spread to the rest of the Middle East."

Marina von Neumann Whitman, distinguished public service professor at the University of Pittsburgh, said: "Should the industrialized countries fail to solve the problem of stagflation domestically, a liberal and coherent international economic system will be among the early casualties and, with it, the economic fortunes of the numerous developing countries heavily dependent on the markets of the industrialized world."

Kurt Richebaecher, chief economist of West Germany's Dresdner Bank, wrote: "The more governments borrow, the sooner the time will come when this debt cannot be increased any further relative to the growing burden of current debt service on income. Such a borrowing process may go on for a long time but nothing is more certain than the fact that this reversal will come one day. Then the opposite process, which was termed 'debt deflation' in the 1930s, will begin."

But the greatest immediate problem was what the second oil shock stemming from the Iranian revolution would do to oil prices and to worldwide inflation and unemployment. The outlook was grave. At the start of the year, the price of a barrel of light Arabian crude oil was $13.34; oil industry experts were now forecasting that by the end of the year it would rise by about 50 percent to $18 or $20 a barrel. Some were looking for an even greater rise. John Swearingen, then chairman of Standard Oil of Indiana, said he expected the price to settle between $20 and $25 a barrel.

But all the experts were too conservative. The oil price kept climbing and, with the help of the Iran-Iraq war, rose above $40 a barrel.

SINKING DOLLAR AND SINKING POPULARITY

And at last President Carter began to move. In April 1979 he announced a plan to decontrol oil prices. This evoked cheer in Wall Street and strengthened the dollar. Paradoxically, the higher oil prices helped the dollar throughout the world, because the oil trade is largely conducted in dollars, and when oil prices went up, oil-importing countries everywhere had to purchase more dollars to pay their bills to OPEC. Further, the oil-price increases had not hit the United States balance of payments as hard as they did countries like West Germany and Japan, more dependent than the U.S. on imported oil.

Nevertheless, the inflation boiled on. At the Federal Reserve, Chairman G. William Miller parried the pressure from Treasury Secretary W. Michael Blumenthal to raise interest rates and tighten monetary policy to slow down the inflation. Carter told Blumenthal to lay off Miller, but it was not clear whether he was really backing Miller or just trying to stop an unseemly brawl between the Treasury and the Fed after the fight broke into the public prints.

In mid-April, Miller told me an economic slowdown was in progress and he had no intention of tightening monetary policy further. He said he didn't think the inflation, which had gone back up to double-digit rates in the first quarter, reflected excessive demand for goods. The revival of business capital spending didn't bother him. "We want to encourage capital spending," he said, arguing that it was the fundamental solution to lagging productivity and inflation. He found "few real shortages" and said that "all in all, you are seeing the signals you would expect to see in the fifth year of an expansion." Climbing energy prices stemming from the upheaval in Iran, he said, would soften the economy: "The more money spent on energy, the less people can spend on other goods, so this will soften other sectors."

But the markets at home and abroad took fright again at the timid Fed and Administration policies, and the dollar went into a new sinking spell; and Carter's political stock was sinking. A *New York Times*/CBS News poll found that Carter's approval rating had tumbled from 42 percent in March to a new low of 30 percent in June, with public concern over the economy and inflation the main cause of his fall. Only 20 percent approved of President Carter's handling of the economy.

What did they want done? A 64 percent majority of those interviewed said they would vote for "someone who supports wage and price controls to limit inflation." Carter continued to declare his opposition to mandatory controls, accepting the warning of his advisers that controls would damage business investment, produce even more sluggish growth, misallocate resources, and, in the end, fall apart and lead to a worse burst of inflation.

What was the alternative? The European central bankers, speaking through the Bank for International Settlements, told the United States Government to push the economy into a recession now to curb inflation and avoid a more serious collapse later. They were urging the American monetary authorities to tighten up monetary policy and raise interest rates to cool off the economy.

And in July, Carter fired W. Michael Blumenthal as Secretary of the Treasury, gave G. William Miller his job, and called in Paul A. Volcker, the president of the New York Federal Reserve Bank, to be chairman of the Board of Governors of the Fed. Volcker was regarded by the banking and business community in the United States and internationally as a hard-nosed central banker who would have the political independence to slow the economy down, probably dump it into a recession to stop the inflation.

Carter knew that this might cost him the White House. But he had delayed his assault on inflation so long and the situation was getting so out of control that he agreed to bring in

Volcker and let him get on with the job. As Robert S. Strauss
put it to me, "He had no choice. He had to appoint Volcker."

KEEPING FAITH

At the end of July 1979, President and Mrs. Carter invited my
wife and me, together with a small group of other news people
and their spouses, to a dinner party at the White House. Such
affairs are generally off the record; they are used to try to let
selected members of the press know what the President is
doing or thinking, without accepting the responsibility of a
clear public statement.

It's a hazardous business for news people to get involved in
these affairs, since the whole business verges on news management, with a certain amount of stroking thrown in for the
favored guests. But it's difficult to say no; a news person
usually welcomes any chance to see and hear a President close
up.

In my case, the deal, which had been set up for me by Bob
Strauss, who had by then been shifted from chief inflation
fighter to chief trade negotiator, was originally supposed to
have been that I would go to the dinner party and at some
point in the evening the President and I would steal away to his
private quarters for an exclusive interview. But the party lasted
so long that Mr. and Mrs. Carter said their good nights before I
could get my interview. Of course I was greatly disappointed;
the conversation at the party had provided some fascinating
insights into what the President was thinking. When my wife
and I got back to the Washington apartment where we were
staying, we wrote out as exactly as we could just what the President and Mrs. Carter had said.

The next morning, I was sitting glumly at a typewriter in the
Washington Bureau of *The New York Times,* trying to figure
out how to make some use of the White House dinner conversation, when a call came in to me from Jody Powell, the Presi-

dent's press secretary. He said the President was awfully sorry
that the interview had not come off, but it had got too late, and
now he was on his way out to Kentucky and Ohio to do a little
politicking. Then Powell added: "The President wanted me to
ask you if you had got what you wanted."

I said, Sure, it had been a fascinating evening, but I didn't
know what I could do with it. Powell said I could use anything
I wanted from the conversation or my side discussions with
him but to treat it all as an interview.

I asked, "Can I quote the President directly?" He said, "Yes,
you can. I wouldn't overdo it, but you could certainly use half
a dozen direct quotes."

So I did, and my story in the August 1 edition of *The Times*
caused a furor.

I led with the President's statement that he expected unemployment to rise during the rest of 1979 and into 1980, when he
was determined to make a fight to hold on to the White House.
The story went on to say that Carter accepted the diagnosis
that the economy was already in a recession but intended to
keep his Administration's policies focused on arresting the rate
of inflation, which he considered "the most serious problem
facing the nation economically—and himself politically."

But none of that caused the outburst; it was the following
paragraph that did it:

"In last night's discussion, the President ranged from the
economy and energy to Middle East peacemaking and Presidential politics. At one point he likened the Palestinian cause
to the civil rights movement in the United States. He predicted
that few Palestinians would actually choose to return to the
West Bank, if given the chance, and doubted that other Arab
states genuinely wanted a new Palestinian state."

The *New York Post* in its afternoon edition that day
splashed all over its front page a story, based on mine, declaring that Carter had likened the United States civil rights movement to "the P.L.O." The *Post*, which had been taken over by
the Australian press lord Rupert Murdoch, was doing its best

to stir up trouble for Carter with the Jewish community—and it was succeeding. Criticism from Jewish leaders poured in on the Carter White House.

In response to one letter written to *The Times* by the national president of Hadassah, Bernice S. Tannenbaum, asserting that President Carter had affronted "the American civil rights movement in comparing this exemplary, nonviolent struggle to the terrorist methods of the P.L.O.," I said, in a letter of my own to *The Times*:

> This is an incorrect version of what the President said.
>
> The President did not compare the civil rights movement to the P.L.O. or any other terrorist group but to the aspirations of the Palestinian people. He specifically said that the United States would not accept the P.L.O. as a negotiator, because that organization does not accept Israel's right to exist.
>
> Mr. Carter spoke sensitively of Israel's security concerns. There was no trace of bias in his entire conversation. He opposed the creation of a separate Palestinian state. He stressed the importance of Israel to American and Western interests in the Middle East and said, as I reported, that some nations, such as France, which had been dubious about his efforts to bring Egypt and Israel together, had come to appreciate how valuable a contribution their combined forces made to the security and stability of the area, whether against radical Arab states or threats of Soviet incursion.

But the story didn't die. In a "Letter from Israel" to the British periodical *The Listener* on September 13, Chaim Herzog, the Israeli Ambassador to Great Britain, said, "Israelis, as indeed many Americans, were horrified by the President's gauche equation of the PLO with the Civil Rights movement."

My colleague Anthony Lewis, who had also been present at the now celebrated Carter dinner party, wrote to *The Listener* to say, "What is gauche is that Ambassador Herzog should thus blandly repeat a thoroughly discredited untruth about what President Carter said at a private dinner in the White

House on the evening of 30 July." After quoting from my own letter, Tony concluded: "That a former ambassador as distinguished as Mr. Herzog, and as familiar with the United States, should choose to believe an ugly and totally unsupported fairytale about the President is surprising and sad."

In his own memoirs, *Keeping Faith,* Jimmy Carter quotes from his diary of August 3, 1979, written four days after our dinner party:

> There's a general feeling that Begin's government is going to go under in the next 60 days because of dissatisfaction in Israel concerning economics, and also because of Begin's health. We don't think this will be good for the peace prospects. Had a long discussion about the Palestinian-UN resolution, and how we could move forward toward peace without committing political suicide. My own preference is that [Robert S.] Strauss take charge of dealing with the Israelis, American Jews, and Arabs. Cy [Vance] said he'd just as soon resign if he was going to be a figurehead, but I think later on he cooled off a little. It's obvious to me that there's no advantage for me or Vance to be in the forefront of this difficult issue. We can set the policy, and Strauss can carry it out and deal with these diverse groups with more political impunity than I can.[1]

Ten days later President Carter accepted the resignation of Andrew Young, his Ambassador to the United Nations, when word leaked out that Young had met with the Palestinian representative to the United Nations, Ambassador Terzi, apparently in violation of a pledge by Henry Kissinger, which Carter had reaffirmed, that the United States would not talk to the P.L.O., which it considered a terrorist organization.

Carter says in his memoirs that Ambassador Young, "as President of the Security Council, met in his apartment with the representative of the Palestine Liberation Organization." This was not accurate. As Young told me, he had actually met

---

[1] Jimmy Carter, *Keeping Faith,* 1982, p. 491.

Ambassador Terzi, the P.L.O. representative, in the apartment of Ambassador Abdullah Beshara of Kuwait, who was serving as secretary general of the Arab Gulf states.

[Carter writes that Young] notified Israel's United Nations Ambassador about the meeting, and the information immediately became public. State Department officials felt that Andy should have informed them more frankly about his actions. American Jewish leaders felt that we were attempting to recognize or negotiate with the PLO, and black leaders believed that Ambassador Young had been unjustly condemned for merely doing his duty as leader of the Security Council. During the furor following this incident, Andy resigned and I appointed his deputy, Donald McHenry, to take his place. Andy had *not* [italics in Carter's text] violated the United States agreement with Israel concerning the PLO, but he should have informed the Secretary of State more fully about the controversial meeting. A mountain was made of a molehill— another indication of the politically charged character of the Middle East dispute.[2]

DAMNED IF YOU DO OR DON'T

But that is not the way Andy Young sees what happened. His story, as he told it to me in a telephone interview on August 15, 1983, from his office as Mayor of Atlanta, was this:

"In July 1979," said Young, "there was a report of the Commission on Palestinian Rights. It should have been considered while Britain was chairing the Security Council. But it was not, and in August it was my month to chair the Security Council, so I was faced with the report of the Commission on Palestinian Rights. The resolution had come straight from Arafat's office. It accepted the U.N. resolutions 242 and 338, acknowledging Israel's right to exist, and it called for a Palestinian state, as we expected it to do. But it contained condemnatory

[2] Ibid., p. 492.

language about Israel. Things were in a state of upheaval in Washington—that was the month when Carter asked Califano, Schlesinger, and Blumenthal to resign.

"I spoke to Cy Vance about what to do about the Palestinian resolution, and he said, 'You're damned if you do and damned if you don't. Postpone it.' "

But Young decided to try to get the offensive language out of the resolution as a way of moving the peacemaking process along. "I spoke to the Syrians, the Lebanese, and the Kuwaitis," he said. "I felt that if we could get rid of the condemnatory passage, the resolution would be as moderate as we could get, and to reject it would break down our credibility. But the Arabs said there was nothing they could do and I would have to talk to Ambassador Terzi about it.

"If Arthur Goldberg had been Ambassador to the U.N. instead of me, nothing would have happened. Technically, there was no violation of our agreement not to negotiate with the P.L.O., because I was acting as president of the Security Council. I said I would try again, even if it required my meeting with the Palestinians. Ambassador Beshara said he had invited the Syrians and the P.L.O. representative to come to his apartment, and hoped to wait until 6:30 P.M. or so to resolve it.

"I said I would stop by and see what I could do. I was reluctant to postpone the resolution. As it stood, the U.S. would have to veto it and not accept a Palestinian state, but for us to veto it would be bad for everybody. We were almost putting the moderate elements into a trap. Basically the resolution said what we wanted—they would accept Israel's right to exist with the quid pro quo of a Palestinian state."

Young said, "You have no idea how many other contacts were going on with the P.L.O., even involving the Israelis. The Palestinians had met with Moshe Dayan at breakfast and with Shimon Peres at the actor Harry Belafonte's house.

Silk: "Why, then, did you resign?"

Young: "I resigned basically because of the big brouhaha after the *New York Post* found out. We were afraid of fanning black and Jewish flames."

Young said a fictional version of such a confrontation between blacks and Jews had been written by Theodore Koppel and Marvin Kalb based on an imagined meeting between Henry Kissinger and Yasir Arafat. "Frankly," said Young, "I could see that occurring—an unruly mob at a police station in Brooklyn. I would have had blacks there defending me."

He said there was so much at stake that could be wrecked by such a confrontation: "the independence of Zimbabwe, the passage of the SALT treaty—my presence would not make it possible."

Young said he sought guidance but none was available. "Cy's mother-in-law was ill and dying."

Further, he thought he "had pushed the Establishment as far as it could be pushed. People at State were upset with me. I'd been taught to do things that were politically acceptable. Take Zimbabwe—I pushed it hard. State would have left it to the British. But both Carter and Vance would end up backing me on that. I was viewed as a politician, not a diplomat. Carter had the support of only a minority of the Democratic Party. He had moved too far to the right."

Young said he was angry and deeply offended when the State Department announced that his meeting with the P.L.O. representative was just a "casual meeting," not negotiations. "Everybody knew that was a lie," said Young. "I told the Israeli Ambassador what had happened and said I would do whatever I could do. I wanted to be straight with people. That has to be the basis of anything we could do. So it was just awkward. That's why I resigned."

BILLS TO PAY

All of this had a significant bearing on economic policy. For a crucial question in mid-1979 was how could the United States best handle the economic problems—intensified inflation, threatened recession, and a worsening of the international balance of payments—set off by the Iranian explosion that was reverberating throughout the Middle East. Carter hoped that winning a peace treaty between Israel and Egypt would ease this country's and the world's energy and financial problems; and he saw resolving the Palestinian problem as vital to a lasting peace.

Taken in isolation, peace between Egypt and Israel would only heighten disaffection among the radical Arab states and the militant Palestinian groups, who would see it as a blow to their prestige and their desire to establish a strong Palestinian state on Israel's border. The radical Arabs and Palestinians would, as a high State Department official put it, be likely to commit "desperate acts" to wreck the peace. One such act would be a move by their allies among the oil workers in Iran to shut down production again, giving another upward push to world oil prices. Pressures would also be intensified, in all probability, on other Arab states, especially Saudi Arabia and Kuwait, to restrict their oil output. It was conceivable that another oil embargo like the one in 1973–74 would be aimed against the United States and other nations regarded as friends of Egypt and Israel.

Even without an oil embargo, however, the United States would have a huge bill to pay. The Saudis, Kuwaitis, and other Arab states had been giving Egypt $2 billion a year in foreign aid, and had threatened to cut that off if Egypt made a settlement with Israel. Saudi Arabia, the biggest donor, had cautiously qualified its threat, saying it would cut off aid only if the "legitimate aspirations of the Palestinians were not honored."

On the Israeli side, there would also be big bills for the United States to pay. It was likely that the initial period of transition would necessitate a higher level of military spending by Israel; the Camp David accord required the withdrawal of Israeli armed forces from Sinai and the turnover of airfields near El Arish, Rafah, Ras en-Naqh, and Sharm el-Sheikh to Egypt for civilian use. The United States was committed to construct two new airfields in the Negev at the cost of more than $1 billion. The strategic redeployment of the Israeli armed forces would impose additional costs, as would the acquisition of new oil supplies as a result of the return to Egypt of the Aima oil field required by the Camp David agreement. President Carter had told the Israeli Knesset: "We know your concern for an adequate oil supply. In the context of peace we are ready to guarantee that oil supply."

But in the long run, peace would come as a benefit, not as a cost, with enormous savings in military spending and a shift of resources to civilian consumption and investment. Both Egypt and Israel were spending about 40 percent of their gross national product on defense. In addition, genuine peace would bring opportunities for cooperation between the countries in trade, exchange of technical skills, transportation, water management, banking, agriculture, solar energy development, and other fields.

If, however, the peace effort failed, United States officials expected Egypt to re-evaluate its entire position and turn in a strong pan-Arab direction. Egypt would have to cope with radical pressures internally as well as externally.

And a failure of the peace effort would mean much heavier economic burdens for the United States in the long run, not only because of the strengthening of the oil producers' cartel but also because of the danger of a strategic shift adverse to American interests. So there were plenty of economic as well as military reasons for Jimmy Carter to give a top priority to efforts to solve the Palestinian issue.

ECONOMICS AND CHARACTER

Thus it is impossible to disentangle economic from political, diplomatic, and national security considerations. And the making of economic policy is also a reflection of the personality and character of the President—and, especially in the case of Jimmy Carter, of his wife, Rosalynn.

During the July White House dinner party, Carter mentioned his concern about the "national crisis of confidence" that was then troubling him. "What's the root cause of it?" someone asked. Mrs. Carter gave her own answer. "You know, I have done a good deal of work on mental health," she said. "And I think that a nation can be very much like an individual who has experienced a psychological trauma. I think the nation has gone through a series of traumas—over Vietnam and then over Watergate. Suddenly the bottom seemed to drop out and there was nothing left to believe in. And I think the nation has not yet worked through those traumas."

Carter himself picked up the Vietnam theme and said he felt deeply that the country was indeed in a crisis of confidence and not just about his Administration; he ascribed that crisis to the nation's failure ever to admit that it had been defeated in Vietnam or that it had been "immoral" in waging the Vietnam war.

He said that he had rejected Stuart Eizenstat's proposal that OPEC be branded as "the enemy," to be blamed for gasoline lines and a much tougher Administration energy policy. He said it would be "unethical" to blame OPEC for our failure to cut back our use of oil and to do the other things we ought to do to take care of our energy needs.

OPEC, he said, was not a monolith, and he opposed any "blanket condemnation" of it. Some countries—and he singled out Saudi Arabia and Venezuela—had been friendly and helpful to the United States. He said he had made direct overtures to Crown Prince Fahd of Saudi Arabia to persuade him to hold the oil price at $18 a barrel and to raise production by one million barrels a day, and his efforts had been successful.

Carter contended that proposals made by some outsiders to use U.S. food exports as a bargaining weapon against OPEC's high-priced oil made no sense. He derided the slogan of "a bushel for a barrel." If the United States tried to cut off food supplies to OPEC, France and other countries would supply it. He also rejected proposals that the United States be ready to use military force to guarantee Middle Eastern oil supplies. That, he said, would only result in sabotage of the oil fields and worse political and security problems than the United States already had in that area. He linked his efforts to bring about peace and cooperation between Israel and Egypt to the security of American oil supplies from the Middle East.

Egyptian and Israeli arms, Carter suggested, would be important not only in securing the Middle East against moves by radical Arab states but also against the threat of Soviet incursions. He was concerned about the report of the C.I.A. that the Soviet Union would be forced to start importing oil soon, and might be turning to the Middle East to satisfy its needs. In that situation he regarded Israeli-Egyptian unity as more important than ever.

He said he did not think stable peace could come to the area without a solution to the Palestinian problem, and hoped "urgently" that American Jewish leaders—here he named Sol M. Linowitz and Robert S. Strauss—would support and help to sell his efforts to work out arrangements that would give the Palestinians autonomy on such issues as schools, police, housing, and immigration on the West Bank.

In likening the Palestinian issue to the "civil rights movement here in the United States," Carter depicted it as a highly emotional issue and a matter of "rights." If the Israelis permitted Palestinians to come back to the West Bank, he said, they would be satisfied with "just the right to do it," but relatively few of the Palestinians scattered through the Arab world would want to return to the poverty of the area.

On the other side, he believed that the Palestinian Arabs would be willing to accept the physical presence of Israeli military units as a safeguard of their national security. He maintained that according to polls he had seen, a sizable majority of the Israeli people favored a generous settlement with the Palestinians, based on U.N. Resolution 242.

He insisted that there would also have to be "give" on the Arab side; he said the other Arab states did not want a new Palestinian state that would be a source of continuing instability and a radical threat even to themselves.

When the talk turned to domestic politics, Carter said he was still "very much alive" as a candidate for re-election in 1980, and said he was the most optimistic of any in his White House group. He said he and his staff had already done a good deal of work planning the 1980 campaign. He said he had met with Senator Edward Kennedy to talk over their differences. Asked how they had gotten along, Carter said, "Well, it was strained, but we eased the tension by laughing a lot."

On the Republican side, the President said he thought the candidate would be Ronald Reagan, though he himself would prefer to run against Senator Howard Baker of Tennessee— not, Carter said, because he thought Senator Baker would be easier to defeat but because he regarded him as a more worthy opponent and a man better qualified to deal with the nation's major problems.

Carter was a remarkable President: one of the most intelligent and sensitive, and one of the most febrile and unsure. He remained the outsider in Washington, suspicious and wary of the Eastern Establishment, many of whose members he had named to his Administration—and several of whom, including Secretaries Califano, Blumenthal, and Schlesinger, he had dismissed. I once asked him how he would characterize the Establishment, and he said: "Arrogant, snobbish, untrusting— untrusting of us Georgians."

Chapter

12

A WALK ON THE SUPPLY SIDE

Ronald Reagan's drive for the White House was powered by two quite different types of conservative supporters. One was a group of right-wing "populists" whose main objective was to slash taxes, eliminate government programs and cut spending except in the military areas, eliminate government regulations, and release the enterprise of private individuals and private business. In California, these were the people who had led the Proposition 13 tax revolt. This group of populists was dominated by small- and medium-sized businesses, homeowners, farmers, retirees, white-collar, and even many blue-collar workers: "Middle Americans," many of them with scant sympathy for those they consider below them on the economic and social scale (especially those on welfare) and not much sympathy toward Big Business. Indeed, many in this populist camp regarded Big Business, Big Banks, and the internationally oriented institutions they supported, such as the Council on Foreign Relations and the Rockefeller-founded Trilateral Commission, as a kind of conspiracy designed to serve the interests of the "liberal" Eastern Establishment. (Early in the campaign, George Bush, though a transplant from Connecticut and Yale to Texas, had resigned from the Council on Foreign Relations to stress his separation from the Eastern Establishment.) These populists represented the radical wing of the Reaganauts.

But within the Reagan fold, particularly after he had secured his hold on the nomination, were a second band: representatives of Big Business, Big Banks, and their professional economic and political counselors who constituted the Republican, if not entirely Eastern, Establishment. The thinking of this group, though not in clear conflict with that of the right-wing populists on every issue, was focused on the importance of checking inflation, stimulating corporate investment, preserving the stability of the international monetary system, balancing the budget, restraining monetary growth, and putting their greatest stress on insuring the stability rather than the rapid growth of the United States economy. These were the old-style conservative Reaganauts. He had not been their first choice as the Republican candidate—they would have preferred Bush or even John Connally—but they were willing to ride with Reagan after it became clear he had the nomination sewed up.

During the campaign, Reagan's pitch was a loose and vague amalgam of these two contrasting conservative approaches, packaged to appeal to a majority of the electorate, angry about inflation, distressed about the economy's slow growth, and unhappy about their taxes, constantly rising as inflation pushed them into higher tax brackets. Jimmy Carter and his economic advisers had kept saying there was no "quick fix" for inflation, including mandatory price and wage controls; they tried, by supporting greater fiscal and monetary restraint, to keep the economy growing below its potential and thereby to sweat inflation out of the system—a slow and costly cure. Reagan and his advisers regarded this as "the economics of despair"—in answer to which they offered their own "economics of hope."

Despite divisions among the economists in his camp, Reagan enthusiastically bought the line of "supply-side economics" forcefully argued by such supporters of his as Representative Jack Kemp of upstate New York, Professor Arthur Laffer of the University of Southern California, and Jude Wanniski, a former associate editor of *The Wall Street Journal* who had become an economic consultant to business. Their contention was that the country had been cast into a slough of despond by "demand-side economics"—not only the economics of John Maynard Keynes but also that of Milton Friedman and his monetarist followers, who now claimed Paul A. Volcker, chairman of the Federal Reserve Board, as a convert to the monetarist cause.

The Kemp-Laffer-Wanniski supply-siders asserted that "demand management," whether employing fiscal or monetary restraints, could not solve the linked problems of inflation, unemployment, and sluggish growth of output and productivity. They insisted that, whether explicitly or implicitly, both fiscalists and monetarists were trying to solve the problem of inflation by creating unemployment, and to solve unemployment by creating inflation. Some of the Republican economists, such as Herbert Stein, who had served as President Nixon's chairman of the Council of Economic Advisers, and George P. Shultz, his Secretary of the Treasury, believed that the supply-siders were dead wrong in their assault on the economics of Professor Milton Friedman, who had made his public political debut as a supporter of Barry Goldwater for the Presidency in 1964 against Lyndon Johnson, and had been a close adviser of Richard Nixon before and after he entered the White House. Jude Wanniski, conceding that Professor Friedman was "a good friend of Reagan's," said the supply-siders respected Friedman as a "free marketeer" but not as a monetarist. "I really believe," Wanniski said early in the campaign, "that Reagan prefers to think in our terms."

Politically, supply-side economics, with its call for big tax cuts, was far more appealing than the hard discipline offered by monetarism. Reagan had bought the supply-siders' idea of a 30 percent cut in Federal income taxes, embodied in the Kemp-Roth bill, which, said Jack Kemp, was not intended as a one-shot spur to consumption but as a means of "restoring incentives" and of increasing the willingness of individuals and businesses to supply the marketplace. Professor Friedman, who wanted to bring down taxes as a means of curbing government spending, for the long-term ideological goal of shrinking the role of government, was willing to go along, as were many other conservative supporters of Reagan, whether they bought the supply-side argument or not.

In his campaign speeches, Reagan hailed Kemp-Roth as a "replica of the Kennedy tax cut of 1964." George Bush, while he was still running his own campaign to get the Republican nomination, denounced Kemp-Roth and supply-side claims as "Voodoo Economics." The supply-siders said that, as Barry Goldwater had rejected the Kennedy-Johnson tax cut of 1964, Bush was rejecting Kemp-Roth. Kemp, Laffer, and Wanniski spent twenty hours briefing Reagan at the Marriott Inn at the Los Angeles airport on January 3, 4, and 5, and emerged convinced that he had accepted their ideas.

Reagan's supply-side populists also said they differed from the Friedman monetarists in their plan to restore a fixed rate between the dollar and gold, ending the floating exchange rate system strongly supported by Friedman—and opposed by their own guru, Professor Robert Mundell of Columbia University. President Carter's economists had also championed floating rates and, like Friedman, favored eliminating gold's monetary role. But Reagan, down deep, was a gold bug, and favored the supply-side line on gold.

Curiously enough, where the "liberal" Jimmy Carter committed himself to achieving a balanced budget in 1981 and treated Kemp-Roth as fiscally irresponsible, the "conservative" Ronald Reagan plunged ahead with his support for a 30 percent tax cut and rapidly rising military spending in the face of a yawning budget deficit and persistent inflation. It was a stroke of great political daring, maybe genius, whatever one thought of his economics.

"An Incredible Morass"

After Reagan's big victory at the polls in November, his supply-siders urged him to hit the ground running, as Franklin D. Roosevelt had done in his celebrated "hundred days" at the start of the New Deal in 1933.

Jude Wanniski gave me a copy of a 23-page memo to the President-elect warning of an "economic Dunkirk" that would face the Administration as soon as it took office. The memo was the work of David A. Stockman, the 33-year-old Michigan Congressman who would become the Reagan Administration's budget director, and Representative Jack Kemp, the 45-year-old ex–Buffalo Bills quarterback who was co-author of the Kemp-Roth bill. The leak was designed to maximize pressure on Reagan to plunge ahead with his program.

Stockman and Kemp warned of a worsening "credit crunch"—a severe tightening of money and credit and a shooting up of interest rates—that would lead to further deterioration of long-term capital markets, a renewed slowdown in consumer spending, and "intensified uncertainty throughout financial markets." They predicted that national output would stagnate or decline in the first half of 1981, and thereby generate "staggering political and policy changes," including a dire budget outlook, intensified pressures for protection against auto imports, a costly bailout of housing and other threatened industries, and rising outlays to support a growing number of jobless workers.

Even without the big tax cuts that both men favored, they said there would be deeper Federal budget deficits, rising government spending, and a hemorrhage of Federal credit, swelling the deficit for the 1981 fiscal year to $50 billion to $60 billion. Further, they said, growing Federal loan and loan-guarantee programs would pre-empt $100 billion in available funds beyond the Treasury's borrowings to finance the official deficit; these spending, deficit, and credit trends, they warned, were "generating market expectations of a chronic and severe Reagan inflation." They foresaw shocks to commodity and oil prices if the Iraq-Iran war continued and warned of an "unprecedented" scaling up of the regulatory burdens on American business, which, they asserted, were just about to strike the industrial economy "with near-gale force," pre-empting billions in investment capital, driving up costs, and leaving companies in "an incredible morass" of new controls and compliance procedures.

The Dunkirk paper said that unless Reagan dealt with these developments boldly the Republicans could suffer an erosion of momentum, unity, and public confidence. It predicted that unless crude oil price controls, refiner entitlements, gasoline allocations, and product price controls were completely ended by February 1 there was "a high probability of gasoline lines and general petroleum market disorder by early spring."

The two Congressmen warned Reagan that a failure to spur early economic expansion would quickly destroy the Republican consensus on economic policy. If the Federal Reserve refused to accommodate the commodity price and credit-demand shocks ahead, they said, the "already-tattered credibility of the post–October 1979 Volcker monetary policy will be destroyed," and this could subject the Fed to enormous internal strife and external pressure, creating conditions for "full-scale financial panic and unprecedented global monetary turbulence."

The chief purpose of the Dunkirk paper, Jack Kemp told me, was to urge President Reagan to demonstrate to the American people that he was committed to a program of vigorous action to combat stagflation, much as President Roosevelt had demonstrated on taking office that he was committed to fighting the Depression. "We haven't hesitated to invoke the name of F.D.R.," said Kemp. He added that his aim was to make the Republican Party the nation's majority party, with broad-based support among working-class people as well as among the middle class and the wealthy.

The supply-siders held that the United States could not solve its complex of economic problems, including inflation, except within a pattern of vigorous growth. This represented a real departure from traditional conservative economics, which seeks to cure inflation by slowing the economy down, whether by raising taxes, cutting expenditures, or checking the growth of the money supply. The failure to stop inflation by such measures in recent years had demonstrated, in Kemp's and Stockman's opinion, that this was an utterly erroneous approach to the problem of stagflation. What they believed, as Mr. Kemp put it, was that "75 percent of the explosion of government spending, government debt, government credit programs, growing pension bills is not the fault of 'big spenders,' as most Republicans like to charge." Rather, he said, "climbing spending results from the weakness and volatility of the economy. It's the fault of the misery index." (The misery index is the name the late Arthur Okun gave to the sum of the indexes of inflation and unemployment: 10 percent inflation plus 10 percent unemployment, for instance, would give a misery index figure of 20.)

Kemp and Stockman sought to explain their thesis by analyzing the $36 billion rise in government spending between the preceding June and November. Of that rise, they said, $5.9 billion was due to higher inflation, including $1.2 billion for indexed Social Security benefits and $4.7 billion to cover a rise in military fuel costs and for Medicare and food assistance. Rising interest rates had pushed up budget outlays by $2.8 billion. Higher joblessness accounted for an extra $9.15 billion to pay for more unemployment insurance, food stamps, Medicaid, and other social benefits. And generally worse economic conditions added $8.25 billion, bringing the extra Federal outlays to $26 billion. This was almost three-fourths, they said, of the unexpected rise in government spending from June to November 1980.

Thus, said the supply-siders, achieving control over Federal spending and Treasury borrowing could not be done "exclusively through legislated spending cuts in the orthodox sense." And it certainly could not be done, they argued, by raising taxes. "Only a comprehensive economic package that spurs output and employment growth and lowers inflation expectations and interest rates has any hope of stopping the present hemorrhage," said Kemp and Stockman.

Reagan was convinced. After the Dunkirk paper was leaked, he stuck with Stockman as his budget director and installed other supply-siders in key posts at the Treasury: Norman Ture as Under Secretary for Tax Policy and Paul Craig Roberts as Assistant Secretary for Economic Policy. But he made a monetarist, Beryl Sprinkel, an ardent disciple of Professor Friedman's, his Under Secretary of the Treasury for Monetary Affairs. And he named a "pragmatist," Donald T. Regan, formerly head of Merrill Lynch, the stockbrokers, as his Secretary of the Treasury to yoke the supply-siders and monetarists together.

The lions and the lambs were expected to lie down together. The first order of business would be to get the big incentive-generating, investment-stimulating, growth-propelling, budget-balancing tax cuts through Congress, together with the rapid buildup in defense spending and the cuts in social programs for which Reagan had campaigned.

GAMES ON CAPITOL HILL

The Great Communicator proved himself to be a master strategist as well in prevailing over the Democrats who held a majority in the House of Representatives.

One of the greatest intellectual achievements of the 20th

century is game theory, developed by the mathematician John von Neumann in 1928 and extended to economics by Dr. von Neumann and the economist Oskar Morgenstern in their classic work *The Theory of Games and Economic Behavior* (1944). Game theory, a mathematical system for analyzing contests where opponents seek to outwit each other and design the best course of action under all circumstances, has had a steadily growing influence in such areas as warfare, arms control, business, and politics.

The contest between the Republicans and Democrats in Congress over Reagan's economic program, including the big multiyear tax cuts, rapid increase in military spending, and cuts in social spending, can be analyzed in terms of game theory. The Democrats, as the accompanying diagram shows, had to choose between two basic strategies: (I) mainly support the Reagan program or (II) attack it and present a tax and spending program of their own.

The Republicans also had to choose between two strategies: (A) fully defend the President's program or (B) compromise with the Democrats, who had a majority in the House (if they held together).

Each combination of Republican and Democratic strategy would produce different pairs of payoffs. The best result, as judged by each party, is represented by the number 4, the worst result by 1, the next-best result by 3, and the next-worst by 2. In each pair, the Democratic outcome is listed first.

The action began in the Senate during the first week of April, when the Democrats played their "mainly support" strategy (I) and the Republicans played the "completely defend" strategy (A); the payoff was to the Republicans' advantage (2, 4). The Democrats succeeded only in avoiding the worst possible outcome of incurring public scorn for pure negativism in the face of the President's electoral victory and popularity, but they still incurred Republican insults for criticizing parts of the President's program and then voting for all of it. The Republicans scored a complete victory.

In the House, however, after observing the outcome in the

Diagram 1
THE TAX GAME

REPUBLICANS

	Support Reagan Completely (A)	Compromise (B)
Mainly Support Reagan (I)	Republicans triumph; Democrats avoid blame (2, 4)	Republicans win but vex Reagan; Democrats share credit (3, 3)
Attack Reagan (II)	Republican program blocked in House; Democrats incur blame (1, 2)	Republicans lose much of program; Democrats look fiscally responsible (4, 1)

DEMOCRATS

Key: 4 = best
3 = next best
2 = next worst
1 = worst

(First number in pair is outcome for Democrats, second is outcome for Republicans.)

Senate, the Democrats switched to a strategy of strong attack (II). They offered a "counterbudget" that would reduce the Reagan fiscal 1982 tax cut by $18 billion, limit it to one year instead of three, close $3 billion in tax loopholes, trim the military by $4.4 billion, and cut the projected deficit of $50 billion in half.

The Republicans responded to this attack by sticking to their "completely defend" strategy (A). With a Senate majority and Presidential vetoes to back them up, the Republicans could block the Democrats' counterbudget.

But if the Democrats stuck to their strategy (II), with their majority in the House, the Republicans could not get their program either, and the result would be a stalemate. Both parties would suffer (1, 2), with the Democrats losing more. A nation sympathetic to the President, especially after the attempt on his life by a mentally sick school dropout, would doubtless be angrier with the Democrats and punish them in the 1982 Congressional elections. But the Republicans would have nothing to show by way of an economic program.

However, if the Republicans responded to the Democratic attack by switching to the compromise strategy (B), they would have handed a political victory to the Democrats while surrendering most of their own program; outcome: (4, 1). This the Republicans would not do. The President's economic spokesmen denounced the Democrats' counterbudget as "the same old tune." Yet they appeared to have moderated their attack to avoid harsher Democratic opposition.

Indeed, it looked as though a Republican compromise was in the making (B) if the Democrats would only moderate their attack and move back toward strategy (I) of mainly supporting the President's program. The mixture of a Democratic strategy (I) and a Republican strategy (B) would give the second-best outcome for each party (3, 3). The Republicans would get most of their program. The Democrats, especially if they limited the tax cut and restored some of the social programs, could claim that they had given the President most of what he asked for but had still served fiscal prudence and social responsibility.

But Reagan would have none of it. His decision to order his three top White House aides—Edwin Meese 3rd, James A. Baker 3rd, and Michael K. Deaver—to repudiate a report that he was willing to compromise showed that he was a natural game theorist, better than the three sub-Cabinet officers who had led Representative James R. Jones, chairman of the House Budget Committee, to believe that the President would accept a one-year rather than a three-year tax cut.

For Reagan had sensed that the Republicans had what game theorists call a "dominant strategy"—one that makes a player better off than his opponent, no matter what strategy his opponent chooses.

The dominant strategy for the Republicans was (A)—to support the President's program completely. For if the Republicans did that, as the matrix shows, they would score higher than the Democrats, whether the Democrats went along with or attacked the President's program.

Actually, if the Democrats attacked and the Republicans stuck with the President down the line, a stalemate might result. But that outcome would be unstable, because the Democrats would be better off to support the President rather than attack him and incur their worst result, suffering public condemnation and risking major losses later.

The only stable outcome of the political game would thus be the (2, 4) payoff in the upper left corner, resulting from the Democrats choosing (I) and the Republicans sticking with (A); that would give the Republicans a complete victory, with the Democrats minimizing their losses by supporting the popular President. And that was the course Reagan took.

To be sure, the real-life game was more complex than this simpler version that treats all Democrats and Republicans as though they were united teams and treats political outcomes as though they were the same as economic outcomes (with different political feedbacks). For instance, some Republicans, such

as Senator Bob Dole and Senator Pete Domenici, were tempted
to break ranks because they themselves were worried about
the effects of excessively deep and prolonged tax cuts on budget deficits, inflation, interest rates, and the stability of the
economy.

Of course, many Democrats thought the best solution from
the standpoint of the country, and not just their own party,
would have been the compromise solution (3, 3) resulting from
the combination of Strategies (I/ B). But Reagan preferred to
win big politically; that was the sure outcome, like money in
the bank. What the economic consequences would be for the
nation seemed far more uncertain, with economists differing
widely in their forecasts.

In fact, the different possible economic outcomes greatly
complicated the political game. If the Reagan forecasts were
too optimistic, the country (and the Republicans) would suffer
later on.

If the Democrats really believed Reagan was wrong, they
might gain the most politically by letting him have what he
wanted—a neat Machiavellian move. Similarly, if the conservative Republicans were right in fearing the economic effects
of excessive and prolonged tax cuts and military buildup, they
might have been doing the President (and the country) a favor
if they had managed to bring off a compromise with the Democrats on his program.

But it was not to be. Reagan went for broke, and Congress,
Democrats and Republicans alike, went along.

FISCAL GRAFFITI

Indeed, more than went along. The Democrats, with the Reagan Administration's collaboration, joined in turning the tax
bill into a Christmas tree that outglittered any of the past. With
Republicans and Democrats vying for the privilege of providing tax breaks to assorted special groups, the bill became a riot

of fiscal graffiti—and a bonanza for the well-to-do and, perhaps most of all, for tax lawyers, tax accountants, and investment advisers.

For openers, there was the 25 percent (scaled down from 30 percent) three-year across-the-board cut in personal income taxes. The effort of Senator Bill Bradley, the New Jersey Democrat, to tilt the bill more toward people earning less than $50,000 a year was easily stymied by the Senate Finance Committee's chairman, Kansas Republican Bob Dole, with the help of three Southern Democrats. The prevailing argument was that tax relief was needed most of all at the highest level for the sake of the national welfare, because the rich were the biggest savers.

The Administration and the Senate held firm on a modified version of the 10-5-3 plan for accelerated depreciation for business, now called 15-10-5-3 because commercial and residential structures would be written off in 15 years rather than ten, while factory buildings could be fully written off in ten years regardless of their useful life, equipment in five years, and motor vehicles in three years. A consortium of business lobbies decided to stick with 15-10-5-3 depreciation despite a tempting bid by the Democrats to give business a different tax break: one-year expensing of equipment outlays plus a five-year phased cut in the corporate income tax rate to 34 percent from 46 percent. As Joseph Pechman, the Brookings Institution's leading tax expert, pointed out, one-year expensing would by itself have eliminated the effect of the corporate income tax on many businesses by cutting the cost of capital nearly in half. But the business lobbies decided that 15-10-5-3, when fully effective in 1986, would be even more generous and seemed surer of adoption.

The Reagan tax experts had originally estimated that the 30 percent Kemp-Roth cut in individual income taxes plus 10-5-3 accelerated depreciation would result in a total tax cut of $148 billion in 1984 and $222 billion in 1986. Such figures still appeared to be in the ball park, since the scaling back of cuts in individual income taxes and of depreciation would be offset, or more than offset, by the many baubles Congress and the Administration added to the fiscal Christmas Tree.

For instance, the Administration offered to raise the estate-tax exemption to $600,000 from the previous $175,000 and the gift-tax exemption to $10,000 from $3,000 per beneficiary. Those changes would reduce estate and gift taxes by $5.8 billion in 1986. Although the cut in estate taxes was offered as a way to protect family farms and businesses, it was made to apply to all other estates as well. And Senator Dole expressed his view that the next move would be to eliminate estate taxes totally for everyone, however rich, presumably in the interests of equity. As the old French gibe went, the rich and poor were equally free to sleep under the bridges; in America, the rich and poor would be equally free to leave a fortune to their children.

This was a far cry from the original case for inheritance taxes, once supported in the name of the democratic doctrine that all people should have a more or less equal start in life; it was even supported by some rich people on the practical grounds that inherited wealth would spoil the young. In his "Gospel of Wealth," Andrew Carnegie wrote that "the parent who leaves his son enormous wealth generally deadens the talents and energies of the son and tempts him to lead a less useful and less worthy life than he otherwise would." The steel-maker added, "Of all forms of taxation, this seems the wisest."

So the rush was on in Washington to cut taxes to provide breaks for almost everybody—businessmen and farmers and investors, decedents and heirs, small savers and big savers (or at least those with assets who were willing to transfer them into pension accounts, savings and loan associations, and other thrift institutions), Americans working abroad, and recipients of royalties from oil and gas wells, as well as benefits to the politicians who would vote for tax cuts for all the above.

As the Christmas Tree tax bill lit up, the most unpopular man in town would be Scrooge, the old-fashioned fiscal freak who still worried about how government would pay its bills without resorting to inflationary finance. The cuts in Federal spending (especially with military outlays rising fast) showed no signs of keeping pace with the tax cuts. But the Great Communicator went far toward convincing the nation that they would.

On July 29, 1981, Ronald Reagan's radical change in United States fiscal policy, aimed at cutting back the role of the Federal Government, came to pass. The Congressional approval of his tax program would translate into by far the biggest tax cut in the nation's history—a cut estimated at $600 billion over three years.

That tax cut followed actions by a House-Senate conference committee to reduce the government's expenditures by $36 billion in the following year and, according to President Reagan, by a cumulative total of $140 billion over the next three years, which Reagan called "the most sweeping cutbacks in the history of the budget."

Those tax and budget cuts certainly appeared to represent the most striking change of direction in the balance between the public and private sectors of the American economy since Roosevelt's New Deal. The aim of the conservative Republicans who made this fiscal counterrevolution—with the help of Democratic conservatives and even some liberals who were carried along in an effort to maintain their political strength—was to revitalize American capitalism and to bring inflation under control.

But the issue troubling not only the President's political opponents but also investors, foreign leaders, and many in the business community was whether his program would cure or aggravate the problems of inflation, high interest rates, and stagnation that had been plaguing the American and world economy. The worry among many economists was that in cutting taxes so steeply Reagan and the Congress had assured big budget deficits for several years to come, and that when the problem of financing those deficits collided with a restrictive money policy aimed at preventing inflation, interest rates would stay high or go higher, curbing investment and economic growth. It looked as though the House of Representatives, having shortly before passed a resolution condemning high interest rates, had now, in adopting the huge tax-cut bill, assured that high interest rates would continue.

PROLIFERATION OF THE RICH

Yet, whatever impact the Reagan revolution ultimately exerted on the overall economy's stability and growth, it had already accomplished its main goal: a massive shift of income to the rich. Supply-side economics, the doctrine that tax cuts should provide incentives for those who would save money, make investments, and spur economic growth, had done its job in providing Reagan and his supporters in Congress with the rationale for writing tax legislation deliberately calculated to provide the greatest benefits to the wealthy.

The theory that in benefiting the rich one benefits the whole society had once been castigated by egalitarians as "trickledown," an epithet used by Democrats to make Republicans wince. But the Republicans winced no more. With the help of the supply-side philosophy, they now openly proclaimed their pro-wealth program as a triumph of progressive economics. The most eloquent expression of that doctrine was voiced by George Gilder in his book *Wealth and Poverty,* hailed as the "Bible of the Reagan Administration." The book had been praised by Ronald Reagan as a vital description of his own philosophy and by David Stockman as "Promethean in its intellectual power and insight." In a key passage, Gilder said, "A successful economy depends on the proliferation of the rich, on creating a large class of risk-taking men who are willing to shun the easy channels of a comfortable life in order to create new enterprise, win huge profits, and invest them again."

But as time passed and the Reagan Administration coped with the politics of the real world, it seemed likely that the Gilder "Bible," like the Dead Sea Scrolls of the Essenes, would go down in history as an apocalyptic text, representative of only one of the sects, the supply-siders, that had fed into the Reagan canon. Doctrinal strife continued to be intense, and the second principal sect remained that of the monetarists, who believed that control of the money supply was the one and only answer to what they believed was the most serious problem facing capitalism: inflation.

A third sect among the Reagan supporters was the conservative Keynesians, who put their greatest stress on the regulation of the total demand for goods and services as the prime means of preventing both inflation and recession; they emphasized the importance of both fiscal and monetary policy in promoting a stable economy. They spurned both the ideological faith healing of the supply-siders and the rigid rules, to be untouched by human hands or discretion, of the monetarists.

A fourth sect of believers composed of simple old-fashioned congressmen of both political parties and masses of lay voters continued to believe in what Herbert Stein has called the "old-time religion of balanced budgets and sound money." President Reagan continued to lure them with his support for a Constitutional amendment requiring a balanced budget, while in fact accepting huge budget deficits; he also lured them with his hinted abiding affection for gold.

A fifth sect, embracing political pragmatism and the protection of special interests as its philosophy, scorned the ideologies of the free traders, deregulators, and antisubsidizers in the Reagan camp to uphold the cause of auto import quotas against Japan, bailouts for Chrysler, subsidies for synfuels, protection for steel, and the appointment of various industry-sponsored foxes to guard various industrial chicken coops in areas ranging from the trucking industry to the U.S. Forest Service to the Department of the Interior and the Environmental Protection Agency. Some of these foxes, such as James

Watt, Anne Burford, and Rita Lavelle, created political problems for the Administration and had to be replaced.

Some political scientists, like Professor Steven Brams of New York University, thought that eventually the Reagan Administration would lose credibility and coherence as it sought to embrace too many disparate doctrines and interests. Murray Weidenbaum, Reagan's first chairman of the Council of Economic Advisers, had sought to bring harmony between the supply-siders and monetarists, without success. After he had been given his walking papers and returned to Washington University, Professor Weidenbaum, who had earned a national reputation as an ardent champion of deregulation, sharply criticized the Reagan Administration for its flabby and contradictory regulatory actions.

But while the real world of the Reagan Administration grew increasingly complex and compromised, George Gilder's book preserved for all time the basic philosophy of Reaganism in its pure form. And the President's tax program had made that philosophy into flesh.

The supply-siders felt that the Administration program was actually quite modest. The percentage of total income taxes borne by those in the $100,000 to $200,000 income class would, according to the U.S. Treasury's calculations, decline from 8.7 percent to 7.1 percent in 1984, and the share of income taxes borne by those with incomes of $200,000 or more would decline from 6.4 percent to 4.7 percent in 1984.

Meanwhile, the share of total income taxes paid by those with incomes from $5,000 to $50,000 would rise from 67.2 percent to 70 percent. The share of those in the $50,000 to $100,000 class would change little, to 18.1 percent from 18.2 percent.

The estate tax had been virtually wiped out; the Treasury estimated that 99.6 percent of all estate-tax returns filed would fall within the $600,000 exemption, and those above it would be greatly reduced. And, starting in 1986, personal income taxes would be indexed against inflation.

The Administration was delighted to make one compromise with the Democrats: It accepted their proposal to cut the top rate on "unearned" or investment income to 50 percent from 70 percent. That would also reduce the rate on capital gains to 20 percent from 28 percent.

On the whole, the wealthy were content. They were happy to see a return of the biblical principle that rural America once expressed as "Them what has, gits."[1]

---

[1] Strong support was given to this interpretation of the Reagan economic program by David A. Stockman, the director of the Office of Management and Budget, in his interviews with William Greider published in the article "The Education of David Stockman" in *The Atlantic,* October 1981. Mr. Stockman said that supply-side economics was just a disguised version of the old trickle-down theory, long favored by conservative Republicans. The old theory in its new garb, he said, was just a "Trojan horse" to aid the rich under the guise of giving a break to everyone. Stockman's comments appeared to confirm what critics of the Reagan program had long asserted, that it was really a means of redistributing income to the top.

In the article, Mr. Stockman disclosed that he knew precisely what the effects of the Administration's program would be. He stated, for example, in April 1981, that "of the 16.5 million people living with an annual income of less than the poverty-line income of $8,140 for a family of four, 15 percent would gain under the Reagan program, 34 percent would have no change in spendable income, and 47 percent would suffer a loss of between 1 and 5 percent."

From all appearances, the budget director, a former divinity student at Harvard, was assailed by moral doubts. At one point he asked Greider, "Do you realize the greed that came to the forefront? The hogs were really feeding. The greed level, the level of opportunism, just got out of control."

Stockman had begun to fight within the Administration for a less unbalanced program—and a reduced budget deficit—long before *The Atlantic* article was published. However, he lost his battles for cutting military spending to Defense Secretary Caspar W. Weinberger. In language more vehement than any Reagan critics have used, Stockman accused the Pentagon of "blatant inefficiency, poor deployment of manpower, contracting idiocy."

But Reagan continued to go down the line with Weinberger and the Pentagon. So military spending rose rapidly. It was slated to climb by over $120 billion from fiscal year 1982 through 1986, as taxes were being slashed.

Chapter

13

BACK TO KEYNES

A specter was haunting the Reagan Administration: Thatcherism. The worst level of unemployment Britain had suffered since the Depression of the 1930s was by mid-1981 grim evidence of the failure of what had been regarded as a brilliant innovation in economic policy. Was her fault one of execution or were there inherent inconsistencies and contradictions that the Reagan Administration was in process of repeating?

When Mrs. Thatcher became Prime Minister in May 1979, she was the darling of conservatives on both sides of the Atlantic. And the Thatcher plan for curing British stagflation had certainly begun with close parallels to the Reagan program:

- Marginal-income-tax rates would be cut sharply to spur savings and productivity growth, with the biggest cuts, both absolutely and proportionately, going to those in the higher income brackets. The real value of government spending—total outlays corrected for inflation—was also to be cut. And the government's need to borrow from the public was to be cut.

• Thatcher was committed to monetarism, the doctrine that holds that the way to stop inflation is to bring down the rate of growth of the money supply to a rate equal to the potential growth of the economy. She elected to do this gradually: The Bank of England, under the domination of her Government, would reduce the rate of growth of the chosen monetary aggregate called "sterling M-3," currency in circulation plus sterling-denominated demand and time deposits in British commercial banks, to an annual rate of 9 percent in 1980–81 and to 6 percent by 1983–84.

How faithfully did Thatcher carry out her plan? On monetary policy she had striven to tighten up the money supply. True, sterling M-3 overshot its target, but this resulted largely from removing the so-called corset from the commercial banks, the special deposit regulations that had limited the extent to which the banks could increase their interest-bearing deposits. However, the money supply narrowly defined, M-1, consisting of currency and demand deposits, was held to a mere 3 percent rate of growth during the first 12 months after Thatcher took office and an 8 percent rate thereafter.

The clearest indication of tight money was the sharp rise in interest rates. The outflow of funds from London to New York, attracted by still higher rates in the United States, helped tighten money further in Britain despite the government's plans to make more funds available by bringing down public-sector borrowing.

But in that Thatcher failed. She had quickly put through cuts in marginal-income-tax rates, bringing the top rate on compensation income down to 60 percent from 83 percent and the bottom rate to 30 percent from 33. And she cut the top rate on investment income to 75 percent from 98. At the same time, to promote a shift from consumption to saving, the government nearly doubled the value-added tax, a kind of sales tax, to 15 percent from 8 percent, which gave a one-shot boost to inflation.

The steep climb in interest rates pushed the economy into a deep slump, and the budget fell deeper into deficit. To curb the growing need for public borrowing, the government raised excise taxes on tobacco, alcohol, gasoline, diesel fuel, road vehicles, and other items. Government spending kept climbing, despite Thatcher's efforts at belt-tightening. She imposed her steepest cuts on public-sector investments. But instead of realizing her objective of bringing down public borrowing to 7 billion pounds in 1980–81, the Thatcher Government ran its borrowing requirement up to 13.5 billion pounds or 6 percent of Britain's gross national product—one of the highet public-debt ratios in the world.

Thatcher's fundamental mistake had been to combine a tight money policy with a loose fiscal policy. This had forced up both nominal and real interest rates. And that produced an extraordinary slump in production and employment. The unemployment rate soared to more than 12 percent, from 5.4 percent when Thatcher took office two years earlier. With the slump, inflation had fallen, but the high interest rates on both government and private bonds reflected the pessimism of the financial markets about the prospects for solving the long-term problem of inflation.

UNDO SOMETHING

As with Thatcherism, so with Reaganomics. Was it all proving to be one more beautiful theory killed by an ugly little fact—that it didn't work?

It began to look that way. Before Reagan and his aides had a chance to savor the full fruits of their budget and tax triumphs of 1981 and enjoy a well-earned vacation from Washington, the stock market dropped, the long-term bond market looked as though it might be permanently dead, interest rates stayed very high, and the economy, which had been remarkably strong in the first quarter of 1981, began to sink into another recession.

The President's own anxiety over these sorry events was reflected in his effort to find somebody or something to blame them on. It was surely not his own fiscal program. "The Fed," Reagan told a California audience, "is independent, and they are hurting us and what we're trying to do, as much as they're hurting everyone else." The White House rushed to explain that by "they" Reagan meant high interest rates, not the Fed itself. But since the central bank's monetary policy was at least partly responsible for the high rates, and since Reagan and his monetarists, led by Treasury Under Secretary Sprinkel, had been urging the Fed to hold the money supply tight no matter what happened to interest rates, it was not exactly clear what the President wanted the Fed to do.

But the Fed was not the only culprit. Reagan also blamed Congress for giving him greater tax cuts than he even wanted. He was later, in the presence of the recession, to blame Congress for not giving him all the tax cuts he wanted in one year. However, since the President had signed the tax bill without complaint—indeed, signed joyfully, handing out scores of pens to all who had played a part in getting the biggest tax cut in history—it would be a little difficult for Reagan to lay the blame for high interest rates and collapsing securities markets upon Congress.

Reagan also blamed Jimmy Carter for the disorders facing him; they were, said the President, "something inherited." But it was his economy now. What would he do about it? His chief economic adviser, Murray Weidenbaum, had a maxim: "Don't just stand there—undo something." Weidenbaum originally meant this advice to apply to government regulations, but it might be extended to the Administration's monetary, budget, fiscal, and military policies. The problem, however, was what could Reagan undo? Monetary policy was firmly in place, unless Reagan wanted to try to replace Volcker at the Fed and possibly Sprinkel at the Treasury with people willing to zip up the growth of the money supply. But that might drive interest rates still higher, since the monetarists had taught the markets to fear a link between rapid monetary growth, inflation, and high interest rates.

Yet if the Fed held the money supply tight in an effort to check inflation in the face of the huge tax cuts legislated by Congress and the looming budget deficits, interest rates would probably go higher anyway. The Fed would be damned if it did and damned if it didn't ease money.

Despite Reagan's public lament over high interest rates, however, there was no reason to think he was urging a different monetary course; he was still clinging to the assurance of his monetarist advisers that before long interest rates would come down. That could happen if the economy slid into deep recession. But even that might provide only a temporary respite once the slump ended; that thought was what was driving the long-term bond and mortgage markets crazy. James J. O'Leary, consultant to the United States Trust Company, warned that the collapse of the long-term bond market looked like a permanent revolution, dangerous to economic growth.

But what could Reagan do to prevent this dangerous trend? If he did not choose to change monetary policy or rescind the multiyear tax cuts just legislated, he had only a few options: He could ask Congress for new tax increases, such as a "windfall" tax on natural gas coupled with gas decontrol or a stiff excise on imported oil; he could try to cut social spending further, a course that would bear a political cost, and an economic cost as well, coming in the midst of a recession; he could cut back plans for huge increases in defense spending; he could accept the next item on his supply-siders' agenda, a return to the gold standard; or he could call for new policy rules that would commit the United States to a noninflationary financial system, as some conservative economists were urging.

Indeed, different groups of advisers were pressing various of these options upon him. But they were not consistent choices and could not readily be compromised. Since Reagan's initial

set of compromises between the supply-siders and the monetarists had failed the empirical test, he was being forced back to
the drawing board. He could not just stand there; he had to
undo something. But what?

ALL NEWS IS BAD NEWS

Easing monetary policy looked, for the moment, like the best
of the options. Treasury Secretary Donald Regan and Chief
Economic Adviser Weidenbaum both began to suggest in their
public orations that the Fed might make the money supply
grow a bit faster, even if Wall Street took fright. Regan, as the
former tiger of Merrill Lynch, clearly felt he possessed the
hard-earned right to show proper disrespect for the wisdom of
Wall Street. He complained that the Street was so nervous it
was turning all news into bad news. If the money supply increased, the Street grew sick with fear of inflation and rising
interest rates; if the money supply fell, it trembled over a coming money crunch and a plunge of both the markets and the
economy.

Weidenbaum was specific on what the Reagan Administration would like the Fed to do. Though insisting he was a
staunch champion of the independence of the Fed, Weidenbaum nevertheless told the Fed, in an address to the National
Associaton of Mutual Savings Banks, that it really ought to
step up the growth of M-1B, the most closely watched measure
of the money supply, to the lower half of its planned range for
the year; that range had been set at 3 percent to 6 percent. M-
1B had been below that band, although some other measures
of the money supply had been above their bands. No doubt
Volcker would have liked all the money supply measures to be
within their assigned band waves—a place for every M and
every M in its place—but the central bank seemed not to have
the skill of its outside critics or their confidence that the various
measures of money could all be properly controlled.

Earlier, Secretary Regan had muzzled the sharpest inside critic of the Fed, Under Secretary Sprinkel, the Administration's top monetarist. But that was when Sprinkel had been publicly censuring the Fed for not being tight enough. Was Regan, with Reagan's backing, now scolding the Fed for being too tight? Or was he really running interference for the Fed, trying to calm down the financial markets lest they make it impossible for the Fed to get out of a box and get the Administration out of a jam?

Weidenbaum seemed to be doing just that. He told the savings bankers that a resumption of monetary growth "should not be viewed as alarming, even though individual month-to-month increases may appear at first blush to be excessive to the untrained observer."

It was not just the untrained observer who saw an effort by the Administration to push the Fed toward easier money. The professional monetarists were starting to pounce. Allan T. Meltzer, professor of economics at Carnegie-Mellon University and a leader of the monetarist Shadow Open Market Committee, self-elected watchdog of the Fed, said there was "fear" that the Administration would put pressure on the Fed to loosen up, contending that "a little inflation won't hurt now." In fact, Meltzer said, this Administration pressure had already begun.

The pure monetarists wanted Reagan to hang tough, but the President and the pragmatists around him were not enthusiastic about a policy that was threatening them with serious losses in the 1982 Congressional elections—and threatening the economy with a steeper slump.

SOLIDARITY DAY

Reaganomics put the squeeze on labor. The unions took to the streets in Washington on September 19, 1981 (called "Solidarity Day," echoing Polish labor's protest, reinforced by a papal encyclical), to oppose what it saw as the antilabor and antisocial policies of the Reagan Administration.

American labor unions were worried that Reaganomics would spell higher unemployment and lower real wages. Commerce Secretary Malcolm Baldridge and a host of private economists had fed those worries by warning that the economy was weakening.

For the Administration and for employers, the worsening economic trend had the benefit of bringing down the rate of wage settlements. This was a timely trend as the coming year, 1982, would mark the beginning of a new three-year bargaining cycle for many major American industries, including petroleum refining, over-the-road trucking, autos, rubber products, agricultural implements, and electrical equipment. Arnold R. Weber, an industrial relations expert and former Nixon Administration wage controller, who had become president of the University of Colorado, observed that the outcome of these wage negotiations in 1982 would determine "the broad framework and tone" for collective bargaining in the subsequent two years. The Reagan Administration insisted it would take a hands-off attitude in the coming round; it was opposed to any form of incomes policy to restrain wages and prices. However, Weber suggested that the Administration's 25 percent tax cut constituted an "implicit" incomes policy, based not on the agreement of workers to some specified standard but on an undefined hope that lower taxes would mean lower advances in money wages.

But the real way the Administration meant to push down the rate of wage increases was by changing the national economic and political environment. The President marked that line by breaking the air traffic controllers' strike and firing the striking workers. Discussing Reagan's tough line in discharging the air traffic controllers, Murray Weidenbaum said: "It is our intention to carry out the law. It is not our intention to jawbone." If management was excessively generous, Weidenbaum argued, it would suffer excessive costs and loss of markets, and if labor sought to raise wages too much, it would suffer higher unemployment.

And as though to set an example for private employers, the President, as employer, announced that he meant to hold the increase in Civil Service pay to 4.8 percent in the following year (while backing a 14.3 percent pay increase for the military). However, Reagan was also considering a three-month deferral of all civilian and military pay increases.

"We are not telling labor and management what to do," the President's economic adviser Weidenbaum said. "We are subjecting them to the fundamental force of market pressures." These presumably included pressures of competition from abroad. But in the case of autos, the Administration's imposition of import quotas on Japanese cars did not put its own principle into effect.

Weakening business conditions induced by tight monetary restraints, which resulted in high interest rates and rising unemployment, seemed bound to bring down the rate of wage settlements; hard-pressed industries were demanding "givebacks" from labor. It looked like hard cheese for labor on Solidarity Day, with stagnation and higher unemployment the chosen remedy for inflation. That was Reagan's real "shadow incomes policy."

ANTI-HOOVERISM

But the Administration was torn. It did not want to risk too deep a recession that could blow it out of the water on Election Day. Besides sniping at the Fed's monetary policy, it began to reconsider its own attitude toward new budget cuts. David Stockman, who had been point man in the attack on the budget deficit, appeared to have been converted to a Keynesian view of fiscal policy by the looming recession and unemployment. At a press breakfast with reporters on October 5, 1981, Stockman said that if a weak economy caused tax revenues to fall short of forecasts, he would not seek additional spending cuts just to keep the budget deficit from growing. Just a few days earlier, on October 1, Stockman had warned Congress that it would have to cast politically painful budget-cutting votes "again and again and again."

But Stockman's zeal for budget-cutting was attacked not only by Keynesians but also by some supply-side economists. Professor Irving Kristol of New York University, considered to be the "godfather" of the supply-siders, warned that budget cuts in a time of economic slump would represent a return to "Herbert Hoover economics." In 1932, with tax revenues falling and the budget deficit widening, the Hoover Administration had tried desperately to balance the budget. The move was dictated not only by fear of budget deficits but by fear of inflation. But the effect of tax increases and spending cuts was to put additional burdens on the economy, restrict private spending even further, and aggravate deflation, which was the reality, not inflation, the more distant threat.

The fiscal and monetary blunders of the Hoover era opened the door to the Keynesian Revolution in economics. While using supply-side rhetoric Reagan's top economic-policy advisers had joined that revolution. The Reaganauts were not willing to risk worsening a slump by Hoover-like fiscal and monetary policies.

Chapter

14

THE GREAT REPRESSION

Hard times were intensifying strains between the United States and its European allies. The Polish crisis erupted and became a critical element in a larger political and economic agony, the 1980s equivalent of the severe testing that the world had faced in the 1930s—and had failed miserably.

A meeting between President Reagan and Chancellor Helmut Schmidt of West Germany in Washington at the beginning of 1982, despite their efforts to paper over cracks in the wall, dramatized their differences on how to respond to the Polish crisis—and how to prevent it from wrecking the alliance.

Reagan, holding the Soviet Union responsible for the military crackdown on the Polish workers, had imposed economic sanctions on the Soviet Union. But Schmidt, asserting that

Moscow was not the prime mover against the Poles, wanted to take a less aggressive tone that would permit West German trade with the Russians to continue. This dispute between Bonn and Washington long antedated the Polish crisis. At the Ottawa Summit Conference in July 1981, a fight had broken out between the German and American leaders over the export of high technology to the Russians, as well as over the planned Siberian natural gas pipeline to supply West Germany and other European countries.

At the start of 1982, the Reagan Administration appeared to be hoping that the Polish upheaval could be exploited to break the Soviet grip on Eastern Europe, if only the United States could make it too costly for the Soviets or their supporters in the Polish Army to try to break the workers' and the church's resistance. But many European critics, and not just in West Germany, contended that policies intended to sustain and worsen chaos and economic hardship in Poland would only make it more likely that the Russians would tighten their grip on Poland and the other satellite countries, a grip that could be broken only by war. These critics also contended that efforts to weaken the Polish economy by withholding food supplies and balance-of-payments support were likely to be counterproductive in weakening the will of the Polish people to resist. The Polish people, they said, would starve, but the Polish and Soviet armies were in no danger of starving.

The British newspaper *The Guardian* warned that the Polish people must not be treated as "dispensable pawns" in Western strategy, adding, "The line between penalizing General Jaruzelski and penalizing ordinary Poles is thin and gray, for however one views it, it is the ordinary Poles who will suffer." The same arguments, the newspaper said, applied to a deliberate severance of bank loans to Poland; it insisted that a nation bankrupt and in default would create a two-edged crisis—for Poland and for Western banking as well.

But the United States made clear to the Europeans that it expected support for its economic sanctions. Under this pressure, the leaders of the Common Market, meeting in Brussels, pledged that they would do nothing to hamper American sanctions against the Soviet Union. However, they took no initiatives of their own.

Chancellor Schmidt stressed his belief that the greater danger to the alliance came not from political differences over Poland but from the economic slump in the West, with rising unemployment intensifying pressures for protectionism and other beggar-my-neighbor policies. The Germans had long made plain their view that mistaken United States economic policies, resulting in high interest rates—"the highest since the birth of Christ," Schmidt said at the 1981 economic summit conference in Ottawa—were the source of rising joblessness throughout the industrial world.

But the Reagan Administration contended that it was persistent inflation that was responsible for the West's economic troubles, and that its economic policies, however painful they might be during the transition, were breaking the back of inflation, bringing down interest rates, and setting this country and its neighbors back on course to stable growth.

While sharing the goal of bringing down inflation—a passion in which the Germans felt they needed no instruction—Schmidt and his Economics Minister, Count Otto von Lambsdorff, insisted that the Reagan Administration's approach, by relying so heavily on monetary restraints, was simplistic and brutal, both toward the American labor force and toward other members of the Western alliance.

If pursued doggedly, the Reagan Administration's mixture of monetary, fiscal, and military policies would keep the industrial world in a state of high interest rates, stuttering growth, and chronic unemployment. This, Schmidt warned Reagan, might cause a plunge into a worldwide depression. A disruption of trade, stemming from the efforts of nations to protect themselves against high unemployment and economic disorder, would intensify the danger of a world economic breakdown.

BITTER TIMES

Indeed, the entire world economy, which had been growing increasingly interdependent since the Second World War, was being subjected in 1982 to the most severe disintegrative pressures since the start of the Great Depression of the 1930s.

In the United States, Canada, and Western Europe, 30 million workers were jobless. High unemployment among young people exacerbated radicalism in Europe. Only in Japan, thanks not only to its strong economic growth and export performance but also to its cooperative labor-management policies, was unemployment held in check.

Elsewhere high unemployment, combined with rising competition for shrinking markets, was intensifying demands of business and labor for protectionism. In the United States, for instance, the Ford Motor Company and the Chrysler Corporation, with the tacit support of General Motors, had already induced the Reagan Administration to exact "voluntary" auto export quotas from the Japanese. Steel producers were pressing for import quotas and charging "dumping" against foreign competitors.

American industries were far from alone, however, in the push for protection. The members of the European Common Market joined with the United States in a new Multifiber Agreement to set tight limits on the major textile exporters: Hong Kong, Taiwan, and South Korea. China, eager to earn foreign exchange by selling its textiles to the West, was being held at bay.

Strains between the so-called North and South—the developed and the developing countries—were worsened by the shifting shares of global industrial production. A. W. ("Tom") Clausen, the former chairman of the Bank of America who had just succeeded Robert S. McNamara as president of the World Bank, said that even with a good recovery from the slump the older countries of Western Europe and North America would account for less than half of world production by 1990, compared with more than two-thirds in 1960. The newly industrialized countries, he said, were likely to increase their share of world output to 25 percent by 1990 from 8.3 percent in 1960. "We have to remind ourselves that there is simply no precedent in history for the dynamic rate of change in the geographic spread of global output in our era, and in the structure and character of world trade," said Clausen.

But the world was far from frictionless, and Clausen's scenario would depend on the industrial countries' maintaining high rates of growth and employment—and also on labor and educational policies aimed at shifting workers from waning industries into others which were expanding. Neither in the United States nor in Europe was that shift of labor taking place smoothly or painlessly. In Europe, not only were jobs scarce for the young and unskilled but the lost jobs in old-line industries such as steel, autos and chemicals were causing nations to send their surplus "guest workers" back to their countries of origin, such as Turkey, Greece, Italy, and Spain. In the United States, the shrinking of job opportunities was also having a major impact on young people, blacks, and other minorities, and provoking rising resistance to immigration from such countries as Haiti and Mexico.

Hard times breed political antagonisms. The Common Market, one of the great achievements of postwar Europe, was under intense strain, with Britain, France, and West Germany pulling apart. The Europeans liked to blame the United States for their troubles, pointing a finger at its big budget deficits, tight money and high interest rates. But the United States rejected the charge, contending that high interest rates, tight money, and sluggish growth were consequences of inflation and the efforts of all governments to check the inflation.

There was merit in both sides' arguments. The world slowdown of the early 1980s had stemmed from measures adopted by all the industrial countries to prevent the oil shock of 1979 from worsening inflation, as the first oil shock of 1973–74 had done.

The skyrocketing of oil prices through the 1970s had also created another serious source of world strain: the mountain of international debt, especially that of the oil-poor developing countries. By 1980, the total debt of the developing countries had reached $440 billion and was still rising fast. Two-thirds of the total was owed to private banks. By 1984 the total foreign debt of the developing countries would climb above $700 billion.

To complicate and spread the world's financial troubles, the oil-producing countries of OPEC and those outside OPEC were now faced with a huge oil glut, thanks to the economic slump and the impact of their high prices on oil consumption and production in other countries. Their external debts also soared.

Thus the world slump was embittering both economic and political relations all over the world—North-South, East-West, within the capitalist world and within the Communist world alike. Inflation hung on, and the fear of worsening it was inhibiting national economic policies to stimulate recovery.

RISKS OF A CRASH

Below the surface of daily events in the spring of 1982, anxieties were growing that the economy was suffering from worse ailments than those of a conventional business cycle. Increasingly one heard the question "Could we have another depression?" And some businessmen, fighting for their companies' survival, thought they were already in one.

Many companies were struggling to stay above water by cutting costs—shutting down plants, laying off workers and managers, trimming outlays on new plant and equipment, cutting wherever they could. Some regions, such as the Great Lakes states and the Pacific Northwest, were very hard hit.

But it was too early to call it a depression. Nationally, by March, unemployment had risen only to 9 percent, far below the peak of 25 percent it reached in 1933. Of course it had taken a few years of continuous erosion for the jobless rate to get that high. In 1930, the year after the Great Crash of the stock market, the unemployment rate averaged 8.7 percent. In 1931 it got up to 15.9 percent and in 1932 to 23.6 percent.

The Fed's Volcker, testifying before the Senate Banking Committee, said on March 2, "There are risks, but I wouldn't characterize them as a depression. I think the probabilities are very strongly on the side of a recovery later this year."

Many businessmen were not so sure. American industry, generally speaking, was in a seriously strained cash position, hard put to cover its debt. The latest data of the Federal Trade Commission, for the third quarter of 1981, had showed a rapid worsening of corporate liquidity since 1979, coming on top of a more gradual erosion of corporate liquidity during the postwar period. The situation continued to worsen as corporate earnings fell and interest rates, despite the recession, moved up again. The picture was particularly worrisome in autos, nonferrous metals, steel, housing, the thrift institutions, banks, lumber, farms and farm equipment, and even among some oil companies. While large companies with strong borrowing power could stay afloat, many small businesses—more than ever before in the postwar period—were going under. One physician I know went to an executive-search firm for help in finding a new corporate post and was startled to have her check returned with "Out of business" written across it by the search firm.

What turns ordinary hard times into a real depression? There are many theories. Professor Daniel Fusfeld of the University of Michigan says that every great depression—such as those of the 1840s, 1890s, and 1930s—had come after a period of stagnation in the world economy. The struggle to control inflation in the 1970s and early 1980s had produced a series of stop-go recessions and a decline in the growth of real income.

But whenever the recessions had threatened to produce a politically unacceptable level of unemployment, inflationary fiscal and monetary policies had floated the United States and other nations off the rocks.

Those who feared the economy was on the lip of a depression in 1982 stressed the fragility of the world financial structure. Julian Snyder, publisher of *International Moneyline,* warned the New York Society of Security Analysts in early March of the parallels between the existing levels of debt and those of the late 1920s, including "an unmanageable amount of consumer installment debt, a heavy burden of agricultural debt, a mountain of home mortgage debt, a huge pyramid of business debt erected on a thin equity base, and a critical mass of international borrowing resting on a continuing flow of credit from the United States."

Another theory is that the conditions for a depression are created by the undermining of real purchasing power in the last stage of a long expansion, when inflationary pressures drive up prices faster than consumer incomes. Such an erosion of real buying power had been going on for nearly a decade. Measured in constant dollars, average weekly earnings in private nonagricultural industry had declined 16 percent from 1973 to the beginning of 1982. Higher taxes, resulting from inflation and "bracket creep," had reduced consumers' real disposable income even further. With more workers, especially women, entering the labor force, total real income had grown, allowing the economy to advance sluggishly; but when that kind of growth gave way to steep recession, the drop in purchasing power worsened, causing sales of such durable goods as autos and housing to plunge, threatening depression.

A classic explanation of depression, putting greater emphasis on business investment, is that of the nineteenth-century Swedish economist Knut Wicksell, who found the root in the relationship between interest rates and the rate of return on capital. When interest rates soar above expected returns on capital, business investment founders, and the economy decays. If, for example, a company must pay 17 percent interest for capital and sees no investment projects likely to come close to yielding such a return for years to come, it stops investing. Booms are built on the opposite relationship. For almost two decades after World War II, the cost of capital was below its real rate of return; investment boomed and productivity and the economy grew apace. But after 1966, the cost of capital gradually moved above the rate of return. For a time inflation, induced by monetary expansion, covered the gap between capital costs and expected returns on capital. But once the government and the central bank decided to stop the inflation by arresting excessive monetary growth, the house of cards threatened to fall.

That house of cards was built of layers of domestic and foreign debt, including the enormous debts contracted in the unregulated Eurocurrency market and from commercial banks by third world and Communist countries such as Poland and Rumania.

Thus financial weakness at home and abroad, high interest rates, low returns on capital, inflationary fears, and falling real income confronted the Federal Reserve with a cruel dilemma: If it continued to fight inflation by holding money tight, it risked a widening gap between high interest rates and real returns on capital, driving income and output further down. But if it accelerated monetary growth to check rising unemployment and rescue failing businesses, it might alarm financial markets. Interest rates might then move still higher, threatening a collapse of the bond and equity markets and of business investment and risking a full-scale economic crash.

MONETARY STRANGLEHOLD

No economic theory, however, can fully explain the events of a particular time and place, with particular human decision makers. Wesley C. Mitchell, the founder of the National Bureau of Economic Research and the outstanding pioneer in the investigation of business fluctuations, held that every business cycle was unique.

How could the American economy in the middle of the Reagan Administration be described? Short-term, it was obviously in a recession that had begun the preceding fall. But this was the second recession since 1980, the third since 1975. The economy had undergone a long sequence of recessions and weak, aborted recoveries.

Was this long, hard spell, then, a depression? The term seemed too strong. The economy had been stagnating, not collapsing. It might become a depression, but the odds were against it.

I called it a "repression"—a chronic state of underemployment and industrial slack that had dogged the economy for the greater part of the past decade, a condition brought on by the repressive actions of governments in the industrial world to cope with inflation, the demands of labor, energy shortages, and currency disorders.

When did this Great Repression begin? Since history is a seamless web, it is hard to date it precisely. But its roots lie in the escalation of the Vietnam war in 1965 and 1966 since that is when a price-stable phase of economic growth gave way to an inflationary trend. President Nixon, the Shah of Iran, and the sheiks of OPEC aggravated the trend. And during the 1970s the main method of checking the inflation was a repressive monetary policy. In the United States the money supply, defined as currency in circulation and demand deposits plus other checkable accounts, was reduced from 21 percent of GNP in 1971 to 15 percent in early 1982.

But this means of arresting inflation had come at a high cost. John Winthrop Wright, head of an investment advisory firm, said: "The United States has suffered through ten years of record-breaking inflation, a surge in business bankruptcies, mostly among small companies, and an unprecedented shrinkage in the auto, housing, savings and loan, and farm equipment industries."

David M. Jones, vice president and chief economist of Aubrey G. Lanston & Co., a leading government securities dealer, declared: "The United States is currently in the throes of a deepening and widening recession. It may turn out to be the worst slump since the Great Depression of the 1930s. The main cause of this cumulating downturn has been the Federal Reserve's excruciatingly tight money and credit policy over the past year or so. This Fed restrictive overkill took the form of an abrupt and irregular series of restrictive responses to unexpected spurts in money demand." While Jones generally commended the Fed's determination to stop inflation, "particularly in the face of an irresponsibly stimulative fiscal policy," he held that the prolonged and excessive Fed restraint would almost certainly produce higher unemployment and more economic pain than would have been required to crush inflation and inflation psychology.

Perhaps the best indicator of what Jones called the Fed's "stranglehold on the economy" was the level of real rates of interest—market rates less inflationary expectations. Since one cannot precisely quantify inflationary expectations, it is conventional to measure real interest rates by taking selective market rates of interest against the annual rate of increase in consumer prices. On that basis, the real rate of interest in the spring of 1982 was over 8 percent compared to 2 percent or less in most earlier years. The spread between market rates on utility bonds and inflation was about 7.5 percent, the highest in the postwar years. One had to go back to the early years of the Great Depression to find higher long-term real interest rates.

This was true all over the world. And the world slump had resulted from similar efforts of other countries to fight inflation, partly in response to climbing oil prices, partly to protect their own currencies against the pull of high interest rates in the United States. Kurt Richebaecher, the economist of the Dresdner Bank, maintained that, although the second OPEC oil shock had triggered the crisis, "we should beware of making it solely or even mainly responsible for our present worldwide economic predicament." Rather, he contended, the emphasis on oil distracted attention from "the real causes and the real culprits—our governments, and in most cases our central banks." Anyone who found that hard to believe, he said, should look at Japan, which had "coped with the oil price jump in masterly fashion despite its unmatched dependence on energy imports." But virtually all other countries were suffering from their own forms of monetary repression.

MONETARISM ABANDONED

In the United States, the time for a change in monetary policy was at hand. At the end of July 1982, close White House and Fed-watchers found signs that the old hard-line monetarism was about to be replaced by a more flexible, pragmatic, and easier monetary policy.

They said that the Treasury's most dedicated monetarist, Under Secretary Beryl Sprinkel, was on the verge of falling and had certainly been forced into unwanted and unwonted silence, and that President Reagan wanted, more than anything, to see those high interest rates come down.

For it seemed impossible to halt the slump and get a recovery going without lower interest rates. Paul Volcker began slowly, confusingly, but surely to increase the growth of the money supply in an effort to deliver those lower rates, even if monetarist orthodoxy had to be abandoned. But that might not be nearly enough unless the still huge deficits in the Federal budget could be shrunk. That was why Reagan, who loathed tax increases, signed a $98 billion three-year loophole-plugging tax increase passed by Congress, to the horror of his old supply-side ideologists. It was the clearest sign of the emergence of a new pragmatism; but the residue of the original tax-cutting spree remained, along with the big defense buildup, and the country was still a long way from being out of the big-deficit, high-interest-rate woods.

At the same time, Congress also pushed for easier money.

Looking back to mid-1982, former Representative Henry Reuss of Wisconsin, who had been chairman of the House Committee on Banking, Finance, and Urban Affairs, said that Congress recognized that the Administration and the Fed would not loosen money except under pressure. Under the Constitution, Congress had the ultimate authority "to coin money, regulate the value thereof"—that is, to regulate the Fed. "For the first time in many years," said Reuss, "Congress intervened to exercise its monetary power." In its budget resolution, it requested the central bank to "re-evaluate its monetary targets." Though the words were gentle, they commanded bipartisan support, and the Fed immediately got the message: In July 1982, it abandoned monetarism and its exclusive focus on the money supply. It "refused to be spooked" when money grew month after month at a rate of 15 percent, way above its earlier target ranges. Interest rates tumbled; the markets refused to be hexed by the monetarists.

In fact, starting in mid-August, stock prices soared. Wall Street's explosion raised hopes that if stocks were rising the resurgence of the national economy could not lag far behind.

But there was wild irony in the picture: The forecasts of lower interest rates that triggered the stock market's upsurge in the third week of August were based on gloomy analyses of the overall business outlook. For instance, Henry Kaufman, the sage of Salomon Brothers, said the economy was "straitjacketed by financial blockages and fear of international competition." Albert M. Wojnilower, a fellow merchant of gloom, had just said flatly that "the business outlook has deteriorated"— capital spending had been slashed again, consumption had fallen, and inventories had resumed piling up. The July 1 tax cut, the second installment in Reagan's three-year program, said Wojnilower, was more like a life preserver thrown to a struggling swimmer than extra stimulus to an economy already at the point of lift-off.

Nevertheless, in the face of these gloomy pronouncements, Wall Street cheered wildly, focusing on the predictions of declining interest rates. Treasury Secretary Regan, the transplanted Wall Streeter, was exuberant too; he would not look a gift horse in the mouth. A rally was a rally, and an enormous rally was an enormous rally. He expressed his appreciation to Henry Kaufman for his help, but said he was right for the wrong reason. The real cause of Wall Street's upsurge was its recognition that the Reagan Administration had restored stability to the economy, Regan contended.

On August 19, waking up after its two-day binge, Wall Street seemed less sure, wondering whether it had not overdone things. The gloomy economic forecasts—and the existing reality of weak business conditions, declining profits, and high and rising unemployment—were still staring it in the face. It was not, after all, just Kaufman and Wojnilower who had turned sour on the prospects of recovery just before the stock market exploded, but the vast majority of other economists as well. Robert J. Eggert, president and chief economist of Eggert Economic Enterprises, had reported on August 10 that the earlier, modestly cheerful outlook for the "after-the-tax-cut" third quarter had faded among the 44 leading economists polled for his "blue chip" composite forecast. And Alan Greenspan, president of Townsend-Greenspan and still a frequent White House caller and adviser, had just declared on August 13 that "the recovery is still not here," and noted that the outlook for 1982–83 "has continued to deteriorate since our last forecast."

However, I concluded that the gloom had been vastly overdone. On August 20, 1982, I wrote in my column that there was good reason to think the resurgence of the stock market earlier in the week had marked an important turning point in the economy: "There has been a drawing back from the brink just before the economy crashed over it." It looked as if the economy would survive the mistakes of the past, now that they were being repaired.

"The decline in long-term rates as well as short-term rates should help lift housing out of its deep slump," I wrote. "The strengthening bond market should help arrest the fall in business investment on plant and equipment, although, given the heavy hangover of excess capacity, it will take months before capital spending recovers. High unemployment will still be a drag on consumer spending, but gains in take-home pay from the net tax cut (even if the tax-increase bill before Congress passes), higher Social Security benefits, and, most important, a gradual rise in output and income as inventory cutting fades will put more money into consumers' pockets and increase their outlays."

Strengthening financial markets, I added, were likely to give a psychological lift not only to Wall Street and Washington but to many consumers and businesses around the country.

All the economy's woes had not vanished overnight, I said. The international financial picture, with Mexico rising to the top of the worry list, remained especially serious.

"But," I concluded, "Wall Street's burst of action this week suggests that the Great Crash is not at hand. And if Congress supports the White House move to produce a more stimulative fiscal policy and the Fed continues to work for lower interest rates, the recovery may soon get under way."

It did—three months later, in November 1982.

Chapter

15

THE MISERY INDEX

Though the Federal Reserve had switched from repression to stimulation, the economy could not be turned around on a dime. Through the summer and fall of 1982, real output continued to sink, unemployment to rise, and more and more businesses to go under.

The biggest danger was international. An avalanche of debt threatened to wreck the world monetary system. At the annual meeting of the International Monetary Fund and the World Bank in Toronto during the first week of September, the mood among government officials and private bankers was more anxious and the warnings more dire than at any such gathering in my memory. Denis Healey, the British Labor Party's shadow Foreign Secretary and former Chancellor of the Exchequer, warned that the Toronto meetings were "the last chance to save the world from a catastrophe even greater than the slump of the 1930s." Countries such as Mexico, Argentina, and Poland, he said, found it impossible to pay their present debts, let alone raise new capital to stay afloat, and many third world countries faced the prospect of economic collapse, political anarchy, and starvation. "The risk of a major default triggering a chain reaction is growing every day," said Healey.

Healey may have been exaggerating, but the seriousness of the debt problems facing the third world and the Western banks that had lent so heavily to them was beyond doubt. The total debt of the developing countries had soared from $97 billion in 1973, just before the OPEC oil-price explosion, to over $600 billion in the fall of 1982. The size of a country's debts alone does not create a crisis but rather the country's inability to pay the interest on its debts. In the midst of a world slump that had cut the demand for the exports of developing countries, as well as their prices, a growing number of countries could not meet their payments out of earnings.

With oil prices down, the problem applied to some oil exporters as well as the oil importers. Mexico, for one, had borrowed like crazy from private commercial banks, which were only too eager to lend on the assumption that the country's vast oil reserves and climbing world oil prices meant that its credit was extremely good. But that left out not only the oil glut and the world recession but the fiscally irresponsible policies of the Government of President José Lopez Portillo.

Unfortunately, the Mexican case was characteristic of a long list of countries as different as Argentina and Rumania, Brazil and Egypt, Chile and Poland. All shared a combination of excess debt, stagnating or falling export earnings, yawning budget deficits, and a decline of domestic savings. The shortfall in savings had forced nations to seek abroad the capital they could not raise at home.

The United States and other lending governments of the capitalist world, as well as Jacques de Larosière, managing director of the International Monetary Fund, and A. W. Clausen, president of the World Bank, were determined not to try to rescue the world economy by creating so much new debt and money as to generate worse inflation. And they wanted borrowing nations to take tough steps to curb inflation—reduce their budget deficits, increase domestic savings, increase their exports, and cut their imports, all of this coming under the head of "austerity"—as the price of getting more loans from abroad.

But too tough a line in making extra resources available to severely strained nations could cause some to refuse to cooperate with the international lenders and private bankers, because of domestic political pressures. Countries with masses in deep poverty and on the verge of starvation could be pushed over the brink.

It would be important for the I.M.F. to have enough money to induce nations that wanted to stay solvent to work with the financial doctors. Support from private commercial banks would also be important to sustain their efforts to work their way back to growth and economic health.

Toronto did produce general if still not precise agreement on increasing the lending agencies' resources. Having peered into the abyss, the nations overwhelmingly declared, "Anything but that!" But the game of adjustment in a world of massive debts, declining trade, overcapacity, and unemployment would remain hazardous and painful.

MISERY REBUFFED

The Republicans suffered losses in the Congressional and gubernatorial elections in November 1982—losses that were clearly linked to rising unemployment. The rise in the civilian jobless rate to 10.1 percent in September—the last number seen before the November 4 election—outweighed the effect on voters of news about declining inflation. President Reagan immediately after the election gave notice that the unemployment rate for October was likely to go "a few fractions" of a point higher. In fact, unemployment in October hit 10.3 percent, with 11.5 million workers jobless. Nor was that the peak. The unemployment rate moved up to 10.7 percent in December, when over 12 million people were out of work.

And though the inflation rate had come down—from 12.4 percent in 1980 to 8.9 percent in 1981 and 4.8 percent at the time of the November 1982 election—the memory of the high inflation rate appeared to have played a role in voters' blame of the Republican incumbents for the poor state of the economy.

Seymour Martin Lipset, a political analyst based at the Hoover Institute at Stanford University, said the 1982 election in the United States fit into a worldwide pattern in which economics dominated politics. Lipset offered evidence that the "misery index"—the sum of the rates of unemployment and inflation at any given time—was a reliable predictor of election outcomes.

In countries where the misery index had been above 10 percent, incumbents had been regularly defeated. But where it had been below 10 percent, incumbents had been re-elected. This principle held in two-party countries whether the incumbents were conservatives or liberals. In Britain in 1979 and the United States in 1980, the misery index was 19 percent, and the voters replaced Labour and Democratic governments with Conservative and Republican ones. The Reagan Administration, with the misery index at 15 percent—10 percent unemployment and 5 percent inflation—had suffered a sharp rebuff, in 1972, although the index was not so high as to provoke a rout.

Similarly, incumbent governments, without regard to left-wing or right-wing political ideologies, had been thrown out in the last few years in Canada, Portugal, Norway, Denmark, France, Greece, Sweden, Spain, and West Germany.

The high correlation of the misery index with the electoral defeat of incumbents, Lipset contended, challenges claims that various elections have produced mandates for the policies of the victors. President Reagan appeared to have overestimated the public support for his fiscal, social, and military policies in 1980, when the electorate was voting against the Carter Administration and voting for "something better." The outcome of the 1982 election seemed likely to bring about a shift to the broad center, where the American electorate felt most at home after brief flirtations with the left or right. The more extreme and abrasive conservative supporters of Reagan had just taken a bad licking. But it was by no means clear whether Reagan himself, in many ways the most ideological of Presidents ever, had accepted the lesson.

Nevertheless, the Republican political theorist Kevin Phillips appeared to have been just plain wrong in warning against a swing to the more extreme right if Reaganomics appeared to be failing. Though distressed about the economy, the voters had expressed their hopes for practical answers, not their fears of collapse unless there were a fundamental "capitalist revolution," in Phillips's words. American voters are simply not very ideological. The heavy rejection of Republican candidates for governorships—the Democrats had won 27 of the 36 at stake—looked like a sharp reaction against Reagan's proposed "new federalism," which voters thought would impose insupportable burdens on the states for financing social programs, unless they were to be cut drastically.

COLD-TURKEY CURE

Although the National Bureau of Economic Research, the closest thing we have to an official dater of business-cycle turning points, said the recession had ended in November 1982, the recovery that month looked feeble or nonexistent. The latest piece of worrisome news was of a 4.9 percent drop in orders for durable goods, the biggest decline in a year. And there were anxieties over the heavy overhang of manufacturing and trade inventories, weak sales in the stores, and rising unemployment.

Companies were still trying to cut their labor and other costs to restore profitability. Hampered by an overvalued dollar, they were struggling to bring down costs to compete more effectively with foreign producers. Consumers were showing few signs of being willing to save less and spend more. Their caution reflected the high unemployment and worries about layoffs still to come. Both households and businesses were reacting sluggishly to declines in nominal interest rates, because rates, after adjustment for lower inflation, remained very high.

But had the long, steep slump been a cure for what ailed business? Or was the cure worse than the disease? Subjective answers would depend not only on one's political and social philosophy but on how particular people and businesses are affected. For the unemployed, the slump is experienced as all cost, no benefit; inflation might drop, but if one's income dropped further, where's the gain? For some businesses, confronting falling sales and mounting debts, a continuation of the recession would mean unmitigated disaster. But for most businesses and the economy in general the recession could work as a restorative.

One way of seeing this is to look at the stock market. The market had climbed by more than 20 percent from August through November and, in the face of flashes of bad economic news, was holding on to its gains. Since the market collectively represents the capitalized value of future corporate earnings, this suggested that, depite the forecasts of a weak recovery by the great majority of economists in November and December, with unemployment expected to hover around 10 percent in 1983, the market was seeing better profits ahead.

An improvement was taking place not only in the quantity but the "quality" of profits. The Standard & Poor's Corporation concluded that the quality of profits, as measured by the share of earnings not due to inflation, was higher than it had been for a decade. Inflation artificially swells profits but worsens their quality in two ways: by creating inventory profits, which vanish when the economy sags and inflation slows and inventories need to be dumped; and by encouraging corporations to make inadequate allowance for the depreciation of capital assets in terms of what it would cost to replace plants and equipment, thereby temporarily swelling their reported profits while reducing their ability to maintain or increase capital and to produce efficiently and profitably.

As recently as 1979, inventory profits had been accounting for about 20 percent of total profits before taxes. By the end of 1982, with inflation down from more than 10 percent to 5 percent, inventory profits were accounting for only about 6 percent of corporate earnings. Standard & Poor's concluded that this improvement in the quality of earnings was one of the more important elements in the market's more liberal stock valuations, with price-earnings ratios their highest in a long time.

The recession had left other constructive legacies. Tighter internal controls, the hold-down in wage costs, cutbacks in hourly paid and salaried staff, higher productivity, tighter inventories, reduced capital spending, would all help companies strengthen their balance sheets and prepare for expansion again. Such adjustments had been taking place under pressure of the recession; they had already produced a rise in corporate profits in the third quarter of 1982, lifting pretax earnings to $170 billion from $162 billion in the second quarter.

But the squeeze is agonizing while you are going through it. That's how the business cycle works—as meliorated or aggravated by the government's fiscal and monetary policies. And the pain cost is worst of all on the unemployed, draftees in the war against inflation.

"QUICK FIXES"

President Reagan was sensitive to the plight of the jobless. As 1982 was drawing to a close, he proposed to solve the unemployment problem by urging every American business to hire "just one person." That proposal did not exactly get off to a flying start, since it collided with an announcement by Bethlehem Steel that it was eliminating the jobs of 10,000 workers in Lackawanna, New York, and Johnstown, Pennsylvania. Unhappily, Bethlehem was not an isolated case. Nearly half the steel industry's 450,000 workers had been laid off, probably half of them permanently.

The Bureau of National Affairs reported in December that hiring projections for the first quarter of 1983 were the lowest recorded since it began to survey employers on the job outlook in 1974. Its new survey found that only 9 percent of the employers who responded planned an increase in their work forces in the first quarter of the new year; if anything, the survey was biased on the optimistic side, since only companies still in business could respond.

Interpreting Reagan's proposal, Edwin Meese 3rd, the President's counselor, said: "This may really involve in some cases not letting someone go that they might have to, by staggering work hours or something like that. That's what the President is talking about."

Clearly Reagan found the simplicity of his hire-one-worker proposal appealing, because, he said, "There are more businesses in the United States than unemployed." According to the Census, in 1977, the last year for which data are available, there were 14.7 million businesses in the United States compared to 12 million jobless workers in December 1982. But 11.3 million of the businesses listed in the Census were proprietorships, most of which had only a few or no employees.

For Reagan it was not just a question of numbers, which have not been his strong point, but the "neighborly spirit" of his proposal. He seemed to see unemployment as what economists call a "microeconomic" problem, in which every individual and business can solve the problem on his, her, or its own initiative. Solutions involving government are decried as "quick fixes."

A reporter reminded Reagan that he had spoken on various occasions of his father's losing his job in the Christmas holidays during the Great Depression, and he asked the President at his final news conference of the year what he thought his father's and mother's reactions would have been if the Congress of that period had passed a $5 billion bill "that would have gotten him back to work right away when you were little."

Reagan replied, "Well, I've always thought my father, God rest his soul, had the common sense that he would know that temporary fixes wouldn't work."

But when his father finally did get a job, the President added, "it happened to be for the government." He and the county supervisor of the poor, Reagan said, "shared a secretary and were in charge of the help—they called it relief in those days—for the people in our community."

Yet his father believed in free private enterprise; he went around town, Reagan said, lining up private jobs for the unemployed, who would come into his office and say, "When is it going to be my turn? When do you get to my turn again? It's been a long time since I've had some work." This was as heartening a scene as ever came off the M-G-M lot.

"And guess what?" the President asked the reporters rhetorically. "The Federal Government then intervened and figured it out that they couldn't take that work, because if they took that work they were denied relief.

"So they were forced onto permanent relief," Reagan said. "They couldn't work."

However, when Reagan took office in January 1981, a person on welfare—Aid to Families with Dependent Children—could keep $30 plus one-third of his or her earnings without loss of welfare benefits. That provision, ironically, was knocked out by the celebrated tax act of 1981, which made earnings from work by a welfare recipient subject to taxation at a 100 percent rate.

COMING ON STRONG

By the early spring of 1983, there was growing evidence that the economic recovery would be hearty. President Reagan, more optimistic than his own economic advisers,[1] said it would soon be bustin' out all over. "Economic recovery is something like a seedling," he said. "What we're starting to see right now are the shoots of an economic recovery." Busily watering those seedlings was Paul Volcker, chairman of the Fed.

Reagan was not alone in his view that the recovery would soon be coming on strong. Suddenly many of the nation's businessmen, bankers, auto dealers, real estate agents, and even some economists sniffed something new and refreshing in the air. Albert T. Sommers, the chief economist of the Conference Board, who had never been regarded as an economic cheerleader, told the House Budget Committee that, far from being "weak, slow, and hesitant," as many economists had predicted earlier, the recovery would be strong, and "only the most improbable fiscal and monetary blunder" could stop it.

The stock market, a reasonably good but far from perfect forecaster of the economy, had called it right back in August 1982. This was no act of nature or of an abstraction called the business cycle. The Federal Reserve, by pouring in money when all looked lost, had turned the economy around and fed the expansion.

But by the summer of 1983, with the recovery picking up steam, the question was: Where would the Fed go from here? The Fed-watchers—those financial hawks on Wall Street who are to the central bank what Kremlinologists are to the Kremlin—were putting Volcker's every word under a microscope. After a long delay, Reagan had reappointed him to the chairmanship of the Fed. Was this a vote of thanks for beating the

[1] Martin Feldstein of Harvard had replaced Murray Weidenbaum as chairman of the Council of Economic Advisers.

inflation down and rescuing the economy just in time? Or a yielding to bankers and others still deeply worried about the shaky international monetary system and the need for an experienced hand like Volcker at the Fed to ensure against systemic breakdown? Probably both.

For its part, the Reagan Administration had no intention of contenting itself with anything so passive as Fed-watching. Its game was Fed-pushing. Shortly before Volcker testified at his reconfirmation hearing before the Senate Banking Committee, Larry Speakes, the President's spokesman, said: "We do not want to see interest rates raised. We'd rather see them come down." Speakes, well versed in the arts of Fed-influencing, said he was voicing only an Administration view, not issuing instructions to the Fed. "We deeply respect their independence," he said.

Monetarism no longer represented the creed of the Administration or the Fed. A cardinal tenet of that doctrine was that the central bank should concern itself only with regulating the money supply, permitting interest rates to swing up or down as the markets took them. But despite the White House's Canute-like view that interest rates should not rise, with the economy gathering force the tide was coming in. "An upward bias in interest rates is now in motion," said Henry Kaufman.

The Fed-watchers were having an exceptionally hard time reading the central bank's intentions. Volcker obviously wanted to head off a revival of inflation, but if he tightened money too much and interest rates went up, the Administration would be after him for endangering the recovery. All the Fed-watchers could be sure of was that the Fed would not raise the discount rate, because the White House had made its objections to that move so clear and forceful.

The real mystery was what policy the Fed was following. Strict monetarism had been locked in the closet because it looked too costly and too risky. A strong and unbending move by the Fed to hit narrow targets for the money supply could risk aborting the recovery, and the White House was simply unwilling to take that risk with November 1984 swimming into view. The one thing it would not tolerate was a rise in the Misery Index.

FUTURE FACTS

Curiously enough, the second half of 1983 began with economists voicing increasing confidence about the strength of the recovery and investment advisers expressing growing concern about the outlook for the stock market. How could the disparity be explained? One key factor might be the way the two professions perceive "reality." The economists, seeking to be "scientific," focus on existing data, such as the latest figures on gross national product or industrial production, and try to build models on the basis of such data. But the investment advisers, seeking to make money, focus on "expectations"—the beliefs and moods of the market—however difficult these might be to measure or incorporate in systematic models.

In the summer of '83, the economists, with the economic data improving, were busy raising their forecasts. As the economic analysts at the Fidelity Bank of Philadelphia put it, contemplating the big leap in real GNP in the second quarter of the year, "Real economic activity has shifted gears and is emerging from the recession at a rate more rapid than had been anticipated." By them.

But the improved data had made many Wall Street analysts wary. They were thinking not only about the current facts of economic life but also about what the market expected to happen, and how the economic outlook compared with what the market had expected the outlook to be when it bought stocks in the past year. Then the great majority of economists had remained cautious or bearish about the economy, while speculators and investors were bidding up the value of equities in one of the most rapid stock market booms in history. Now with the economists singing the praises of the recovery, many stock

market advisers had begun to sing what Greg Smith of Pru-
dential-Bache Securities called "the second-half blues."

"Now, at best," said Smith, "companies will deliver 'expected' results, and the most cyclical companies will probably
fall short of expectations. This introduces overall risk to the
stock market for the first time this year." But not all the investment advisers agreed. Some saw a strong uptrend continuing.

The economists were more unified on the outlook for the
coming year than the investment advisers. This was a normal
state of affairs. In a memorial article on Keynes, Paul Samuelson, M.I.T.'s Nobel laureate, noted that the dictum of the
economist Roy Blough, a member of President Truman's
Council of Economic Advisers, had stood the test of time:
"Economists are like six Eskimos in a bed. You can be sure
only that they'll all turn over together." The reason the economists turn over together is that they all look at the same data—
and react to it on the basis of similar economic models of how
the economy works.

Not so with the investment advisers. Their models are ill-
defined. They are as much concerned with psychology as with
economics. And their information about "expectations" is
hazy, shifting from day to day with all the winds that blow
through the canyons of Wall Street. Yet the market had been a
lot better at sensing and predicting the turnaround in the
economy than the economists.

Keynes, who on the 100th anniversary of his birth in 1983
was being hailed as the most influential economist of the century, was also a successful stock market speculator. He did not
despise what the market knew, however it knew it. Professor
Samuelson, though no stranger to the market game, clearly
preferred Keynes the economic scientist to Keynes the intuitive
speculator. Samuelson made sport of those who believe that
the "real McCoy of Keynes" is to be found in the subtle nu-
ances of his perceptions—the notions of "bearishness," "ani-
mal spirits," "liquidity," and "the ineffable importance of
expectations"—rather than his systematic and measurable
concepts and equations.

But analysis based on existing information may not necessarily be preferable to intuition and expectations, admittedly more uncertain than the "hard" data but possibly more relevant. And a "scientific" model of the economy drawn from conventional data may not necessarily be superior as a predictor of the real world to a conceptually more realistic approach that draws on fuzzier information about expectations but processes a vastly larger amount of information about companies and industries.

Imperfect as it is, the market is a useful, though wavering, mirror of expectations.

Chapter

16

THE SOVIET CONNECTION

I can't be sure why I had felt so little desire to go to the Soviet Union for so long. Part of the reason, I suppose, was my feeling that, not knowing the Russian language and having focused on the United States and other capitalist economies for so many years, I did not see what I could contribute that Sovietologists and foreign correspondents based in the country couldn't do better.

There was an even more serious reason for my not wanting to go: my disgust over the Soviets' treatment of human beings, the ugliness of a system that treats people like things. Who needed it?

But soon after Yuri Andropov succeeded Leonid Brezhnev as the Soviet leader in November 1982, I changed my mind and decided the time had come for me to try to go and see with my own eyes what was going on. Andropov had made reinvigorating the Soviet economy a top priority. Did the former head of the K.G.B. really mean to change the system, and if so, which way would he go—toward liberalization or back toward Stalinism?

Another question I wanted to look at for myself was whether, as some high officials in the Reagan Administration contended, the Soviet economy was a basket case, or could be made one if the United States revved up the arms race and forced the Russians to cut back on civilian investment and consumption in order to compete. Would aggravating their economic weaknesses force them to trim their military programs and adopt a less aggressive foreign policy?

But would the Russians be willing to cooperate and give me access to some of the people I wanted to see? Eugene Shershnev, an elderly man who was the economic counselor at the Soviet Embassy in Washington and a longtime associate of Ambassador Anatoly Dobrynin, said he thought Moscow would let me in and let me talk with economists in Moscow and Novosibirsk, Siberia, a major center of economic and scientific research. I submitted lists of people I wanted to see, and after months of delay Moscow finally came through with visas and appointments for me with government officials and economists at the principal academic institutes in Moscow, Novosibirsk, and all the way out to Yakutsk in northeastern Siberia.

So I spent the month of May traveling across the Soviet Union, listening to much franker talk than I had expected to hear—and talking my own head off.

No Soviet economist I met denied that their economy is having severe problems and that the rate of growth in national output has slowed down markedly in recent years. The Soviet economists expressed their familiarity with C.I.A. and other American estimates of their growth rates and said they showed trends consistent with their own, though the American figures were slightly lower than theirs.

Calculations by two of the leading American specialists on the Soviet economy, Daniel L. Bond and Herbert S. Levine of Wharton Econometric Forecasting Associates, are that the average annual growth of Soviet gross national product slid from a peak of 5.2 percent during 1966–70, the period of the Eighth Five Year Plan, to 2 percent during 1981–82, the first two years of the Eleventh Five Year Plan. The Soviet economists' own calculations are that their GNP growth rate declined from 7.5 percent in 1966–70 to 2.5 percent in 1981–82. Soviet living standards, according to the Wharton estimates, are only about one-third of ours. And the gap is widening, not narrowing.

What ails the Soviet economy? I want to approach the answer to that question by giving you a sense of what their economy looks and feels like today.

Let's start by going shopping, not in the big department stores or Beryoshkas (foreign-currency stores) of Moscow or Leningrad, which so many tourists know, but in the general store of Neryungri, a town of 45,000 out in northeastern Siberia. The store is housed in a plain wooden barnlike structure. At five o'clock in the afternoon of a normal working day, the store is jammed with workers, men and women and some children, waiting in long lines to get up to the handful of saleswomen.

Behind the counters running around the walls, goods are piled on shelves in no discernible order—brassieres and panties next to children's toys, fabrics next to souvenirs, fountain pens and clocks next to shirts and pants, pots and pans next to shoes and socks. In one corner of the room are sofas, chairs, tables, and small refrigerators with the brand name of "Candy" that look like something out of a 1924 Sears catalogue. Everybody seems to be buying like crazy, as though rubles were going out of style.

The whole hectic and messy scene—the long lines, the doggedly waiting customers, the shoddy goods—was as familiar as a recurrent dream, familiar from other visitors and foreign correspondents; yet it struck me harder than I expected—because it was the thing to be explained, the heart of the mystery of the Soviet economy. Was this hidden inflation, with government controls turning pressures on prices into perpetual queues? Or was it prosperity Soviet-style—the lusty demand-side economics that kept the rickety supply-side from breaking down? Or was there some deeper mystery involved?

We go to the biggest Moscow bookstore to buy a Russian-English dictionary. But it has no Russian-English dictionaries. We try another bookstore: no luck. We try in Leningrad, Novosibirsk, Yakutsk: still no Russian-English dictionary. Where the hell are the Russian-English dictionaries? Have they been banned by the K.G.B.? Do the scholars and journalists and diplomats grab them all and hoard them? Why don't the bookstores order more? Why don't the customers order more? Is the explanation that bureaucrats in the cultural ministry get their brownie points not by giving customers what they want but what the state wants them to get?

In search of economic freedom, we go to the free market, housed in an old warehouse in Moscow. Actually, the building includes some stalls with government-controlled goods cheek by jowl with free-market goods. Business is lively in both kinds of goods; the government goods are common and cheap, the free-market goods expensive and rare. On the free-market counters you can find flowers ($5 for one rose), fruits, meat, vegetables (the vegetable-craving wife of a foreign correspondent once paid $31 for a cauliflower). The only vegetables we ever got in restaurants were cucumbers, potatoes, and cabbages. You get to feel like a veggie junky in need of a cauliflower or string-bean fix.

My wife takes out her camera to shoot pictures, and a small plump Russian lady wearing a white apron and cloth cap runs up, red-faced, furious, hollering at us that we are not permitted to take pictures. Our Moscow bureau chief, John Burns, tells the lady in Russian that he has taken pictures there many times, and says she has no right to interfere. Where is her authorization? The busybody lady does not retreat but keeps protesting—a real fighter. What state secrets is she protecting? How have we offended her?

We go to a toy store, the biggest in Moscow, close to Lubyanka, the K.G.B. headquarters with the prison in the basement. We want to buy a present for Mischa, the son of our guide and interpreter, normally an economic commentator for Novosti, the Soviet news agency. But we run out of time waiting in line. Poor Mischa! Too many Russians want presents for other Mischas.

We are walking back to our hotel and see a line forming off Gorky Street. What are they selling? Oranges? Cucumbers? Cabbages? All three! The line quickly grows halfway down the block. Are these free-market oranges, cucumbers, and cabbages? No, they are government-controlled goods, sold by a lady on outpost duty from the store down the block.

At last, like everybody else, we go to GUM, the mammoth Moscow department store in the shadow of the Kremlin. More mobs, more lines. It is a hot day, and the crowds are blocking the intersection of aisles, trying to buy ice cream from the ladies in the white aprons. There are four separate ice cream queues, each with an ice cream lady dishing it out some of the time, each without a lady some of the time. Where do the missing ladies go? To pick up another tray of ice cream cones in a back room. Why do the people in one queue not change to another queue when the ice cream lady leaves? Because each lady will have only a few dozen cones on a tray, and by the time you change from one line to another and get up to the head of the queue, the cones will have run out, so you might as well stay where you are.

The congestion worsens. It is hot, and the ice cream cones are melting fast.

But there are other things to buy, if you can wait through each of the three lines necessary to make any purchase—one line for telling the clerk what you want, a second for paying the bill, and the third for picking up your purchase.

Same system in the music stores. Same in the groceries. Same everywhere.

"WESTERN ECONOMISTS ARE LUCKY"

Why do people put up with it? Why are the goods so shoddy? But why is business so good? Why are there shortages all over the place?

Because it is a shortage economy. Government price fixing is partly responsible; prices are generally set below the level at which supply would equal demand. But there is excess demand not just for particular goods but for goods in general.

Shortages are aggravated by the rigidly controlled production and distribution system, and by the inertness of Soviet business organizations, fouled up by red tape and comatose from the lack of competition, yet secure in the knowledge that they will not fail.

A Hungarian economist, Janos Kornai, says all Communist economies are shortage economies, and blames this on the "soft" conditions facing their businesses. The Communist business firm does not have to keep costs below selling prices and make a profit or go broke. Its survival and growth depend mainly on its ability to acquire labor, materials, machinery, trucks, space on freight cars, whatever, not on its efficiency or profitability. The managers' success commonly depends not on how well they manage but who they know out there, and up there.

Soviet managers use expediters or pushers (*tolkachi* is the Russian word for what in the United States Army we used to call "dog-robbers") to procure material or equipment. With its soft budget, the Soviet enterprise develops an insatiable appetite for resources. Each enterprise seeks to solve its problems by taking labor, materials, equipment, and capital away from other businesses and industrial sectors. But since all businesses are doing it to each other, they collectively succeed only in intensifying the shortages, bottlenecks, waste, and low productivity of the entire system.

How can this sloppy and disorderly system be fixed? Soon

after he took office in November 1982, Andropov made a first pass at the problem by going to the shop floor of the Sergo Ordzhonikidze machine-tool factory in Moscow to talk with the workers about the need for harder work and greater discipline. Curiously enough, Ordzhonikidze, the man for whom the factory was named, shot himself in the 1930s in a vain protest against Stalin's terrorist methods.

Was Andropov symbolically saying, "Yes, we need greater discipline, but we are not going back to Stalin's ways"? Or had he just chosen a handy plant to put out the message that he would mix toughness toward goof-offs and drunks with bigger material incentives for people who worked harder?

"Discipline," an economist at the Institute for Economic Studies of the Academy of Sciences in Moscow told me, "is only one of the ways of intensification." ("Intensification" is the Soviet buzzword for measures to raise the productivity of labor and capital.)

"In the past," he went on, "discipline meant treating people harshly, putting them in jail. That won't work any more. We cannot go back to the Stalin era. Now we have to find ways of giving greater incentives for work.

"You Western economists are lucky. You can count on the discipline of the market. Managers know their businesses will fail if they don't manage better, make better products. Workers know they will lose their jobs if they don't produce or if their employers fail."

This was a fantastic thing to hear there at the heart of the Soviet planning system. But whether the Soviet economists knew how to fix it was another matter.

I heard the same question expressed by other economists. Said one in despair: "We've tried everything—this incentive, that incentive, bigger incomes if they will overfulfill the norms, threats if they won't. We put out 'punishment books' if customers are dissatisfied with services. But nothing works. What should we do? What should we do?"

Some observers contend that the Russians simply lack a

work ethic like Americans or Japanese, and that if harsh discipline is not imposed on them, as in the Stalin era, nothing will work. But the economists I spoke with consider that stupid. They see low productivity as a result not of the national character but of the way the system is organized and of conflicts among goals.

Andropov had proposed to change the way the system is organized. He aimed to give greater authority to plant managers and reduce rigid central control. When Andropov died in February 1984, he was succeeded by a protégé of Brezhnev, Konstantin U. Chernenko, who had been an Andropov rival. Customarily in the Soviet Union a new Secretary General praises his predecessor's achievements, especially, as is usually the case, when he has just died. Nevertheless, Mr. Chernenko did not hesitate to call attention to the economic failures at the end of the Brezhnev era, and promised to advance by "collective efforts" the work begun by the Andropov regime.

But there is no sign that anyone in the hierarchy is prepared to change the fundamental goals of the Communist system; and it is those goals that are creating the major barriers to increased productivity and growth. For the goal of more efficient use of human and material resources is running smack up against the goals of jobs-for-all and no-business-failures.

Nikolai V. Baibakov, chairman of the State Planning Committee, on August 17, 1983, had told top Soviet officials that two major tenets of Soviet economic doctrine would not be changed by Andropov's proposed reforms: Moscow would continue to support money-losing plants rather than close them, because the Communist approach was to turn such plants into profit-makers and save jobs; and the government would not tolerate unemployment, even of a temporary nature, since Soviet law requires that any worker who is dismissed be found another job.

The Andropov reforms barely had a chance to get off the ground, but Mr. Chernenko also meant to have a go at it. "The system of economic management, the whole of our economic machinery," he said, "needs a serious restructuring. Work in this direction has only been started."

"The Failures of Success"

Full employment is obviously a worthy goal in itself, in the West as well as the East. Its fulfillment provides the Russians with their strongest appeal to workers in other countries, especially in times of high unemployment in the West. Economic instability, underutilization of industrial capacity, and unemployment are the abiding problems of the capitalist West, and they have led in recent years to sluggish growth and the wastage of human resources.

But the wastage of labor in the Soviet Union, seen in its entirety, looks even greater—and even more demoralizing. I am thinking of those ladies sitting around the lobbies of hotels watching and waiting; the vast numbers of secret agents employed in bugging and spying and informing on people for a living; the oversupply of militiamen stopping cars, watching the streets, and patrolling in front of office buildings, residences, and compounds of diplomats and foreign correspondents. (The full-employment goal appears to dovetail with another: achieving maximum internal security—or perhaps it should be called nursing national paranoia.)

But the biggest wastage is the horde of supernumeraries in factories, in offices, and on farms who even if they were pushed out of a job here (it sometimes happens) would have to be put into one there.

The system produces a sour and corrupt or semicorrupt national mood. One gets used to but never accepts the grumpiness and inertia of those in undesired and undesirable jobs: the key ladies in the hotels sitting day and night doing a little snooping or selling you a bottle of mineral water or sending a woman to pick up the laundry, snoozing when there is nothing else to do; the invisible men, their coats over the backs of chairs in offices (signifying that the coat owner is present and nominally at work, though actually soemwhere else—shopping? visiting a friend? hiding in a bath house or movie theater? who knows?); the incredible waiting times in restaurants and the surliness of the waiters and waitresses (my favorite line, spoken in pidgin Russian by a waitress at the National Hotel in Moscow in response to a plea for an omelette, not the fried or boiled eggs that were always put out: "Omelette—nyet!!!").

I came to recognize some of the subtler side effects of the combination of no-competition and jobs-for-all: the inescapability of ear-splitting live music in restaurants from Leningrad to Yakutsk (full employment for musicians); the climate of laziness—the gardener sprinkling flowers while sitting in a truck holding the hose in one hand and a book in the other, or the men taking down the flags and pictures of Lenin after the Victory Day celebration spending hours, days, wearily moving their cherry pickers from location to location; the filthy conditions of public toilets (who wants to work in a toilet when you are sure of getting a job elsewhere?); the endless waits in airports as Aeroflot in its mysterious and unfathomable ways decides when to fly or whether to fly and whether to change you from one flight to another one, whether you want to change or not; the hordes waiting and sleeping on benches in the airport steerage-class hall while Aeroflot makes up its mind; the widespread drunkenness on and off the job; the impossibility of getting anything done on time.

"We understand these problems," the economist Yuri I. Bobravov, of the Institute of United States Studies in Moscow, told me. "They are the failures of success." The success includes full employment, slowly rising living standards, and the elimination of extreme poverty—no mean achievements against the background of the country's tortured history.

Yet the Soviet economists themselves stress that the methods used to achieve past successes, when the country lacked virtually everything and could be run on a forced-draft basis by Moscow, have lost their effectiveness and are in fact breeding stagnation and decay. A group of economists based at the Siberian Division of the Academy of Sciences in Novosibirsk noted in a critical document prepared in April 1983, shortly before I visited there, that scholars had attributed the slow-down in economic growth to many different factors: harder mining conditions, more frequent dry years in agriculture, lagging investment, an aging and wasting transportation network and capital stock, flagging work discipline, and so on.

But the Novosibirsk economists said that while all those factors did indeed play their part the effect of each was generally limited to a particular economic sector, and the deteriorating indicators applied to virtually every branch of the economy and region of the country.

"Therefore," they concluded, "there must be a common cause underlying these phenomena. In our view it lies in the outdated nature of the system of industrial organization and economic management or simply the inability of the system to insure complete and efficient utilization of the workers and intellectual potential of society."

Thus the old Soviet system is running down. Russian economists told me the Soviet Union must now enter a new stage of its development. Always careful to cite Communist authority to buttress their views, they referred me to an article by Andropov, published in the journal *Kommunist* on March 14, 1983 to commemorate the 100th anniversary of the death of Karl Marx, in which Andropov said the Soviet Union had entered "the beginning period of the developed Socialist society."

The new stage will be tricky to traverse. Professor Georgi E. Skorov, deputy director of the Institute of U.S.A. and Canada Studies, said: "Our society is not philanthropic. We are people of labor. But there are some traditions it is difficult to overcome."

It will be particularly difficult for the Soviets to end overfull employment—with more jobs than workers to fill them—and not just for the political and ideological reasons stressed by state planning chief Nikolai Baibakov. The Russians also have powerful economic reasons for maintaining what Western

economists call a "taut economy"—one in which industrial capacity and labor are used to the hilt, to enable them to handle
the problems generated by their clumsy, rigid price-controlled
system.

Franklyn D. Holtzman of Tufts University, an outstanding
American scholar of the Soviet economy, observes that, while
eliminating tautness might solve some of the problems that
plague the Soviet economy, it would aggravate others and
would make urgent an even more fundamental reform of the
system than Soviet leaders and bureaucrats would tolerate.

A high degree of tautness prevents the emergence of massive
gluts of poor goods that would develop if Soviet consumers
were not ready, willing, and able to buy whatever they can get
their hands on. The same applies to plant managers and the
likely emergence of gluts of capital goods if tautness were eliminated. And the emergence of massive gluts of both consumer
and capital goods would in turn lead to mass unemployment,
which Communist ideology forbids.

To cope with the problem of gluts of unsalable products and
idle workers, the Soviets would need to use countercyclical fiscal and monetary policies and build a welfare system to support the unemployed—like that in the Western capitalist
countries. More than that, to head off the gluts or cure them
they would need to liberate businesses to make their own adjustments—to improve the quality of their goods, change the
product mix, cut labor and other costs, set their own prices to
meet consumer demands, and fire managers (no matter what
their Communist Party status or protection).

It would also appear to mean a drastic reduction in the
power of the big shots at the top of the Soviet system. They
would fight it.

A EUPHEMISM FOR FREEDOM

Andropov had assured his fellow hierarchs that his changes in
the economic system would be made cautiously and carefully,

and in a way that would *strengthen* economic planning and control at the top. In Chernenko's first speech as General Secretary he indicated he too means to shake up the apparatus (whose creature he has been) and to impose discipline not just on workers but also on party bosses, ministers, and bureaucrats.

The key political-economic issue in any country, Communist or capitalist, is who controls what is produced and who gets what. The economic experiments announced by the Andropov regime in its decree of July 26, 1983 did mark a shift of power toward the managers of corporations and economic enterprises—and away from the middle levels of the state bureaucracy. The decree called for a broadening of "the rights of enterprises in planning and economic activity, to ensure their truly proprietorial interest in achieving a high level of production efficiency." Truly proprietorial interest! Remarkable language indeed for the leaders of a Communist society. Chernenko has gone a step further, urging economic executives at all levels to demonstrate independence and to engage in "well-justified risk-taking" for the sake of increasing economic efficiency and raising living standards.

During my trip to the Soviet Union, the economists I met with asserted that there should be both greater autonomy for managers but greater control at the top. What they had in mind was that the central planners would gain greater control if the powers of the middle-level bureaucrats in the ministries and government agencies "who were in business for themselves," as we say in Washington, were drastically reduced or eliminated.

The Novosibirsk economists in their confidential April memorandum that leaked to the Western press said that "the consensus among Soviet economists" was that there had been a weakening of the power of the State Planning Committee, representing the state interest, and a parallel decline in the powers of the "lower entities"—the industrial corporations and other economic enterprises.

"In stark contrast," their paper said, "the powers of the

functionaries of the intermediate levels of management, the ministries and agencies, have grown out of proportion, giving rise to departmentalism, to disproportions in the economy, to a growth of economic activity outside the formal economic structure"—the last phrase apparently referring to the Soviets' peculiar kind of official underground economy, in which bureaucrats make out like bandits.

In reassuring the Soviet big shots that their powers would not be reduced, Baibakov, remarkably enough, cited the controls exercised in capitalist countries by high government officials and by managements of large corporations as proof of the need for strong central controls.

In their search for economic reform, the Soviet leaders and economists appear to be seeking their own version of a "mixed economy." They see current capitalism as an effective mixture of business and government, not as the atomistic model of Adam Smith, with government pursuing a policy of laissez-faire.

The Soviet economists I met seem to have been careful students of what they take to be the best Western models, which they mean to adapt to Communist use. The decree of July 26 calls for "the development of democratic principles in the management of the economy" and for "enhancing the role of labor collectives in managing enterprises" (shades of participatory management in West Germany, France, Japan, and other capitalist countries). It calls for "the broad introduction of autonomous financing," allowing Soviet businesses to use their own profits, depreciation reserves, or borrowed funds to expand on their own, without central government control over their use of money.

The Soviet leaders and economists are deeply worried about their system's weakness in making scientific and technological innovations, which are the heart of economic growth in this era of the "research revolution."[1] The Andropov experiments proposed to give selected enterprises the right to draw on a special state fund for innovation to cover the increased costs of plan-

---

[1] See L. Silk, *The Research Revolution* (New York: McGraw-Hill, 1960).

ning and design while the innovation was being prepared and to give innovators extra financial incentives for taking risks. The July 26 decree states: "The material interest of specialists and workers in expanding the products list and in increasing the output of machinery, equipment, and instruments for export is being stepped up."

But Andropov appeared to some observers to be putting his toes in the water timidly. The new experiments, starting in January 1984, were to be limited to the Ministry of Heavy and Transport Machine Building, the Ministry of Electrical Equipment, the Ukrainian Republic's Ministry of the Food Industry, the Belorussian Ministry of Light Industry, and the Lithuanian Ministry of Local Industry. However, Andropov declared that his changes eventually would be applied throughout the economy.

Although these proposals fall well short of a radical transformation of the Communist system, Andropov and his economists had hoped that in giving greater autonomy to economic enterprises and in providing greater material incentives to producers, they would be able to increase the efficiency of the system and thus gradually to reduce the overall tautness of the economy—which is the source of overfull employment, hidden inflation, shortages, low morale, low productivity, corruption, and all the rest. The Party's hopes were rising that Andropov had found ways to break the stagnation into which the Soviet economy had lapsed—and, indeed, the economic performance had improved in 1983. Industrial output reportedly increased 4 percent, compared with only 2.9 percent in 1982, and labor productivity in industry rose 3.5 percent, though this may have been only a one-shot improvement resulting from the crackdown on loafing, absenteeism, and corruption. Nevertheless, Chernenko plans to continue the Andropov program, calling for a 3.8 percent rise in industrial output in 1984, and agricultural output is supposed to rise 6.4 percent, compared with 5 percent in 1983.

But there is no thought of reducing the power and privileges of those at the top or changing the political system. The first and most powerful sense I had of the nature of that system came in the late afternoon of a sunny day, driving back into Moscow from a trip to the country. We had driven past the grand estates and villas of high officials in that carefully policed area that American correspondents in Moscow call "Westchester." Suddenly, militiamen were stopping all the traffic, waving us off to the side of the road. Then big black limousines without license plates came roaring through, traveling at 100 miles an hour or more, followed by smaller black cars. The members of the Politburo were on their way home from a hard day's work at the Kremlin. But we couldn't see them behind their curtained windows. Finally, when the limos and the guard cars had passed, the militiamen waved us on.

I asked Vladimir, my Novosti guide, how he felt about the leaders in their limos, with their villas and fancy apartments in town, dachas at the Black Sea and so on? "That is state property they are using," he said.

The feudal, hierarchical, military style of the Soviet system reaches down through the system, layer after layer. It is hard to tell whether one is witnessing power hunger, officiousness, or fear.

One sees rank-pulling and power-wielding every day in scores of ways. It is hard to believe that such a society is headed for democratic reforms and a diffusion of economic and political power that would weaken control at the top and lessen it significantly for party officials, bureaucrats, the secret police, and the military.

I seriously doubt that such a political structure is compatible with an effective economic system—not in the modern post-industrial world. The best Soviet economists don't think so, either. The Novosibirsk group said that in the past "people were regarded as 'cogs' in the economic mechanism, and they behaved accordingly—obediently, passively—like machines and materials." Now the Soviet economy needed people who were more cultivated, who possessed social and spiritual values and who wanted, and should be granted, "greater leeway." Is "leeway" a euphemism for "freedom"? Why do they need a euphemism for freedom? Because the economists know that their masters are still determined to solve the economy's problems by "technical" means.

FEAR OF WAR

Central economic planning has important advantages for a nation at war, whether the country is Communist or capitalist. That's why the United States used production controls, price controls, wage controls, material allocations, rationing, the draft, and so on during World War II.

In a sense, the Soviet economy is still on a wartime basis, and the military has the first and foremost claim on national resources. But the weak performance of the Soviet economy has created serious problems even for the military. Sluggish technological progress makes it hard to keep their military modern and effective in competition with the United States.

The shrinking supply of competent labor, the depletion of natural resources and energy in the European part of the country, and the aging of the capital stock in industry and transportation have not only helped slow economic growth but made it hard for the military to claim the resources it wants; in fact, the military's growing claims have themselves been another factor in slowing Soviet economic growth.

Until recently, Western experts estimated that Soviet military expenditures were growing by 4 to 5 percent a year, but that figure has lately been scaled back by American intelligence sources to 2 percent a year. Even at such a low rate of increase, Soviet military demands could halt growth in civilian consumption during the second half of this decade. If Soviet military expenditures were to grow by as much as 7.5 percent—roughly in line with the pace President Reagan set for American military spending—Soviet consumption would drop.

Accelerated military outlays would be even more damaging to investment in new plants and equipment and would aggravate the decline of productivity. According to estimates of Wharton Econometric Forecasting Associates, at a 7.5 percent rate of increase, military procurement would gobble up more than the entire increase in machinery production during the second half of the 1980s. Herbert Levine and Daniel Bond of Wharton believe that bureaucratic pressures from competing claimants for investment equipment make it "unlikely that a 7.5 percent rate of growth of defense expenditures could be maintained for very long, except in extreme circumstances."

Soviet officials and economists support this reasoning, while declining to give detailed military estimates of their own. Vsevolod Y. Budavey, deputy director of the Economic Research Institute of the State Planning Committee, told me, "We are not responsible for the share of national output going to the military, but our principal viewpoint is clear to every specialist on the economy—that reduced defense expenditures will give us more opportunity to fulfill social programs and develop the eastern regions in Siberia where production costs are so much higher than in the rest of the country. For these reasons we will be glad to see a lessening of tensions, which would give us more resources for economic development."

I asked Budavey what Soviet planners would do if the United States stepped up its military production.

"Andropov has answered the question," he said. "Our main problem is to get a balanced economy. In the process of balancing we certainly will have obstacles and difficulties. But by careful planning, we intend to preserve our defense potential and fulfill our defense programs without unbalancing the economy. We do not deny that the arms race and the Soviet response to the American challenge will press hard on our resources.

"But if the American position is tougher, Soviet policy will also be tougher. Certainly, if some principal steps are made to press us, we will find funds for new programs."

I interpreted him as saying that, if they were forced to, the

Soviets would give the military priority and squeeze their civilian sector harder. However, Budavey added, "We will do our utmost to avoid a dangerous situation. We are not pioneers in the arms race."

Soviet ministers, when asked what effect stepped-up American pressures would have on their economy and arms programs, responded with a mixture of toughness and moderation. Alexei Manzhulo, a deputy minister of foreign trade, said this was not the first time the United States had tried to make the Soviet economy collapse. "It began in the time of our Revolution," he said. "Truman tried after the war, when our country was in ruins, our power stations broken by the Germans. Now we are three or four times stronger than we were then. We can do whatever we need to do." But he insisted that a conflict between the United States and the Soviet Union made no sense: "Everybody stands to lose," he said.

Boris A. Runov, a deputy minister of agriculture, got hot under the collar when I brought up the subject of American military and trade pressures on the Soviets. In World War II, Runov had been a sapper—a human mine detector. "In the sappers," he said, "we used to say, 'You can make a mistake once.'" Cooling down, he said, "You see, I didn't throw an ashtray at you. I didn't throw you out of here."

Off the record, a Soviet official said the Soviet Union would not allow itself to be dragged into economic debilitation by an American military buildup. But that did not mean, he said, that they would yield to American military threats. Instead, he said, the Soviets would "lower the threshold for the use of weapons." Asked whether that was meant as a threat to launch missiles on warning, he said, "Let's just agree that arms control is more urgent than ever before."

The fear of war in the Soviet Union, in my view, is pervasive.

UNPROFESSIONAL IN POLITICS

So is the fear of internal dissension and rebellion. That is the only way I can make sense out of all the repression I saw; it must be experienced to be believed.

Repression has not only painful human costs but heavy economic costs as well, however difficult they may be to estimate quantitatively. What is the cost of inhibiting the imagination and daring of creative people by spying on them, cutting their communications with colleagues at home and abroad, knowing that their colleagues have been victimized for insisting on human rights and freedom?

In one of the institutes, at a seminar with a dozen economists, I was asked by one scholar what I thought were the best and worst things about the Soviet Union. I said the best things were the Kirov ballet, the circus, and some of the individual people I had met, and the worst things were the spying, the treatment of Andrei Sakharov and other dissidents and Jews who wanted to leave the country, my inability to get reading material I wanted and needed—in short, the lack of freedom.

When I finished, the man who had asked the question looked at me solemnly and said, "*Xorosho*—Good."

Neither he nor anyone else in the seminar tried to refute me. They were silent and sorrowful. Later they asked me to stay longer and join their institute for a year: "You would fit in."

On the other side, I was deeply depressed by the sight of militiamen patrolling the entrance to the apartment building in Moscow where Mrs. Bonner, the wife of Andrei Sakharov, the Nobel Peace Prize–winning physicist and political dissident, live. Her husband, exiled to Gorky, was constantly harassed by the secret police.

"Why were the guards patrolling Mrs. Bonner's house?" I asked Valentin A. Koptyug, the head of the Siberian Division of the Academy of Sciences in Novosibirsk.

"Did it ever occur to you that they were guarding her from the anger of the people?" he replied.

"What did Sakharov do to warrant such anger? What has he been charged with?" I asked.

Academician Koptyug, his face reddening, replied, "Really, Sakharov was an outstanding scientist. He was three times honored as Hero of Socialist Labor. He made big contributions in different fields of physics. But today his potential as a physicist is finished. So he put his mind to other things.

"We respect professionalism in all things. We consider it inadmissible to deal with anything unprofessionally, including politics. If a person begins to deal with politics unprofessionally, we do not take him seriously. We do not respect him."

"What does it mean to be unprofessional in politics?" I asked. "In our country, anybody can take part in politics without being a professional."

Koptyug did not answer the question, a habit Soviet officials have in dealing with questions they do not like. He said Sakharov was free to leave the Soviet Union whenever he wished, but did not want to. When I said that was not my understanding, Koptyug said he would have proof of his freedom to leave delivered to me before I left Novosibirsk. The proof never came.

Such are the ironies of the Soviet system. One minute you're up, the next you're down, even in the same locale. I had had one of my grimmest encounters with a top Soviet scientist at Akademgorodok in Novosibirsk—the very place where a group of economists had written the most devastating critique of the Soviet industrial system for what it does to human beings.

"The type of worker that such a system cultivates," they wrote, "not only falls short of the needs of developed Socialism, but also fails to match the requirements of modern production. His common traits are low labor and productive discipline, an indifferent attitude toward work, a shoddy quality of work, social inactivity, a well-pronounced consumer mentality, and a low code of ethics."

That characterization of the effects of the Soviet system can apply not only to ordinary workers but to some intellectuals and high officials.

LIBERALIZATION WITHOUT FREEDOM

Some Soviet officials think the basic solutions to their economic problems lie in providing greater material incentives and rewards. But will material rewards be enough? Or will the Soviets be forced to a much wider degree of freedom than they are now contemplating—or see their efforts to reform the economy fail?

The government officials I spoke with expressed strong opposition to linking trade and other economic issues with human-rights questions, including the rights of dissenters and Jews to emigrate, insisting that these were internal matters in which we had no right to meddle.

But in a stagnating economy, the Soviets are compelled to seek greater foreign trade, especially in high-technology products—either that or steal them, as K.G.B. agents have been trying to do. Like it or not, they know that if they want more trade with the United States they must make concessions on human-rights issues, as they have done in letting the group of Pentecostalists, long protected in the American Embassy in Moscow, leave the country. But they are giving ground grudgingly, like horse traders. Top Soviet leaders have not yet seen the crucial importance—for their own sake and for the sake of their country's social, intellectual, and economic development—of moving more boldly to create a free society.

There are strong institutional barriers to it, rooted in Soviet ideology. Lenin, whose picture one sees everywhere, wrote: "Since there can be no talk of an independent ideology formulated by the working masses themselves in the process of their movement, the only choice is either bourgeois ideology or socialist ideology. The spontaneous development of the working-class movement leads to its subordination to bourgeois ideology," by which he meant Western democracy. Instead, Lenin declared, the masses would have to be led by a Communist Party possessing the attributes of secrecy, centralization, specialization, exclusivity, and, above all, a membership composed of "professional revolutionaries."

Every morning when I looked out from our balcony in the National Hotel across to Red Square at the long lines of people forming to visit the tomb of Lenin—with the militiamen controlling them, keeping everyone within the painted lines of the Square—I thought of Lenin's principles and how alive they are.

Can those professional revolutionaries in charge of the Soviet Union, with their huge bureaucratic apparatus, now reconstitute the basic elements of what Lenin denounced as a "bourgeois" society, with its proprietorial interests, its competitiveness, its flexibility, its freedom to innovate, as they are now seeking by governmental decree to do—but without moving toward greater economic and political and personal freedom?

I don't see how. Either the economic experiments will fail or the Soviet leaders will have to give up more and more of their highly centralized power to control human lives.

Karl Marx had prophesied the ultimate "withering away of the state" after the revolution. He had called for "converting the state from an organ superimposed upon society into one completely subordinated to it." Instead, Marx's worst fear for a Communist society had been realized: The politicians and bureaucrats and generals had, instead of building a free, open, and democratic society, reconstituted state power and used it to suppress the people.

This inhumane system is failing economically. I have been over into the past and it doesn't work.

Chapter
17
SOVIETOLOGY AND AMERICANOLOGY

I returned from the Soviet Union with a heightened sense of the enormous gulf between Andropov's Russia and Reagan's America. Indeed, the trip forced me to rethink my attitude toward the Reagan "capitalist revolution."

The philosophy of the Reagan Administration seemed to me in some ways akin to that of Herbert Spencer, the nineteenth century sociologist, who took it as axiomatic that the continued expansion of the role of government reduces the field of individual initiative, prevents the development of self-reliant, thoughtful, and altruistic people, and eventually produces infantile adults who expect the state to feed and care for them.

But the Reagan philosophy violated the Spencer creed in one important respect: Reagan's heavy stress on the buildup of military power. Spencer, with his libertarian philosophy, saw the growth of both military and civilian powers of the state as threats to a free society based on ethical principles and competitive markets. To be sure, Spencer recognized that warlike neighbors justified the maintenance of military forces, but he hoped that they would be used only for defensive purposes.

⁄ Reagan had sought to justify as essentially defensive his support of greater overt and covert forces in Central America and his long-range plans for major increases in military expenditures and a buildup of United States and allied forces in Europe, Asia, and elsewhere along the perimeter of the Communist world. So deciding whether the Reagan Administration had in fact been consistently Spencerian would require judgment on whether its military programs were truly defensive and whether the degree of the planned buildup of nuclear and conventional forces exceeds the actual threat.

Professor William L. Miller of the University of Georgia, a leading authority on Spencer, has found him to have been a remarkable social prophet who foresaw the coming of totalitarianism in the twentieth century. He thought the course of social evolution ran from hierarchical, coercive military societies to free industrial societies, but feared that if movement toward libertarianism was interrupted and a sustained period of rising government ensued, a totalitarian state would evolve. Writing in 1877, Spencer warned that military totalitarianism, once reinstituted, would be more nearly complete than the early versions and would consequently be more likely to endure. The Soviet Union has certainly shown remarkable powers of endurance in the face of external attacks and internal failures.

The top authorities of a military society seek to integrate the economic with the military. As an ideal, the military strives for autonomy; lest it find itself without needed matériel in wartime, the military feels it cannot allow specialization of production and free trade, even if this leads to inefficiency and high costs. But, of necessity, it seeks high technology from abroad, lest it fall too far behind the industrial societies to maintain its security.

In his *Principles of Sociology,* Spencer predicted that, internally, the industrial sector of the military society would continue to be a "permanent commissariat, existing solely to supply the needs of the government-military structures, and having left over for itself only enough for bare maintenance." Long before the Soviet Union was created, Spencer predicted that the leaders of the military state would try to suppress individual initiative and reserve decision making to themselves.

But he did not anticipate that these economic principles might lead to such an unsatisfactory economic performance of the state that even its military leaders would back away from excessive central control. In Moscow, in mid-July 1983, Andropov had proposed that greater autonomy be granted to factory managers and that greater individual initiative and innovation by Soviet enterprises be encouraged. Yet the contradiction remained: The Andropov plan was seeking to grant greater autonomy to enterprises in order to strengthen power at the center of the society.

The capitalist societies are still far from approximating Spencer's ideal for the industrial society. He worried that selfishness and crime would persist in a free society, but thought they could be held in check by two forces—competitive markets and a department of justice. He would almost certainly have been disappointed with the present state of altruism in the United States and other Western societies. And his worries about crime have been borne out.

Spencer did not think a hybrid mixing of the military and industrial societies was possible or desirable. He thought the military society would either destroy the industrial or vice versa. But he established so absolute an antithesis between the military and industrial societies that he refused to see the possibility that in the struggle for existence different societies might come to embody major aspects of each other, either to parry external threats or to deal with serious internal strains, whether of unemployment or excess demand, gluts or shortages, too rapid change or too much rigidity, excessive repression or excessive crime.

This is not to say that the military society of the Soviet Union and the industrial society of the United States are convergent; they are more like oil and water, one essentially market-dominated and free, the other government-dominated and serflike.

Yet in a curious way the leaders of both societies are engaged in an evolutionary game that Spencer, not Darwin, christened "the survival of the fittest." That process of conflict and evolutionary adaptation is being conducted in two different environments, within the capitalist and Communist societies, and in the world shared by them. The operative word in that common world is survival.

THE MILITARY BOOM

The biggest growth sector in the world economy is military spending. Unlike other growth sectors, however, the rapidly growing military production and international arms trade does not nourish economic growth but retards it.

Nobody knew this better than the Government of Israel, which in 1983 was devoting over half its budget to military spending and receiving $1.7 billion in military aid from the United States, along with $850 million in economic aid—but whose economy was in serious crisis, with inflation running at an annual rate of more than 200 percent and the shekel deteriorating rapidly. In 1984, the rate of inflation climbed to 400 percent.

The Reagan Administration, seeking greater military cooperation from Israel in an effort to bring stability to Lebanon, had proposed to ease Israel's financial burdens by not requiring repayment of any of the military aid—half of the military aid had hitherto required repayment with interest. The United

States wanted to cut its military aid to Israel to $1.3 billion, but the Israelis were holding out for the whole $1.7 billion.

Ironically, Israel's President, Chaim Herzog, warned the United States of the destabilizing economic and political effects of the arms trade on third-world countries. He warned the Americans against relying on military aid as a means of cementing an alliance and getting other countries to pursue political aims consistent with the donor's. Herzog was apparently cautioning the United States against making similar mistakes in providing huge military support to Israel's foes in the Middle East. Israel itself had had poor results from its own arms sales and military aid to other countries.

Historically, economists in both capitalist and Communist countries have put the blame for the arms trade on the economic interests of profit-seeking military producers. Lenin contended that imperialism was the final phase of capitalism. Even President Eisenhower warned against the influence of the "military-industrial complex."

But the Communist countries, and not just the Soviet Union, have themselves become major arms suppliers all over the world, and not just to other Communist countries. For instance, North Korea has supplied $800 million worth of arms to Iran, which is engaged in a war with North Korea's ally Iraq, causing Baghdad to break relations with Pyongyang. North Korea is also supplying arms to a long string of other countries.

North Korea and Israel only begin the list of countries that have been committing increasing shares of their countries' budgets to military programs. A study by the Stockholm International Peace Institute finds that 31 third-world countries increased their military spending from 1965 to 1975 by 100 percent or more as a share of gross national product; these included Chile, Egypt, Iran, Kuwait, Syria, the Philippines, Iraq, Honduras, Nigeria, Zambia, and Zimbabwe. A great many others, including Jordan, Lebanon, Indonesia, Ethiopia, Morocco, and El Salvador, increased their military outlays as a share of GNP by 25 percent to 100 percent in the same period.

In a study for the Swedish Agency for Research Cooperation, Milton Leitenberg of Cornell University finds that the major third world arms recipients and purchasers were no mere targets of either capitalist or Communist imperialism, but "have continuously clamored for more weapons and more weapons all through the years." A report on this study published in the *Nordic Journal of Latin American Studies* states that it is increasingly clear that in the industrial countries, high rates of economic growth, investment, and employment are inversely related to high levels of military expenditures. Soviet economists whom I had interviewed in Moscow and Novosibirsk regarded their own country's rising military expenditures as a drag on growth.

Could the United States wreck the Soviet economy by pressing them into a faster arms race? Admittedly, with their economy growing at a very low rate, they are in a zero-sum game among the three big claimants for national resources: military spending, investment outlays, and consumer spending. If the military grows faster than overall growth to keep up with United States military spending, the others must take less, and economic growth will slacken further. Thus, though the United States could aggravate their problems of choice by pressing them hard by an arms buildup, it seems likely that one way or another they will respond to that military challenge, whether by squeezing the civilian sector harder or by adopting a nuclear and conventional military strategy that would add to the hazards of life on earth for everyone.

Obviously, the arms race is economically costly to the United States as well. Strikingly, the industrial country with the strongest economic growth rate in the world, Japan, devotes the smallest proportion of its resources to military purposes. Indeed, the United States in effect acknowledges this by pressing Japan to increase its military outlays.

The developing countries, once considered to be different from the industrial countries with respect to the effect of military spending on growth, now appear to have suffered at least as much.

If neither the industrial nor the developing countries benefit from their heavy military commitments, why do they do it? To explain this, one needs to construct a theory of irrational expectations and passions. But passions, whether political, religious, or ideological, plus the drive for power of particular cliques, military or civilian, may join with the "rational" economic interests of arms sellers. However, as the Communist cases show, this cannot be related simply to the quest for profits.

Unraveling the mystery of what is causing the military to be the fastest-growing sector of world trade will require deeper analysis than it has yet had. There are not many developments so hazardous to world stability, economic and political.

FORECASTING IN CLOUDLAND

Official economic analysis and forecasting in the United States and the Soviet Union have certain similarities. Both are shaped by politicians eager to prove the success of their economic stewardship. Both are marked by internal battles among policymakers. Officials in both systems hate leaks of information, since information is power.

But there are differences. United States official economic reporting and forecasting are heavily constrained by the competition of private economists, analysts, businessmen, and reporters, where the Soviet variety can exist in a cloudland of its own.

Internal policy fights go on over the economic forecast in the United States, but with the budget for fiscal year 1985 due, Treasury Secretary Donald T. Regan, Budget Director David Stockman, and then chairman of the Council of Economic Advisers Martin S. Feldstein buried their hatchets and put out a common set of numbers. They predicted a rise in real gross national product of 4.5 percent in 1984, measured fourth quarter to fourth quarter. This was roughly in line with private forecasts. But all were low; real GNP grew at a sizzling rate of 8.8 percent in the first half of 1984.

How about the economic scene in the Soviet Union, as reported by the Andropov regime? Alas, not only the forecasting in Moscow but even the backcasting was murky, as usual. An American Sovietologist, Philip Hanson, said that even knowledge of what had been happening in the Soviet economy during the preceding year would "probably be limited to official figures on industrial output and the livestock sector of agriculture; so there is not a great deal to go on." Nevertheless, it did appear that 1983 was a considerably better year than 1982, partly because 1982 was so weak.

How about Soviet military outlays? The United States Central Intelligence Agency had cut its estimate of the annual growth of Soviet military production since 1975 to 2 percent from its earlier estimate of 4 to 5 percent. The Russians apparently gear their military spending to the growth of total production. Hence, the step-up in total output by nearly 4 percent in 1983 could presage a step-up in Soviet military spending.

What would be the shape of Soviet economic policies for improving performance in the coming year? Trying to read the disputes among Soviet politicians and bureaucrats makes interpretation of the disputes within the Reagan Administration, or between Republicans and Democrats, seem like child's play.

Did Andropov favor the paper attributed to the economist Tatiana Zaslavskaya and the Novosibirsk group criticizing Soviet industrial organization? Did Chernenko oppose it? Obviously, the true story was far more complex. A journal published by the Soviet Academy of Sciences cited academician Zaslavskaya's paper, but the Soviet intelligence agency, K.G.B., launched a hunt for whoever leaked the document, "Problems of Improving Socialist Production Relations and the Tasks of Economic Sociology," to American newspapers.

Soviet policies on agriculture were swinging to and fro, first hailing, then sharply criticizing the new "group contracts" with farm brigades. The government recognized the high productivity of private plots but, probably for that reason, had frozen them as a threat to the collective system.

Half a century ago, Will Rogers, the American humorist and sage, said: "Russia is a country that no matter what you say about it, it's true. Even if it's a lie, it's true." It was a breakthrough in Sovietology.

Chapter

18

WHAT HAVE WE LEARNED?

What have we learned from all these events?

We have learned that Presidents must not subordinate major economic decisions to immediate political advantage.

Inflation was kicked off in the United States during the Vietnam war when President Johnson, with the economy approaching full employment, delayed for political reasons the difficult choice among three possible policies: raising taxes to pay for the war, cutting his Great Society programs, or curbing military spending and getting out of Vietnam. He finally chose to raise taxes, but too late—the inflationary cat was out of the bag. And President Nixon aggravated the inflation with his New Economic Policy of August 15, 1971, simultaneously

WHAT HAVE WE LEARNED?

launching a highly stimulative fiscal and monetary policy aimed at ensuring his re-election, clamping on wage and price controls, suspending the convertibility of the dollar into gold, and embargoing sales of certain American farm products. When the controls were lifted after Nixon's landslide electoral victory in 1972, the suppressed inflation burst forth.

But it is silly to pretend that the problem of getting stable economic policies oriented toward the long run is a simple one, given the nature of democratic politics and the powerful pull of the political-business cycle. Gerry Ford and Jimmy Carter both tried to practice fiscal prudence in the last years of their administrations.

Jimmy Carter: "The team (Mondale, Miller, Schultze, Eizenstat, Strauss, McIntyre, and others) came down unanimous in asking me to approve a tax reduction and a moderate spending program to assuage Kennedy and to stimulate the economy. I was adamantly against it and, after considerable discussion, prevailed. I think everyone left convinced we had made the right decision: to hold firm; to oppose any tax reduction in 1980 . . . not to deviate from our strict commitment to a restrained budget."

President Reagan took no such chances in 1984. There was broad consensus among economists that he was taking undue risks of imposing inflationary strains on resources by his huge budget deficits, stretching into the future, as David Stockman put it, "as far as the eye can see." The supply-siders still contended that concern about budget deficits was vastly exaggerated and that it would be foolish to try to reduce them by raising taxes. Reagan, on that point, still marched with the supply-siders, whether for political-business-cycle or ideological reasons, or both. He has remained determined not to raise taxes and not to reduce the planned rapid buildup of military spending. And the economy boomed in 1984.

But most outside economists and investors worried that deficits of a trillion dollars or more through the rest of the decade would create severe inflationary pressures as economic expansion proceeds and would absorb far too large a share of national savings. And if tight money was again employed to keep those inflationary pressures from getting out of hand, the result would be another escalation of interest rates, a choking-off of investment and another slide into recession or depression.

WRAPPED UP WITH THE WORLD

We have learned that the United States must pay more heed to the international economy in setting its domestic economic policy.

President Nixon, ignoring this rule, slammed the gold window shut to prevent the further outflow of United States gold—but set off waves in the world economy that accelerated inflation and eventually ended the Bretton Woods system of fixed exchange rates. The end of Bretton Woods was a major cause of the breakdown of the golden age of growth, bringing high currency instability in the world, trade restrictions, and stagflation in the world economy.

Today America's economic problems are all wrapped up with the world's: the enormous Federal budget deficits, the high rates of interest, the international debt problem which the high interest rates aggravate, the gaping and still growing imbalance in the United States' international accounts aggravated by the overly strong dollar resulting in turn from the big budget deficits, the strong forces of protectionism here and abroad, the political instability that stems from economic instability.

The defense against a multiplying international banking crisis would depend on the central banks' willingness and ability to be lenders of last resort, that is, to lend generously to banks whose loans go bad and whose capital is in danger of being wiped out by the defaults of major foreign borrowers.

Foreign central banks, like the Federal Reserve in this country, accept that responsibility, without saying in advance exactly how they would discharge it for banks on their home territory. The situation is less clear for foreign branches and other overseas and offshore financial institutions. The latest version of an agreement among the central banks of the major industrial countries states that the agreement "does not address itself to lender-of-last-resort aspects of the role of central banks." This responsibility of the central banks in the international area needs to be clarified and strengthened.

This is not to say that the decision on which banks to rescue and how much money to pour into the system would be easy or costless. On one side is the danger of pouring in too much money, rekindling world inflation; on the other is the danger of supplying too little money, endangering the private banks and intensifying the financial, economic, and political problems of the debtor countries.

The world debt crisis cannot be solved within the context of economic stagnation. Debtor countries must be able to increase their export earnings if they are to service their existing debts and attract new capital needed to support economic growth. But there the economic policies of the industrial countries and the debtor countries may be in conflict. The industrial countries prefer moderate growth to ward off the danger of renewed inflation; the developing countries want a more rapid recovery to expand markets for their exports and create jobs and income for their people.

But a banking collapse would ruin both rich and poor. The collapse of the Credit-Anstalt in Austria in 1931 did not "cause" the Depression, but it badly worsened it, bringing Hitler's accession to power and World War II in its train. The solution to the international debt crisis will depend not only on rolling loans over and creating more debt to keep the developing nations afloat but on promoting a more vigorous economic recovery in the industrial world. Domestic and international policies are intertwined.

High interest rates and the huge American trade deficit could bring on a deluge of protectionism and wreck the world trading system as other countries retaliated. Foreign governments blame high American interest rates for holding down their own recoveries and for draining their financial resources. But untangling this skein could be tricky; some leading international financial experts fear that at some stage the process of a strengthening dollar will be reversed and then the fall of the dollar could deal a new shock to the world monetary system.

So the domestic monetary and fiscal policy of the United States must be seen as the key element in the world financial system. The need to close the Federal budget gap is pressing, for international reasons. The level of dollar interest rates aggravates the strains on the international financial system— strains apparent in the heavy debt burdens of many developing countries and in the persistent and growing flow of capital into the United States, with its counterpart of a widening trade deficit.

NEEDED: A BALANCED MIX

We have learned that, in any effort to correct the effects of a careless budget and fiscal policy, tight money must be used with great caution.

There is no doubt any longer about the potency of monetary policy in checking inflation. But in the process of squeezing inflation down in the past decade, tight money has taken an enormous toll in lost production, jobs, investment, economic growth, and—let us not forget—in the health and self-respect and family troubles and very lives of the people who have paid the price for high unemployment and economic instability.

There is still a school of economic thought, led by the Nobel laureate Milton Friedman, that insists monetary policy should be applied according to a simple rule: That the money supply be increased year by year—or, if possible, month by month or day by day—at a rate consistent with the national growth of productivity. Following the rule, says Professor Friedman, will permit inflation-free growth over time, though it will not necessarily rid the economy of cyclical fluctuations in production, income, and employment.

In the fall of 1979, the Federal Reserve began an experiment in what Paul Volcker called "practical monetarism," heeding Professor Friedman's call for more attention to the gradual growth of the money supply and less to the level of interest rates. But when tight money produced the recessions of 1979–1980 and 1981–82, Volcker and the Fed swung to much more rapid rates of monetary expansion than sanctioned by the central bank's "target ranges" and paid more heed to interest rates. Thereby, discretionary monetary policy—with the support of the Reagan Administration—was used as a powerful tool for getting the economy out of deep slumps. All but the most orthodox monetarists have cheered the moves. As Professor James Tobin of Yale, a Nobel laureate who eschews monetarism, put it, "Our Federal Reserve finally took mercy on the economy and suspended its monetarist targets. Its easing of monetary policy saved the world financial system from dangerous crisis and averted further collapse of economic activity."

One had to be a very dedicated theorist to have persisted on so dangerous a course so long. Theorists may, right or wrong, have the courage of their convictions; but there is a strong case to be made for opportunism in response to political pressures when economic disaster becomes a clear and present danger. Far better to avoid the need for such last-minute switches and rescue operations by adopting a balanced mix of fiscal and monetary policies in the first place.

THE CASE FOR AN INCOMES POLICY

We have learned that a better way must be found for combining high employment and growth with price stability.

With a sizable part of the labor force still unemployed, this problem may not loom immediately ahead, but if the recovery continues long enough, it will. Mandatory price and wage controls, last used by President Nixon, have proved rigid and inefficient. Resisting overstimulus while controls were in place proved impossible for the Nixon Administration. When the controls were finally lifted, inflation accelerated. The controls proved to be only a temporary and costly solution.

But economic slumps and high unemployment are a costly way of undoing inflation, too. Thus many economists have been trying for years to devise some form of voluntary "incomes policy" to hold back price and wage increases with less pain and less market interference. Arthur Burns had been urging an incomes policy when President Nixon leapfrogged past him to mandatory controls.

The tricky problem is to restrain the overall increase in wages and prices without obstructing changes in relative prices, which in a market economy steer labor and capital to their most efficient uses. President Kennedy's Council of Economic Advisers spelled out a solution to that problem by setting out guidelines for a general rate of wage increases in line with productivity gains, but with high-growth industries and low-growth or declining industries to follow higher or lower rates of wage settlement. The solution seemed to be working until President Johnson's excessively stimulative fiscal and monetary policies wrecked it.

The late Sidney Weintraub of the University of Pennsylvania and Henry Wallich, a governor of the Federal Reserve System, have proposed a tax-based incomes policy that would hold forth the incentives of lower taxes for industries that abided by noninflationary guidelines, or, conversely, the disincentives of higher taxes for those that didn't. This has attracted considerable support among fellow economists, but not much among politicians.

Henry Wallich has now offered a new incomes policy proposal; he suggests "taking a leaf from the Japanese" with a system of two-step wage increases, the second step of which would be a bonus. "With a bonus in prospect," says Wallich, "the first step can be more moderate. The second step would reflect price and profit developments in the intervening period." He proposes a dialogue between business and labor, both of whom have much to gain from such a plan.

Indeed, there is growing interest among both business and labor in profit-sharing arrangements or other ways of rewarding workers in good times and encouraging efforts to raise productivity without building in an inexorably rising floor under costs. Some see this approach prevailing at the national level in the form of a "social contract," with rewards in social programs as the means of inducing wage restraint.

It is often said by conservative critics that such an effort to build an incomes policy is politically unattainable or, if it could be attained, would be counterproductive as an interference with the free-market system. But there have been spells of strong growth and price stability, not only in the United States but in Japan, West Germany, and Austria, in which something like a social contract prevailed and made its contribution to longer-term growth and price stability.

It cannot be stressed enough, however, that no incomes policy can work for long unless it is undergirded by a noninflationary budgetary and monetary policy.

ECONOMIC FORCE VS. MILITARY FORCE

We have learned that, for the sake of stronger and more stable economic growth and of well-being at home and abroad, and indeed for the sake of human survival, we must curb the arms race.

This is not to suggest that the United States can unilaterally renounce power—the power to defend itself and its interests and to help prevent aggression against free people elsewhere in the world. But the events of the past two decades demonstrate the need for a new and more profound understanding of the constraints on national power.

Those constraints have been due in part to the fear of escalating local wars into nuclear wars, and in part to a complex of political and social developments. The cold-war coalitions have been greatly weakened, raising the risk that in the event of war superpowers would not have the support of their allies. Friendships and adversary relationships among nations have grown more complex and ambiguous. Economic issues have risen to the top of the diplomatic agenda. And as the political scientist Seyom Brown has observed, there has been an important increase in the international power of nongovernmental institutions—multinational business corporations and various kinds of scientific, environmental, technological, labor, and cultural communities which have been creating their own global networks and which may either support or conflict with national policies.[1] In the midst of the arms race, much of the business community in the West favored increased trade with the East, and even prevailed over the extremely hostile attitudes toward the Soviet Union of the Reagan Administration in the case of the natural gas pipeline to Western Europe.

In this world of complex coalitions and interests, the essence of power is changing from the direct use or threat of military force to gain national ends to various other kinds of promises, such as offers of economic and technological exchange or access to resources. To be sure, the old military-threat system remains and may be of decisive importance if issues over aggression or national survival develop. But fear of setting off a nuclear holocaust—and the spread of highly efficient "conventional" means of warfare, such as missiles and rockets, to small countries—has greatly weakened the ability of the superpowers to prevail.

Economic strength, balance, and flexibility have become critical elements in the conduct of foreign policy. In the equation of national power, the war game has been partially superseded by economics, the "peace game," in the pursuit of national interest. If the United States is to strengthen its power

---

[1] Seyom Brown, *New Forces in World Politics* (Washington, D.C.: Brookings Institution, 1974).

to achieve its own interests, it must be prepared to play the international peace game through trade, aid, foreign investment, exchange of technology, measures to strengthen and stabilize the international monetary system—and its own economy.

At the end of World War II, it was recognized that for the United States to achieve its international goals of rebuilding the world economy and preserving a secure structure of peace, high employment and economic growth would have to be maintained at home—to create the needed conditions for America's world role, to provide the resources needed by others, and to maintain an open and growing market for the goods of other countries. The world economic and financial crisis today requires a comparable effort on the part of the United States to keep its economy operating at a high level of employment, while curbing the inflation and high interest rates that have worsened the problems of others. International inflation stems from national sources, and the United States has been as great a culprit as any nation in breeding these evils. What is needed is the political courage, in the broad public interest, to curb the special-interest pressures that unbalance the budget, distort and waste national resources, including the arms race but by no means limited to the arms race.

THE AMERICAN MIX

We have learned that radical change, whether to the left or the right, is anathema to the American system; the economy is mixed and is going to stay that way.

The battle of special interests for extra shares of national resources through influence over government is an inevitable aspect of the mixed economy—and makes it inflation-prone, deficit-prone, and corruption-prone. Some would solve the problem by getting rid of the mixed economy and reverting to laissez-faire capitalism. That was Reagan's proclaimed mission—except in the area of military production.

But his Administration, with its rightist ideology, has only served to demonstrate that the mixed economy of the United States is extremely durable. In fact, it has been here from the beginning of the Republic.

The tension between free enterprise and strong government is the leitmotif of American history. American politics is full of contradictions that are bewildering to most foreigners and perhaps even to Americans themselves. At times, Americans seem to treat their President as though he were a monarch; certainly he is always the nation's top celebrity, sought after and celebrated by the media and the common people. But at other times, as in the wake of Watergate, Americans seem uncomfortable with the "Imperial Presidency," as Arthur Schlesinger, Jr., called it. Americans periodically turn suspicious and wary of their political leader, and indeed are normally so of most politicians and bureaucrats. Recognizing this public antipathy to government, first Jimmy Carter and then Ronald Reagan cast themselves as outsiders resident in the White House, foes of the Washington establishment they were elected to head.

The American people have long oscillated between two philosophies of government, the Jeffersonian and the Hamiltonian. Thomas Jefferson thought the way to ensure that the United States would stay a nation of free individuals was to keep the economy essentially agrarian. He feared that factories and big cities would make people corrupt and slavish. He wanted to limit the role of government as much as possible, to keep the country free. But Alexander Hamilton believed in the importance of a strong United States Government capable of promoting national economic development and of ensuring the country's freedom and independence in a world of potentially hostile states—many of them headed by foes of democracy.

This conflict of political philosophies goes on not only between different interest groups but within the American mind.

Under President Reagan, the Jeffersonian view of the role of government has been dominant, at least in the domestic area. By slashing taxes and social expenditures, and by seeking to transfer Federal responsibilities to the fifty states and to the private-business and voluntary sectors, Reagan hoped to shrink the "welfare state"—while expanding the military state.

This policy trend, denominated "conservative" in the American political lexicon, represented a reaction to the perceived failures of the "liberal" consensus which was dominant through most of the preceding half century. That earlier liberal era had had its triumphs: the conquest of the Great Depression, victory in World War II, the achievement of full employment after the war, the reconstruction of Western Europe and Japan, the establishment of the postwar international monetary and trading system, and the containment of Soviet expansion.

But public confidence in the strength and integrity of the United States Government was eroded by a string of failures: Vietnam, the race riots and urban burnings, Watergate and the resignation in disgrace of President Nixon, the energy crisis resulting from the inability to control OPEC countries, the Soviet invasion of Afghanistan, the Iranian upheaval and the Ayatollah Khomeini's humiliation of President Carter and the United States. The liberal era was also discredited by the failure of some major programs to live up to their hyperbolic advertising, such as the Great Society, the War on Poverty, and détente with the Soviet Union. Public perception of the ineffectiveness or wrongheadedness of the Federal government was compounded by chronic inflation and unemployment, sluggish growth, the falling dollar. All those events gave rise to apprehensions that the United States had lost its strength and vitality.

Though the Carter Administration marked the beginning of a conservative reaction to the perceived failures of liberalism, Reagan's landslide victory at the polls in 1980 seemed to seal it. But even though Reagan himself claimed he was ushering in a new conservative era, reversing, as he said, fifty years of liberal failure, the future shape of American politics would obviously require his Administration to demonstrate that it could cope with the complex problems of a new age.

If the Reagan approach failed, would there be an early return to liberalism? Some observers, such as Daniel Yankelovich and Larry Kaagan of the public-attitude research firm Yankelovich, Skelly and White, thought that a Reagan failure would not necessarily mean a return to the liberal consensus but more likely would result in a further swing to the extreme right. If Reagan could not forge a program appropriate to the world of the 1980s, and if a constructive opposition program did not materialize, they prophesied that the country would move "toward the strongly ideological right, with its villains, scapegoats and calls for righteous authoritarianism." They warned that a Reagan failure on the economic front could destabilize American society for years to come and unleash social havoc. And a serious failure in foreign policy, they said, "could leave the United States so vulnerable in its national security that it might even be panicked into some frightful military adventure leading to a nuclear confrontation."

But there are strong constraints inherent in the American system that militate against swings either to the radical left or the extreme right. One of the most important of these is the deliberate dispersion of political power by the Founding Fathers, who in the Constitution separated the executive from the legislative, and both from the judicial branch, and also divided power between the Federal Goverment and the governments of the several states. To govern such a system, politicians, including the President, have to bargain continuously, as James MacGregor Burns puts it, in a "vast system of brokerage and accommodation that would give something to everybody—liberty to the individual, desired laws or appropriations to groups, and governmental balance and stability to the whole."

Besides the formal structure of government, there is the political party system, which in the United States has always consisted of essentially two parties. Since the Civil War, the Republicans and Democrats have given the nation a remarkable degree of political and ideological stability, because both parties include conservative and liberal elements, although the

Republicans as a party are more conservative and the Democrats more liberal. But their rhetoric customarily differs more than their actions.

During his first year in office, President Reagan was able to command significant majorities of both houses of Congress, despite a Democratic majority in the lower chamber, for his big tax cuts, reductions in social spending, and increases in military outlays. But starting in his second year, he ran into much greater opposition from liberals and moderates in both parties. Despite his own determination to "stay the course," his economic program became less radically rightist through the rest of his term.

There can be, of course, no certainty that a serious threat from the far right or far left could never succeed, but the odds appear heavily against it. When the Reagan program appeared to be failing, with rising unemployment and hardships eroding the Republicans' political support, there was no evidence of a further shift to the right in Washington or the nation. Quite the contrary, the pressures stemming from Congress, labor, minority groups, the press, academic institutions, environmental groups, and others pulled the Administration back from the right-wing policies it had adopted in bestowing large tax benefits on the rich while raising taxes and drastically reducing or eliminating programs of benefit to the poor and working class.

Americans have a strongly ingrained sense of fairness. Though it may sometimes be obscured, especially in times of boom and inflation, hard times and suffering seem to bring it out. Roosevelt's measures to help the poor and unemployed won broad national support and made the Democrats by far the majority party for many years. In the Depression, radical groups, including Communists, Nazis, and various fascist groups, did gain some supporters, but they lost all potential for revolution or radical change in the system once Roosevelt emerged, appealing to the sense of fairness of the American people and with a program to implement it. Essentially, Roosevelt rescued the capitalist system, though he certainly strengthened the role of government in it and put "a safety net" under those people at the bottom. We must bring those left out into the mainstream of society.

Today there appears to be even less likelihood of a radical shift than there was half a century ago, because the American system now has greater stability, thanks to the construction of income security programs, increased knowledge of how to prevent major economic breakdowns, and widespread understanding in all classes of society of the horrors that a totalitarian regime would bring. This knowledge has been drummed into the American mind by the still vivid memories of what terrors and crimes Hitler and Stalin committed, and the havoc other totalitarian dictators continue to wreak today. The nation, with the strong voice of the press to educate it, remains far less blasé about dictatorships than does Reagan and far less willing to lend them political and military support.

Most congressmen and their constituents, both conservative and liberal, have shown stiff resistance to becoming more deeply involved in El Salvador, even where the risks of national defeat appear small. The Vietnam experience has not been forgotten. Nor is the nation spoiling for war in the Middle East or elsewhere in the world. Americans are not, unless severely provoked, a war-loving people. They are more likely to act as a check on an aggressive administration than a spur to it.

FIGHTING ON WITH A FREE ECONOMY

After the long postwar spell of growth and prosperity, we learned that the major weakness of the capitalist system remains its tendency to swing from boom to bust.

But progress in economics since the Great Depression, reinforced by strong political motives, makes it probable that a similar national and international catastrophe can be avoided.

With all its anti-Keynesian rhetoric, the Reagan Administration held on to its big deficits, rising military outlays, and tax cuts to prevent recession from becoming depression. The Reaganites did not rely solely on their so-called supply-side tax cuts (which actually stimulated consumption on the demand side, with little immediate effect on investment) to stop inflation or depression. Rather, they supported an activist monetary policy, first to knock down the inflation and, when unemployment soared, to check the slump and stimulate recovery. To their credit, they did not adopt a reactionary do-nothing economic policy but used macroeconomic tools, like every preceding postwar Administration, Democratic and Republican, to stabilize the economy.

And despite Reagan's earlier reluctance to support the International Monetary Fund and the World Bank, when the chips were down and foreign disasters loomed, he made what he called an "unbreakable" personal commitment to get funds from Congress to support those international bodies—and delivered on that commitment despite strong populist agitation around the country against "bailing out the banks" or, as the right-wing populists charged, rescuing Communist debtors.

Similarly, the Reagan Administration's strong denunciation of an "industrial policy"—specific government actions to lend support to particular industries in trouble or to aid the growth of new industries—was not always matched by its performance.

Heated debate persists among economists, politicians, and businessmen whether an industrial policy, or more precisely what kind of an industrial policy, makes sense. Adlai E. Stevenson, the former Democratic Senator from Illinois, told a Congressional committee that the best industrial policy for the United States would be to get government out of the market, not more deeply into it—a view many conservative businessmen (when not in trouble themselves) would warmly support.

The United States may already have the most aggressive industrial policy in the world, Stevenson said: "In proportion to its GNP, probably no government resorts so freely and expensively to business assistance by loans, guarantees and grants, target and trigger prices, import quotas and tariffs, industry regulation, research assistance, tax expenditures and the like as the United States Government." Far from assisting industry, he added, the Government has sometimes crippled it.

Nevertheless, there remains strong support, especially within the Democratic Party, for an industrial policy that would help provide jobs for unemployed labor and help troubled industries and regions. An industrial policy that focused on improving the education and technical training of the labor force would certainly make a good deal of sense. It is in the area of primary and secondary education that the Japanese appear to have their main advantage over the United States.

Government undoubtedly has a vital role to play in complementing private investment in plant and equipment with public investment in education, research and development, agriculture, transportation, water resources, and other vital national needs. In fact, it has been playing that role for the past two centuries in furthering national economic development.

But no industrial policy can succeed in the absence of a vital and competitive market economy which serves human welfare better than if it were planned. That is the fantastic paradox and deep insight into the nature of human societies with which Adam Smith has endowed us. There is nothing like a trip to the Soviet Union to drive that lesson home. Soviet economists themselves, even some planners and top officials, are coming to understand that lesson, and are cautiously starting some new experiments to loosen up their system to encourage change and innovation and to provide greater autonomy and incentives for workers and managers—but without abandoning the repressive apparatus of the Communist system. If the Soviets cannot build a freer society, in my view, they are doomed to economic stagnation, social bitterness and indignity, and ultimately a failed society, frustrated, hostile, and suspicious toward all others, even within their own bloc.

We are incredibly fortunate to have preserved our own free system, which, with all its obvious faults and problems, is probably still the freest and most stable in the world. It had to be to survive the follies and blunders of our political leaders. As Adam Smith said, there is a lot of ruin in a nation.

But we cannot rest too easily on that doctrine. In this century we have been through too many disasters and near-disasters to permit complacency.

Even if economists fully agreed on the lessons to be gleaned from the troubled past, it does not follow that politicians would join in the agreement or enforce its prescriptions. Inevitably it is they, not their economic advisers, who will call the shots—or the shocks.

Living in a shock-prone world, we must stay flexible and adaptable, to roll with the punches of history. And stay in the fight.

STATISTICAL APPENDIX

TABLE A

INFLATION, UNEMPLOYMENT, AND PRESIDENTIAL
ELECTIONS, 1946–1984

Yearly Change in Unemployment Rate and Inflation (Real GNP Deflator)	Presidential Election Years (%)	All Other Years (%)
Less unemployment and less inflation	40	10
Less unemployment but more inflation	20	34
Less inflation but more unemployment	30	38
More inflation and more unemployment	10	17
	100	99
	(10)	(29)

Source: Economic Report of the President, 1984

278

TABLE B

ANNUAL CHANGE IN REAL DISPOSABLE INCOME PER CAPITA IN RELATION TO THE POLITICAL NATURE OF THE YEARS, ALL POSTWAR ADMINISTRATIONS EXCEPT EISENHOWER'S

	No Election (%)	On-year, Incumbent President Not Seeking Reelection (%)	Midterm Election (%)	On-year, Incumbent President Seeking Reelection (%)
1946			−2.6	
1947	−5.9			
1948				3.4
1949	−1.5			
1950			5.9	
1951	0.9			
1952		1.1		
1961	1.0			
1962			2.6	
1963	1.9			
1964				5.6
1965	4.8			
1966			3.9	
1967	3.0			
1968		2.8		
1969	1.5			
1970			3.0	
1971	2.4			
1972				2.9
1973	5.7			
1974			−1.7	
1975	1.0			
1976				2.6
1977	2.9			
1978			3.8	
1979	1.6			
1980				−0.6
1981	2.2			
1982			−0.4	
1983	2.3			
1984 (estimate)				4.4
Median	1.9	2.0	2.8	3.7

Source: Economic Report of the President, 1984

TABLE C

GROSS NATIONAL PRODUCT, 1960–1985
(BILLIONS OF DOLLARS)

	Current Dollars	1972 Dollars
1960	506.5	737.2
1961	524.6	756.6
1962	565.0	800.3
1963	596.7	832.5
1964	637.7	876.4
1965	691.1	929.3
1966	756.0	984.8
1967	799.6	1,011.4
1968	873.4	1,058.1
1969	944.0	1,087.6
1970	992.7	1,085.6
1971	1,077.6	1,122.4
1972	1,185.9	1,185.9
1973	1,326.4	1,254.3
1974	1,434.2	1,246.3
1975	1,549.2	1,231.6
1976	1,718.0	1,298.2
1977	1,918.3	1,369.7
1978	2,163.9	1,438.6
1979	2,417.8	1,479.4
1980	2,631.7	1,475.0
1981	2,954.1	1,513.8
1982	3,073.0	1,485.4
1983	3,309.5	1,534.8
1984*	3,648.5	1,623.4
1985*	3,932.6	1,667.8

*Forecast, Data Resources, Inc., April 1984
Source: Department of Commerce

TABLE D
UNEMPLOYMENT AND INFLATION, 1960–1985

	(1) Unemployment Rate, All Civilian Workers (%)	(2) Changes in Consumer Price Index, December to December (%)	(3) = (1) + (2) Misery Index (%)
1960	5.5	1.5	7.0
1961	6.7	.7	7.4
1962	5.5	1.2	6.7
1963	5.7	1.6	7.3
1964	5.2	1.2	6.4
1965	4.5	1.9	6.4
1966	3.8	3.4	7.2
1967	3.8	3.0	6.8
1968	3.6	4.7	8.3
1969	3.5	6.1	9.6
1970	4.9	5.5	10.4
1971	5.9	3.4	9.3
1972	5.6	3.4	9.0
1973	4.9	8.8	13.7
1974	5.6	12.2	17.8
1975	8.5	7.0	15.5
1976	7.7	4.8	12.5
1977	7.1	6.8	13.9
1978	6.1	9.0	15.1
1979	5.8	13.3	19.1
1980	7.1	12.4	19.5
1981	7.6	8.9	16.5
1982	9.7	3.9	13.6
1983	9.6	3.8	13.4
1984*	7.4	4.8	12.2
1985*	7.2	5.2	12.4

*Forecast, by Data Resources, Inc., April 1984
Source: Economic Report of the President, 1984

TABLE E

FEDERAL BUDGET OUTLAYS, RECEIPTS, AND DEBT, FISCAL YEARS 1960–1985
(BILLIONS OF DOLLARS)

Fiscal Years	Receipts	Outlays	Surplus or Deficit	Off-Budget Outlays	Total Deficits	Year-End Gross Federal Debt
1960	92.5	92.2	+0.3	—		290.9
1961	94.4	97.8	−3.4	—		292.9
1962	99.7	106.8	−7.1			303.3
1963	106.6	111.3	−4.8			310.8
1964	112.7	118.6	−5.9			316.8
1965	116.8	118.4	−1.6			323.2
1966	130.9	134.7	−3.8			329.5
1967	148.9	157.6	−8.7			341.3
1968	153.0	178.1	−25.2			369.8
1969	186.9	183.6	+3.2			367.1

Year						
1970	192.8	195.7	-2.8			382.6
1971	187.1	210.2	-23.0			409.5
1972	207.3	230.7	-23.4			437.3
1973	230.8	245.6	-14.8	0.1	-14.9	468.4
1974	263.2	267.9	-4.7	1.4	-6.1	486.2
1975	279.1	324.2	-45.2	8.1	-53.2	544.1
1976	298.1	364.5	-66.4	7.3	-73.7	631.9
1977	355.6	400.5	-44.9	8.7	-53.6	709.1
1978	399.6	448.4	-48.8	10.4	-59.2	780.4
1979	463.3	491.0	-27.7	12.5	-40.2	833.8
1980	517.1	576.7	-59.6	14.2	-73.8	914.3
1981	599.3	657.2	-57.9	21.0	-78.9	1,003.9
1982	617.8	728.4	-110.6	17.3	-127.9	1,147.0
1983	600.6	796.0	-195.4	12.4	-207.8	1,381.9
1984	670.1	853.8	-183.7	16.2	-199.9	1,591.6
1985	745.1	925.5	-180.4	14.8	-195.2	1,828.4

Source: Department of the Treasury and the Office of Management and Budget

INDEX

ABOUT THE AUTHOR

Leonard Silk is the Economics Columnist of *The New York Times.* Prior to joining *The Times* in 1970, he was a Senior Fellow at the Brookings Institution. He has served as a member of the President's Commission on Budget Concepts and as a member of the Research Advisory Board of the Committee for Economic Development. Mr. Silk is a five times' winner of the Loeb Award for Distinguished Business and Financial Journalism.